Social Enterprise in Anytown

John Pearce
with a chapter by Alan Kay

CALOU ... ONDON

Published by
Calouste Gulbenkian Foundation
United Kingdom Branch
98 Portland Place
London W1B 1ET
Tel: 020 7908 7604
E-mail: info@gulbenkian.org.uk
Website: www.gulbenkian.org.uk

Reprinted 2005

ISBN 0 903319 97 7
978 0903319 97 3

British Library Cataloguing-in-Publication Data
A catalogue record for this book is available from the British Library

Designed by Andrew Shoolbred, cover designed by Onvisual, www.onvisual.com, illustration by Sima Vaziry
Diagrams by Technical Art Services
Printed by Expression Printers Ltd, IP23 8HH

Distributed by Central Books Ltd, 99 Wallis Road, London E9 5LN
Tel: 0845 458 9911, Fax: 0845 458 9912
E-mail: orders@centralbooks.com
Website: www.centralbooks.co.uk

Contents

Preface

For some twenty years, the Gulbenkian Foundation has adopted what has now come to be called the 'investor' approach to social enterprise. From the earliest days of our report *Whose Business is Business?* (1981), we have taken a strong, and I hope, supportive interest in the development of social enterprise, encouraging individuals and communities to investigate and evaluate its value and usefulness. The author of this book, John Pearce, was one of the pioneers in the field, well known for his involvement and skills, and particularly for creating Community Business Scotland.

Ten years ago, the Foundation commissioned *At the Heart of the Community Economy* (1993), subtitled *Community enterprise in a changing world.* The author then, as now, was John Pearce, but even he could not have imagined exactly how the world would change. Social enterprise is now increasingly recognised, with university courses, the DTI's report *Social Enterprise: A strategy for success,* published in July 2002, with an introduction by the Prime Minister, and the term 'social entrepreneur' approvingly on everyone's lips. As John himself notes in his introduction, at times the pace has been breathtaking.

This book updates the earlier one, but also shows how much more sophisticated social enterprise has become in practice, with two 'how to' appendices, one on the now widespread exercise of social accounting and audit. In his final manifesto, John Pearce stresses the need for a shared vision, addresses the values of social enterprise which set it apart from straightforward business, and celebrates that difference. There is now no need for special pleading – this is for real.

Paula Ridley
Director

Introduction

The world of social enterprise is changing with great speed. The pace has been at times breathtaking.

Some of the landmark changes which have occurred during the 18 months in which these pages have been researched, discussed and written, include the appointment of a junior minister with responsibility for social enterprise; the setting up of a Social Enterprise Unit in the Department of Trade and Industry; the publication of a monthly magazine *Social Enterprise*; the publication of a Social Enterprise Strategy for England; and, as these pages were being finalised, the publication of the review on charity law with proposals to recognise social enterprises as 'community interest companies'.

Social enterprises are not only on the map, but are being courted by government to play a key role in modernising and reforming public services. The sector is steadily growing and its contribution to the economy is now much more clearly recognised.

At times of such ferment and change it is possible to lose sight of the underlying principles and to focus on managing the short term at the expense of the long term. There are important questions to ask and answer. What actually are social enterprises? Are they simply businesses with a social purpose? Or are they the harbingers of a change in the way society works? What are the values on which they are based? Can they be both servants of the state and independent bodies? Will government ever really let go and hand control of services and assets to community level? Have social enterprises the capacity to be big businesses? Where do they fit with private-sector corporations and public-sector agencies? Is the capital available to invest in serious growth and expansion?

These are some of the questions which the following pages seek to ask, and to some degree answer. Sometimes there are no answers, but the questions are important because they focus attention onto what social enterprises stand for and what it is realistic to expect them to do.

Chapter 1 is a story, a make-believe of how it might be if social and community enterprises were to be a significant and growing force in the economy of any town. The examples in the story are based on what has happened somewhere or is planned. Can such developments happen everywhere?

Chapter 2 positions social enterprises as part of a wider social economy, which itself is part of a third system in the global economy. It is emphasised that the third system, and therefore social enterprises, are qualitatively different from first-sector private business and from second-sector public agencies.

Chapter 3 explores the defining characteristics of social enterprises and the values more generally of the social economy. Chapter 4 looks at the nature of social enterprises, defining them according to nine dimensions and four areas of work.

Chapter 5 discovers the different origins of social enterprises – how they come into being – and looks at the way language reflects what people think about social enterprise. Chapter 6 examines the concept of social capital and its importance to growing the social economy, while chapter 7 focuses on the community development approach to creating community enterprises and recognises the importance of 'happenstance'. One particular community development approach is briefly described and a description of how that approach may be implemented can be found in Appendix i.

Chapter 8 discusses how the development of social enterprises may best be supported and argues in favour of a mutual approach, with the support structures belonging to and accountable to social enterprises themselves. Chapter 9 argues that the financing institutions for social enterprises should also belong to the social economy and not be controlled by the public sector or by the banking system. Social enterprises are not businesses; they are social enterprises. They require social enterprise plans, not business plans. They require support and financing mechanisms which reflect their values.

Chapter 10 suggests that there should be a recognised legislative form for social enterprises, based on six defining characteristics, and that a registration and regulatory system should be established for social enterprises, as much to be clear about what is *not* a social enterprise as to know what is. Social accounting and audit is proposed as the appropriate system whereby social enterprises may account for their work, and chapter 11 outlines a model process which is now well established in practice and explores some important contemporary issues regarding social accounting and audit for the social economy. The social accounting model is more fully described in Appendix ii.

Chapter 12 glances briefly at the global context and emphasises the importance of global networks in the worldwide Social Enterprise Movement.

Chapter 13 attempts to draw out the key points from the preceding chapters and present them in manifesto format in order to focus attention and stimulate further discussion.

In 1991 the Calouste Gulbenkian Foundation (CGF) gave me the opportunity to review the then current state of community enterprise, its historical origins and influences, values and practice, and issues of importance. I was able to discuss these matters with some 30 consultees drawn from activists and practitioners, support organisations and funders, and academics and thinkers. The result was *At the Heart of the Community Economy*, published by CGF in 1993.

In 2001, on the initiative of Andrew Robinson, Head of Community Development Banking at NatWest and The Royal Bank of Scotland, CGF together with the Banks offered me the chance to reflect on what has happened in the world of community and social enterprise over the decade since *At the Heart of the Community Economy*. It was an opportunity for which I was, and remain, most grateful, and especially for the support and encouragement of both Andrew and Paul Curno, then Deputy Director of the Foundation. Again I met and talked with some 26 consultees, whose names are given on page 184. I am most grateful to all those people for generously giving up their time to talk over some of the issues. No quotations have been attributed but the comments of my consultees are noted in inverted commas in the text.

I also attended conferences – in Cardiff, London, Edinburgh, Newcastle, Brisbane (Australia), Wellington (New Zealand) and Gavle (Sweden) as part of my exploration of social enterprise, and over the course of 18 months had casual conversations with many whose views were always of interest.

An early version of the Anytown story was first published as a New Sector pamphlet but it has been extensively updated and extended here.

Much of the thinking around the position of the social economy within a third system has evolved through a series of transnational European projects organised through the Technical University and the European Network in Berlin. I am grateful to those European colleagues with whom I have been able to share thinking over the years, especially Karl Birkholzer.

Part of chapter 5 is based on a paper given to a conference held within the Commonwealth People's Centre in Brisbane (October 2001); part of chapter 7 originates from a lecture given to community development workers in Dundee and subsequently published in the journal of the Scottish Community Development Centre (2001); part of chapter 11 is based on a paper given to a conference of Social Audit New Zealand, also in October 2001; and part of chapter 12 on a paper given to a conference organised by COMMACT India in January 2002. The five stage social audit model has been published in the *Social Audit and Accounting Manual* (2001) which was also supported by CGF.

I have received patient support from Felicity Luard at CGF and am grateful to Alan Tuffs for his comments on the first draft and for the original designs on which the diagrams on pages 22, 49 and 169 were based, and to Jane Barry for copyediting the text.

My special thanks, however, go to my friend and colleague Alan Kay who has been my collaborator on this project and who wrote chapter 6 on Social Capital, based on an action research project in which he and I have been engaged. We have debated the ideas and conclusions over many hours and Alan has read and commented very wisely and fully on the drafts as they have emerged.

Notwithstanding the generous assistance I have received, the responsibility for the final text and its interpretations is mine.

John Pearce
Harburn
October 2002

1 Social enterprise – how it works in Anytown

This story is about the potential of social and community enterprise; it is a model of what could happen in any town.

The story fuses together many real-life social and community enterprise activities and initiatives into an ideal: a vision of the powerful force social enterprise could be in the economy. It shows how different types of social and community enterprise can interrelate and collaborate and it seeks to shift the debate towards a recognition of the true potential of social enterprise and the common values which inspire its different forms as they already operate throughout our society. Taken together, these enterprises, whether they call themselves community businesses or development trusts, community companies or community co-operatives, social enterprises or voluntary enterprises, social firms or social businesses, community housing associations or co-operatives, credit unions or community trading organisations, represent a powerful other way of doing things in their quest for social and community benefit rather than personal wealth.

All the events in this tale have either really happened or are being planned, but they did not all happen within the time frame of one story, were not made to happen by the people of a single community, and did not all happen in one place. But they could.

Anytown faced many of the problems of a modern town hit by industrial decline, recession and high levels of unemployment. There were few opportunities for young people and a rising sense of hopelessness which showed itself in increased crime and vandalism, empty, boarded-up houses, increased drunkenness on the streets, domestic violence and a growing drug culture.

Twenty years ago a group of local people came together because they were increasingly concerned about the rising level of unemployment. After some informal discussions at the tenants' association committee and at the Community Council, a small action group formed itself to explore 'What we can do, rather than wait for someone else to do it'.

A vision and an agenda for action

The group persuaded Anytown Council to fund a series of Community Futures Workshops, a community development process through which representatives of different stakeholder groups in the town were able to get together to build a community profile, to identify the key problems facing the town, brainstorm possible ideas for tackling them and come up with an agreed vision for the future and an agenda for action. One main recommendation was to create a local body to take forward the ideas for action. A steering group was elected with the mandate to set up some form of community company 'to get things moving'.

Anytown Council was sympathetic to ideas of community organisation and action and certain councillors and officers were particularly excited by the idea of community enterprise. They decided to employ a community enterprise officer with the remit to liaise with the steering group and give them the support they would need. After about a year of discussions and planning, Anytown Community Enterprises (ACE) came into being.

Anytown politics

Anytown Council is rather unusual. Although Labour is the biggest group of councillors it cannot be described as uniformly New Labour. Some councillors are veterans of the old metropolitan county councils which sought and experimented with ways of developing a local, socialist economy until they were abolished by central government. These councillors still use the word 'socialism' and remain committed to the idea of the state's shaping the direction of society and of the kind of economic development which puts people before profit. There has also always been a sizeable Co-operative Party group on the Council which blends its support of the traditional co-operative principles and the consumer movement with a more recently adopted enthusiasm for embracing social enterprise and recognising a common heritage of mutual and self-help philosophy. There is also a small caucus of Liberal Democrats and Green Party members on whom the Labour group sometimes has to depend for a majority in key votes, especially when some of its own members are uncertain about the new social enterprise policies being advocated. The Lib Dems and the Greens ensure that 'localisation' and environmental issues are kept high on the agenda.

The consequence of this curious political mixture and the drive coming from the Labour group leadership has been a political commitment to developing the social economy of Anytown as a way of doing things distinctively different from anything that the private or public sectors have to offer. In Anytown the social economy, and especially social enterprises, are recognised as a sector not only to be promoted but to be used as the preferred means of developing the local economy and delivering local services. This political commitment has featured in successive local election manifestos, sometimes to the despair of head-office party officials. Over the years, senior Council officials have been appointed who share this political purpose and are keen to turn it into workable strategies, and sometimes to find ways around the constraints of central government which might otherwise thwart local political intentions.

ACE Workspaces

The first ACE initiative was to convert a disused primary school into a workspace, that is, small offices and workshops made available to small (especially new-start) businesses on easy-in-easy-out rental terms. At the time such ideas were quite new to Anytown and a lot of the old guard on the Council, especially the architects, had to be convinced that this was a sensible idea and that businesses would actually consider setting up in a former school. Despite these misgivings, the school was leased at a peppercorn rent to ACE and converted with an urban aid grant. The project was a resounding success, almost before it opened its doors. There was clearly a strong demand for appropriately-sized workshops for new-start businesses within a supportive framework.

The workspace attracted a lot of attention and over the next few years the Council identified other redundant schools which it invited ACE to develop and run. Now ACE has four former schools running as workspaces in the town, which gives it just enough square footage for the workspace enterprise to break even. After five years of paying the peppercorn rent, ACE was able to agree the purchase of the former school buildings at an agreed unimproved valuation. This has given the company an important and gradually increasing asset base. ACE has become the Council's equal partner in this area of workspace provision and is seen as the key provider in the town.

Two years ago, following an introduction arranged through the Council's Economic Development Unit, ACE teamed up with a private developer to build a new business park on the edge of town. The basic deal in this first joint venture with a private business was that ACE would operate a management contract as well as having a small equity stake in the development. Having been part of the project from the start, the community enterprise has had a strong influence on the style of the development. ACE was also careful to negotiate a first option to purchase should the local developer ever wish to sell.

Workspace is not just about property management, however. ACE's reason for going into workspace was originally in order to help local people set up in business, enabling them at least to earn their own living and maybe to employ one or two others as well. It was seen as a very practical way of both creating some new local jobs and of slowly expanding the local economy. Therefore the ACE Workspaces have always provided advice and training to existing and potential tenants as well as that informal 'hand-holding' which is so important when people step out into the world of self-employment for the first time, sometimes from the 'grey' economy.

A few years ago ACE persuaded the Council and a charitable trust to fund a special self-employment training programme which, with the agreement of government departments, runs a pilot scheme, known as Enterprise Rehearsal (ER), in which long-term unemployed people are able to start up in business while still receiving benefit. They have to register with the ACE Self-employment Trust and their earnings are credited to their account with the Trust to be drawn on when and if they finally launch themselves into business without the support of benefit. This scheme has been very successful in making it possible for the long-term unemployed to try out a business idea without the fear of losing their benefit income. It fosters enterprise, and has revealed that there are many ideas out there waiting to be tried if the right support structure can be put into place.

In particular it has made it possible for some people operating illegally in the grey economy to come out into the open. When more than two people have been involved, several of the ER participants have been encouraged to set up their small businesses as workers' co-operatives.

All the workspaces also provide basic office services not only to their tenants but also to individuals and organisations who need to have access to photocopying, fax, wordprocessing and so on. ACE members receive these services at a discounted rate. The first workspace, known as the ACE Enterprise Centre, is located quite near the town centre and is still the headquarters of the ACE group. It is a hive of activity day-to-day as people come and go to make use of the various business services, to attend training courses, to use some of the conference and seminar space which is available for local organisations to rent by the session and to enjoy the internet café. A notable feature is the large and well-used community notice-board and the banner above with the ACE slogan 'There *is* another way!' [1]

In addition to basic office services the ACE Enterprise Centre also offers a full management service to small businesses and several make use of this for regular management accounting, debt collection, assistance with mail-shots and other marketing initiatives. Small business advisers hold regular surgeries at the Centre and tenants can make appointments to see them.

Supporting social enterprise

Also located in the Enterprise Centre is the Anytown Social and Community Enterprise Team (ASCET). Originally the development workers of ASCET were employed by the Council but some years ago it was agreed to set up an 'arms-length' company initially formed in partnership by the Council, ACE and the Anytown Co-operative Retail Society. ASCET's job is to provide support, guidance and encouragement to people in Anytown wishing to set up any form of social enterprise: for example, neighbourhood co-operatives, credit unions, community enterprises or workers' co-operatives. The team works both with groups and with individuals; it provides information, facilitates networking, arranges training, offers or organises specialist expertise as needed, and helps directly with legal structures, business plans and funding applications. Recently ASCET has been restructured as a mutual social economy intermediary organisation with a multistakeholder membership based on clients and supporter members. The three founder organisations retain a seat on the management committee.

Over the years the distinction between social and economic projects in Anytown has become progressively more blurred. The social economy strategy seeks social benefits from business and expects economic gain from social projects. Many of the town's voluntary organisations have taken office and workshop space in the Enterprise Centre so as to take advantage of the facilities available and to keep in touch with other parts of the expanding social economy. Indeed, one plan which has just hit the drawing board is to develop a new purpose-built workspace in the town, Social Economy House, which will act as a home for the growing social and community enterprise sector. The idea is to seek funding from the national lottery to finance such a project, although, as ACE activists have pointed out, if the lottery were itself run as a social enterprise company, there would be more money available to support charitable activity in the country and perhaps more incentive for people to buy tickets each week!

The ACE structure

ACE is a community-based social enterprise with a large and growing membership. Considerable effort is made to keep the members involved and informed and ACE is now in the happy position of being able to employ a part-time membership liaison officer. A quarterly newsletter (*ACE Times*) is sent out to all members and occasional members' meetings are arranged (ACEvents), especially to discuss any tricky issues which emerge from the annual social accounting and audit process. Very recently ACE has included a members' section on its website with an interactive bulletin board to encourage comment, discussion and suggestions.

The ACE Group's board of directors is mostly elected by the members and such is the importance of ACE now in the town that there is always competition for the three places which become vacant each year. A far cry from the early days when only a handful of people attended the AGM and it was a constant headache to get new people to come onto the board! All new directors are given an induction course so that they can quickly understand the workings of the board and of the group of companies as well as their responsibilities as directors. Training may include familiarisation with social and community enterprise for directors who come from a business background and are not conversant with the social economy, or a course in understanding accounts for those new to financial management. Each new director's training is tailored to suit his or her needs. A minority of places on the board is reserved to be filled through nomination by other stakeholder groups. Currently four bodies are allowed to nominate: the Anytown Housing Association, AnyLETS, Anytown Co-operative Retail Society and the Council.

ACE employees have two representatives on the board, elected annually by all members of the group's workforce. Because the ACE group's main company is a charitable holding company, the employees are not able to be directors and vote, but they receive all papers and attend and speak at meetings just as if they were full members of the board. The ACE group is made up of a family of subsidiary companies and projects, and in all these subsidiaries there is provision for employees to elect at least one member onto their company's board. Similarly, where appropriate, there is always provision for customers or beneficiaries to be represented on the board of the subsidiary company or on the management committee of any project which directly affects them.

ACE Training

In the days of the government's job creation scheme run by the then Manpower Services Commission, ACE managed a Community Programme (CP) which ran a number of community benefit projects. ACE found these to be a very good way of getting long-term unemployed people back into the way of working and made sure that their projects were interesting and included a training element. When the CP closed, ACE set up ACE Training and has since been involved in a succession of training programmes, cleverly 'surfing' the ever-changing funding initiatives announced from Brussels and London. ACE Training has run various courses, including some in the areas of community care and administrative skills. One very successful outcome has been the establishment of a community care co-operative, Anyhelp, through which most of the domiciliary care in the town is now organised. Anyhelp is a 'secondary' co-operative which arranges work contracts for all the self-employed carers who are contracted to the co-operative – which indeed they own.

In association with the Industrial Common Ownership Movement (ICOM) ACE Training has operated vocational training schemes for the long-term unemployed and for women returners to the labour market, funded through the European Social Fund. Work placements for trainees have usually been with companies in the ACE Group or with tenant businesses in the ACE Workspaces. ACE now provides the secretariat for a Women's Business Network in Anytown and the surrounding district. Currently ACE is involved with a European Union-funded programme to provide specialist training in the social economy on a regional basis. Part of this has recently involved running awareness courses about the social economy for business advisers working in the Small Business Service and in local authority departments.

For the past four years ACE Training has managed an Intermediate Labour Market (ILM) programme, where trainees learn on the job in a real job, are properly paid and undertake vocational training (usually day release). ACE co-ordinates the programme by supporting other local social enterprises and voluntary organisations to take ILM workers as a means of helping build a new business from scratch. One such enterprise, Anytunnel, is a new independent social enterprise set up to develop a heritage centre, including a shop, a café, and a museum and entertainment venue, in a series of extraordinary underground tunnels which were originally built beneath Anytown by a local philanthropist as an early job creation scheme for unemployed soldiers returning from the Napoleonic wars. ACE is always careful to ensure that ILM workers are not simply used as cheap labour to subsidise an otherwise failing project.

ACE Security

In the early days of ACE's existence one of the biggest problems in the two main housing estates in the town was the level of vandalism and damage to empty council housing. As soon as a house became empty it was wrecked, at great cost to the housing department and the community because vandalised houses could not be let and became yet another eyesore in what were already rather grim areas. After discussions with local residents, members of the ACE board came up with the idea of a community security squad which would employ local people and keep an eye on empty council properties by patrolling the streets 24 hours a day and seven days a week.

It was at first a difficult idea to get across both to the Council and to the police but at last ACE was given the go-ahead for a pilot contract. Training was organised at the local further education college. Local men (no women at that stage) were recruited. Communications equipment and simple uniforms were purchased and a base was set up in one of the empty houses. This proved an instant success. The impact of neighbourhood security went far beyond just keeping an eye on council houses; the whole community became a safer place as crime was reduced, graffiti artists ceased to practise their talents, people could walk about safely at night, the guards kept informal contact with the elderly and the housebound, problems with street lighting were reported instantly to the housing department, used syringes were picked up, emergency services could be called upon at any time of day or night, and doctors were no longer fearful of paying night-time visits.

Neighbourhood security contracts now cover all the public-sector and social housing areas of the town. In some places they are now more like estate caretaking, with security but one of a whole range of tasks carried out to keep the area clean, tidy and safe. Housing associations and some private residential communities have started to buy into the services, for which ACE Security always recruits local people; this, after all, is part of the secret – local people doing local work. For a while this enterprise went through a difficult period when the government introduced Compulsory Competitive Tendering which was designed to strip away any 'non-commercial' factors from the awarding of public-sector contracts. Despite this, Anytown Council officials managed to find ways around and through the rules to keep the neighbourhood security services intact. As soon as the new Best Value regulations were introduced Anytown was quick off the mark to use that regime to strengthen community services, which cannot be measured in money and productivity alone.

In addition to neighbourhood security, the company now provides a full range of security services throughout the town for the private sector. Indeed its reputation is such that it has virtually squeezed out the poor-value security companies by providing a quality service for which companies are willing to pay the proper rate. After some time ACE Security bought a long-established locksmith's retail business in the town; this was not a success, however, and after making a loss the company decided to sell it on. ACE's directors now think that running a town-centre shop is not one of the things community enterprises are good at.

ACE has been criticised for its development of security schemes and estate caretaking (and for its related landscaping enterprise, ACE Scapes) because they are low-wage businesses with relatively low profit margins. The ACE board points out that it pays comparatively well for the industry; that the jobs are the sort which local long-term unemployed people can do and in which they take a real pride, that the services provided are essential, valuable and valued; and that the company has a strong training policy through which it is always looking to improve the skill level and therefore employment potential of individual members of its workforce. And after all, creating employment for over 120 people who were previously among the long-term unemployed is no mean feat! Many ACE employees go on to other jobs in the wider labour market after their spell with ACE. In this sense ACE Security and ACE Scapes are providing the same labour market benefits as ILM schemes but without the subsidy payments. ACE does not pretend that these types of business can solve the fundamental problems of the local economy, but it does argue that they are suitable to have under community control, combining, as they do, business with service, and that community enterprise has in fact demonstrated that it is very good at running such businesses.

Social firms in Anytown

Another enterprise, AnyKleenerStrips, was created in partnership with the local mental health association and provides employment especially for people who are or have been suffering from mental ill-health. The business offers a specialist laundry service for sports clubs in the city and through clever marketing has cornered a regular trade throughout the year. The laundry employs as many as 20 people, but never all at the same time as some people work only part-time and others are erratic in their attendance. Despite these problems the business survives and gives a chance to live a near-normal working life to people who otherwise would not be able to hold down a job. This was the first 'social firm' in Anytown. Since it was set up, two others have been formed, all coming under the umbrella of Anyonecanwork Enterprises, committed to creating employment for people with a disability. The two new businesses are a town-centre guest house, which also has facilities for small conferences, and a gardening service which can be contracted to keep private gardens tidy and to maintain the grounds of various local bodies and companies.

AnyWaste

ACE has adopted a policy of being conscious of its environmental impact and is now working out what that should mean in practice. It has made a start with reducing, reusing and recycling some items and now intends, with help from Friends of the Earth, to examine all its current activities in terms of environmental impact and then develop practical strategies. Discussions with the Council are also leading to some exciting new developments in the light of the Council's recent commitment to a 'zero waste' policy. A new social enterprise, AnyWaste, will be established to undertake kerbside collection of all recyclable materials and to uplift bulky items for refurbishment and re-use from domestic premises. A major recycling centre is to be established on the edge of town where ACE is negotiating to take over the management of the country park which includes a golf course. This could become a major development and include a garden centre (a joint venture with a private company), a regular farmers' market (in association with the local producers' co-operative), new allotments (in association with the Allotments Society) and a new leisure and sports complex (also a joint venture).

ACE trumped

Not everything that ACE has attempted has worked out. Some years ago it established a pottery business, ACE Pots, manufacturing to the design of a potter who had been brought up in Anytown but who had trained and made his reputation in the far west tourist belt. The idea was that ACE Pots would make pottery items for sale to tourist shops in the west. The operation soaked up a lot of capital to prepare and equip the premises. There were technical problems in getting the product to look right. Worst of all was the failure to carry out adequate market research. There wasn't a market. To make things worse, the cost of transport from Anytown made the ACE pots expensive relative to local producers in the tourist belt. A harsh lesson, then, but a salutary one. Luckily ACE was able to lease the fully equipped pottery to a local couple who make their own design pottery commemorating the industrial heritage of Anytown, for which there seems to be a small but growing specialist market.

Social enterprise childcare

Located in the ACE Enterprise Centre is a commercial day nursery for children: ACE Tots. ACE Tots has been set up as a joint venture with a major local private company, ANY plc, and one of the 'privatised' government agencies, Nonquang. The capital cost of developing the nursery has been split three ways between the sponsors, ACE raising its share from the Anytown Community Enterprise Investment Fund (ACEIF). A quarter of the nursery places are reserved for ANY plc and Nonquang to allocate to their employees. For this service they pay a weekly rate sufficient to permit ACE Tots to offer the remaining places either free or at a discount to tenants and to trainees.

In fact, the ACE Group has become involved in childcare provision throughout the town in quite a big way. The Council is keen to see a comprehensive network of different kinds of childcare established and has given ACE funding to employ a childcare development worker. The result is a wide range of initiatives: playgroups, after-school care, playschemes and a childminders' co-operative. Few of these are commercial in the strict business sense, except the childminders' co-operative, but they all operate to a strict pattern of businesslike efficiency even when they depend on volunteer staff and community effort. The books have to balance in all community enterprises. Most of the projects are set up as local neighbourhood enterprises with their own local management committee but draw on the ACE Group's management services team.

Subsidiarity in Anytown

For many years now the ACE Group and the Council have been implementing a policy of 'subsidiarity', devolution to local level. One consequence of this policy has been that the Council has recognised the ACE Group as a key social enterprise in the town and therefore as its natural partner in setting up and running schemes or projects which need to be undertaken on a town-wide basis: things like provision of workspace, security, estate caretaking, or enterprise training. The decision to wind up the Council's own community enterprise team and transfer the staff and funding to ASCET was another example of decentralising and allowing control to pass to the community. Although ACE can be seen to be playing a large and growing role in the economy of the town and as the Council's natural partner for many developments this does not mean that all social and community enterprise in the town is run by or controlled by the ACE Group. Far from it. What has emerged is a growing range of social and community enterprises, some created as subsidiaries of the ACE Group, some as joint ventures with other bodies and yet others as quite independent projects. Some of these, but not all, are tenants of ACE Workspaces and/or make use of the services which the ACE Group supplies through its management services team.

One development of particular interest has been the growth of several neighbourhood enterprises in different parts of the town, running businesses such as local launderettes, community cafés, second-hand clothing shops and food co-operatives as well as the childcare enterprises. One especially successful initiative is the pensioners' pub in the town centre, run by pensioners for pensioners and serving low-cost bar meals, snacks and tea and coffee in addition to licensed drinks.

These neighbourhood enterprises have their own management committees and most draw management services from the ACE Group on a contractual basis. Most, too, operate with volunteer labour although some have paid workers as well – the pensioners' pub for example has a paid daily cook but all the rest of the work is done by pensioner volunteers. In this way important community and neighbourhood services can be provided at low cost, but the enterprises still obey basic trading rules. In Anytown they are considered to be an important part of the local economy, providing services, holding money locally (plugging the leaks) and making slender incomes go that little bit further. They have also been a good training ground for people who have learned about business for the first time and gained the confidence needed to consider having a go at setting up on their own or with others.

Credit unions are another form of social enterprise which is promoted in Anytown. There are currently three community-based credit unions in the town and it is expected that at least two more may be set up. Another credit union serves the local Council workforce. The community-based credit unions are based on relatively small neighbourhoods and are now under pressure to amalgamate as one town-wide union. There is considerable local opposition to this and ASCET is trying to evolve a pattern whereby each credit union can retain its local identity but at the same time share economies and opportunities of scale by working together and with support from the ACE management services team.

Operating out of the ACE Enterprise Centre is the Anytown Local Exchange Trading Scheme (AnyLETS). Known locally as 'the grey pound scheme' because it is co-ordinated by a group of active pensioners, AnyLETS facilitates the exchange of goods and services between individuals for 'grizzlies'. Essentially a multilateral barter system with computerised record-keeping, the scheme allows people to trade their skills for goods and services which others can provide. For some people this is an important way of expanding their domestic economy. For others it offers the chance to test out their ability to provide a service which eventually might become the basis for a small business. For yet others, it allows them to turn a hobby to advantage or to reduce their total dependence on one source of income.

Social housing

A major issue which the ACE activists were concerned about right at the beginning, 20 years ago, was the double problem hitting many local young people: no job and no home. It took a few years and many sessions in the pub after board meetings before this problem was tackled but eventually an exciting idea emerged. Why not set up a scheme which would allow young people to build their own flats, learning construction industry skills at the same time, and then to live in and manage their own homes at the end of the process? And so they did just that. The first scheme was to renovate a couple of terraced houses and turn them into one-bedroom flats, and these became the first properties of the Anytown Youth Homes Housing Co-operative, now with more than 50 flats in the scheme. Their first new-build project, some years later, developed a Foyer to provide student-type accommodation for young people who are not students but are in need of short-term housing. Along the way 12 former trainees set up a small general building workers' co-operative which works throughout the town and often wins contracts from the ACE Group, in particular for carrying out the maintenance work on the workspaces. The Co-op uses the ACE management services team to do its accounting and debt collection and is based in an ACE Workspace.

A further group of former trainees was helped to set up the first self-build co-operative in Anytown. They used the famous Walter Segal design and that first initiative has been the inspiration for 10 other self-build groups in Anytown.[2] The Council has always been supportive of this concept and willing to identify (or persuade private developers to identify) suitable parcels of land for self-build within new housing developments.

That early involvement with the young persons' housing initiative led ACE to think about getting even more involved in housing issues. Surprisingly, at that time there was no local housing association and the large national and regional ones that did operate in the town were perceived as being remote and insensitive. Discussions with a number of other people in the town led to a new steering group being set up to guide a feasibility study into establishing the Anytown Housing Association (AHA). A number of opportunities presented themselves: renovation of older terraced properties, the building of special needs housing for elderly and handicapped people and the development of some empty sites in or adjacent to the two main public-sector housing estates. And so the AHA was born, an organisation quite separate from the ACE Group but with a number of common members and directors and sharing offices and administrative services at the ACE Enterprise Centre.

In its 15 years of life so far AHA has become an important provider of social housing in the town. Recently there has been a stock transfer ballot and the Council tenants of Anytown voted by a large majority to be transferred to AHA. The Council has welcomed this move as it will permit new investment in the town's housing while keeping the social housing stock in local, common ownership. As a mutual society the AHA will involve tenants in the management of their houses, achieving a level of participation the Council would never have been able to match. Everyone in Anytown is relieved that the houses have gone to the local association and not to one of the more anonymous regional or national associations.

ACE Developments

An exciting departure for both ACE and AHA was to set up their own development company, ACE Developments. This company initially came into being as a way in which the local community could put together a new private housing development on a prestigious site near the town centre. ACE Developments was able to organise a package which included social housing developed by AHA and several small private developments all undertaken by local building companies, including one by a self-build group. It is ACE policy always to use local contractors and businesses whenever possible: shop locally for local jobs. Indeed ACE and AHA have always decided against setting up their own in-house building organisation, preferring to give contracts to local small firms, some of them workers' co-operatives.

A current development has earmarked a site for a town swimming pool. The people of Anytown have always wanted a swimming pool but all proposals to date have fallen by the wayside. The present scheme will be run as a social enterprise and the swimming pool development will include an industrial history centre, café and entertainment area and fitness suite. These proposals have involved a wide range of local community organisations such as the sports clubs, local history societies and local schools. Anytown Pool Enterprises (APE) is being established as a separate social enterprise to run this integrated leisure development facility for the town. Its constitution is based on directors being appointed by other local community organisations, including the ACE Group and AHA, working alongside a small group of independent directors.

Meanwhile Anytown Council is in the process of transferring all of its other sports and leisure facilities to an industrial and provident society, Anytown Leisure. The structure involves both employees and users in management – a multistakeholder model. In this way public assets remain in community ownership while management and employees can get on with the job of providing a better-quality service. Financial support from the Council is in the form of contracting for the services to be provided and agreeing clear performance targets with the co-operative.

AnyTune, a Council-initiated social enterprise, was formed as a co-operative of teachers of musical instruments at a time when the Council had to cut the school music service because of budget constraints. AnyTune now contracts directly with the schools in Anytown and farther afield and with private clients. The result is a thriving social enterprise and more music in the air than ever before!

The Council owns the local football stadium, which is leased to Anytown Football Club (AFC). Following the demise of ITV Digital, AFC has been going through a difficult patch, but the plan now is to re-form the club as a mutual society, with supporters – members and fans – represented on the board. AFC will soon be yet another member of the social enterprise family in Anytown.

Any other ideas

ACE Developments has other ideas in the pipeline. One imaginative project is to bring back into productive community use the derelict land under the raised section of the town throughway which was built some years ago, an area which has remained something of a concrete jungle, a no-go area in the evenings and at weekends. Part of the development is likely to include a terminus station for the Anytown and Otherton Light Railway Society, a social enterprise based in nearby Otherton which is refurbishing an old industrial railway line and runs a steam train service throughout the summer as a tourist attraction.

A quite different kind of development which is well advanced in the planning phase is to establish and run a specialist daycare and respite centre for elderly people with Alzheimer's. It is likely that this too will be a joint venture of voluntary sector organisations, with ACE Developments acting as the catalyst and ACE Management Services having a service contract to manage the centre which will otherwise be an entirely independent social enterprise.

Some years ago a new manufacturing business was set up as a joint venture with a large multinational, Califoods, which has a local plant. The business idea came from the management team at the local factory. Originally, they put it forward within the company as an idea to be developed but it was turned down as not being directly relevant to main company policy. After one of the management team heard the ACE manager speak to the local Rotary Club he arranged a meeting to see if the idea could be developed locally for the benefit of the community. Califoods management in California gave permission for the idea to be 'given away' and the corporate social responsibility department became very enthusiastic about the idea. The result was a brand-new high-tech food processing plant developed by Califoods and leased to an operating company, ACE Fresh, which was jointly owned by the ACE Group and Califoods. The agreement was that after all costs had been deducted, including a management services fee to the ACE Group and a royalty payment to Califoods, profits would be paid into the Anytown Community Enterprise Investment Fund (ACEIF). Sadly this venture did not turn out as hoped. Despite the promising calculations in the business plan, the market simply was not there and after nine months ACE Fresh closed down. The experience has made ACE much more cautious about the claims of business plans produced by consultants.

Any profits

ACEIF was set up as an independent body by ACE, the Council and the local Co-op to be the main source of financing for the local social and community enterprises. It suits the Council to do this at arm's length and it has sometimes been possible to off-load year-end 'slippage' funds into ACEIF rather than use them for unnecessary equipment just for the sake of spending the budget. After many years of successfully making loans to local community, co-operative and social enterprises, ACEIF has recently discovered that it is a Community Development Finance Initiative (CDFI) – a new-fangled term, imported from the US, for a local loan fund. ACEIF receives a string of visitors nowadays wanting to know how they manage to make the Fund work. One of ACEIF's secrets is local knowledge and the consequent peer pressure which may be exerted on borrowers. But there is also the framework of support and, perhaps most important, the belief in Anytown that social enterprise works.

ACEIF and the Anytown Co-op have been trying to develop a way of increasing the funds available to ACEIF so that really big investments in new projects may be made, some as equity or patient capital. They have started talking to the Co-operative Bank about how to get more of the Anytown social enterprise funds recycled into investment in local social enterprise. One idea is to have a loan guarantee equivalent to an agreed percentage of social enterprise funds on deposit with the Bank. The other is to establish an investment fund to which social investors can contribute (including profitable Anytown social enterprises) and which will specialise in taking equity investments in social enterprises. It is early days yet, but the social enterprises of Anytown want to create their own financing institutions rather than have to go to the standard banking system which they feel simply does not understand the social economy.

The ACE Group itself has quite clear rules about how its profits may be used. Each year at least 50% of profits must be retained as reserves or for reinvestment in existing or new businesses of the group. Usually more than 50% is used in this way. Of the remainder, half is used to fund a profit-sharing bonus scheme for the employees of the group and the other half is divided equally between ACEIF and a charitable Community Benefit Trust Fund which the ACE Group has established. Trustees of the Fund are elected annually at the AGM and include representatives of the workforce, who after all generate the wealth. The Fund makes its own independent decisions about what to support. Most years the emphasis is on the elderly and the young, but last year they gave a substantial grant to a new hostel for single mothers. The Trustees also act as the ACE Group's social committee and organise an annual programme of social events aimed at involving workers, members, directors and their families and friends in one way or another. The ACE Christmas Party has acquired quite a reputation!

Any added value?

ACE and all the social enterprise sector in Anytown are committed to monitoring each year how well they have achieved their intended objectives and what their stakeholders think about their performance. Each year they produce a set of social accounts which are verified by an independent social audit panel. The social accounting and audit process was introduced some years ago with assistance from the Council who paid for training and for developing a model process which is manageable and which can be adapted to suit the needs of different types and sizes of social enterprise. Now, social accounting, including reporting on environmental impact, has become simply the normal way in which social enterprises in Anytown manage their affairs, report on their performance and engage their stakeholders in shaping the direction and work of each enterprise. Through the social accounts the social enterprises account to their stakeholders, including the Council and other funders who have all agreed that verified social accounts will suffice for reporting purposes. Indeed the funders now recognise that they get a much fuller picture of the added value created by all the social

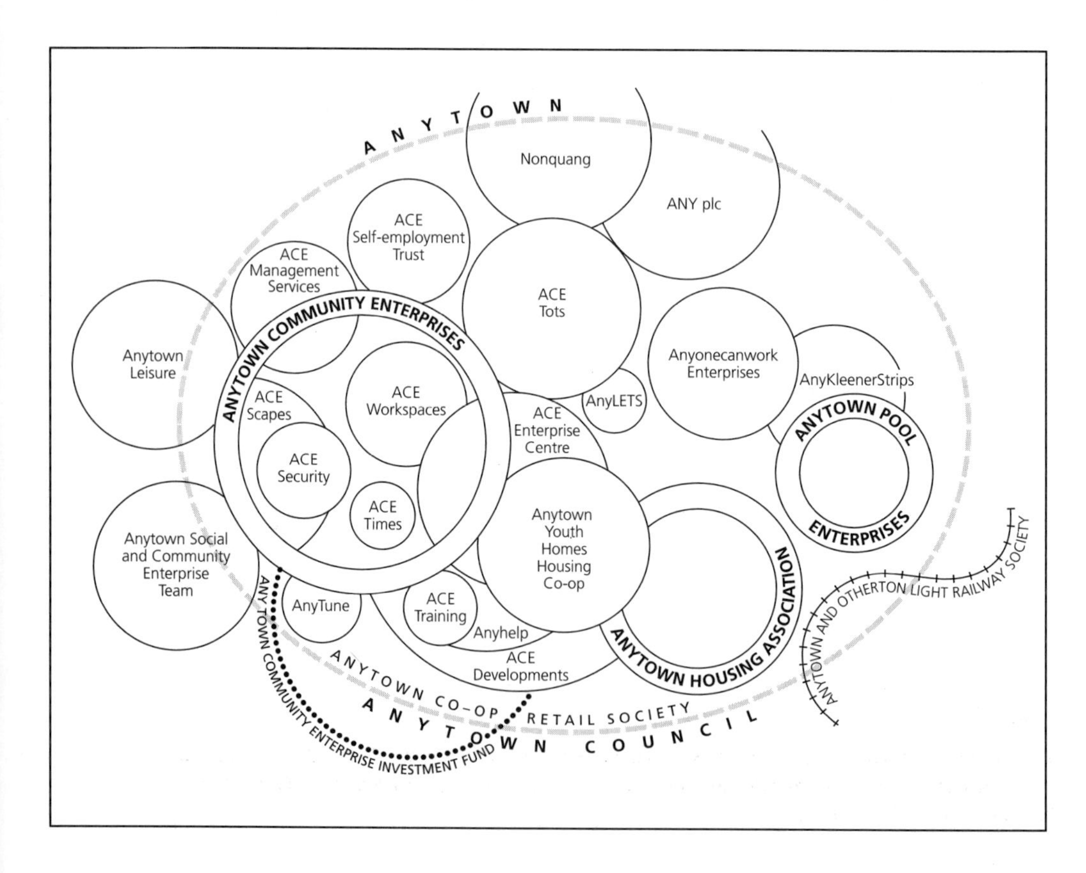

enterprises, with the result that Anytown Council has now decided to undertake a social audit of its own activities and impact. It will be the first local authority in Britain to do this.

Anywhere

Anytown has an intricate network of social economy organisations, all of them enterprising, some more obviously commercial than others, some more successful than others, all having to pay their way, many intertrading and some independent. Some organisations have large memberships, others small. Many have overlapping membership and operating areas. Many residents are either involved with or use several of these community enterprises in the course of a year. All are committed to community ownership and to the reinvestment of profit into the community. All are seeking to better the quality of life for local people rather than to create personal wealth for individuals.

Such is the story of Anytown. It is a story of what social, community and co-operative enterprises can do.

Everything described in Anytown is happening somewhere and everything is possible.

NOTES

1. The slogan 'There is another way!' was that of Coin Street Community Builders in London and for a number of years was displayed on a banner strung across Upper Ground in London SE1.
2. www.segalselfbuild.co.uk

2 Positioning the social economy

The term 'social economy' is relatively new to the English vocabulary, having entered the language from the French little more than a decade ago. Now the social economy, and the social enterprises which populate it, are in common parlance, even if their exact meaning remains elusive. This chapter seeks to develop an understanding of what we might mean by the social economy and to position it in relation to other elements or dimensions of the local, national and global economies.

Three systems

The diagram which follows has been developed over a number of years and results from discussions between partners in a series of transnational European research and action projects. [1]

First, it divides the economy into three systems each of which can be seen to be based on quite different principles or values. The word 'system' is preferred to the more usual 'sector' because each system is essentially about a different way of managing the economy, about a different 'mode of production'. The word 'sector' implies, rather, that there is one homogeneous economy which can, like Gaul and for convenience, be divided into three parts. Second, the diagram shows the different 'levels' in the economy through concentric circles from neighbourhood (in the centre), through district and regional, to national and international.

The first system, otherwise referred to as the private sector, is profit-driven, based on the capitalist principles of maximising return for private shareholders and, at worst, ruthlessly using human and natural resources to achieve that end. The first system operates through the (allegedly) free marketplace, meeting (and perhaps inventing) needs through the production of goods and the provision of services by companies. The primacy of concern for shareholders is enshrined in the legislation which provides the operating framework for these companies. The system embraces the micro-enterprises and small businesses of the local level through to the largest of multi- and transnational corporations which dominate world trade and which epitomise contemporary market capitalism with a scale and power of operation never before seen and exceeding that of many nation states. The first system is founded on competition, celebrates individual gain and maximises profit ahead of other considerations.

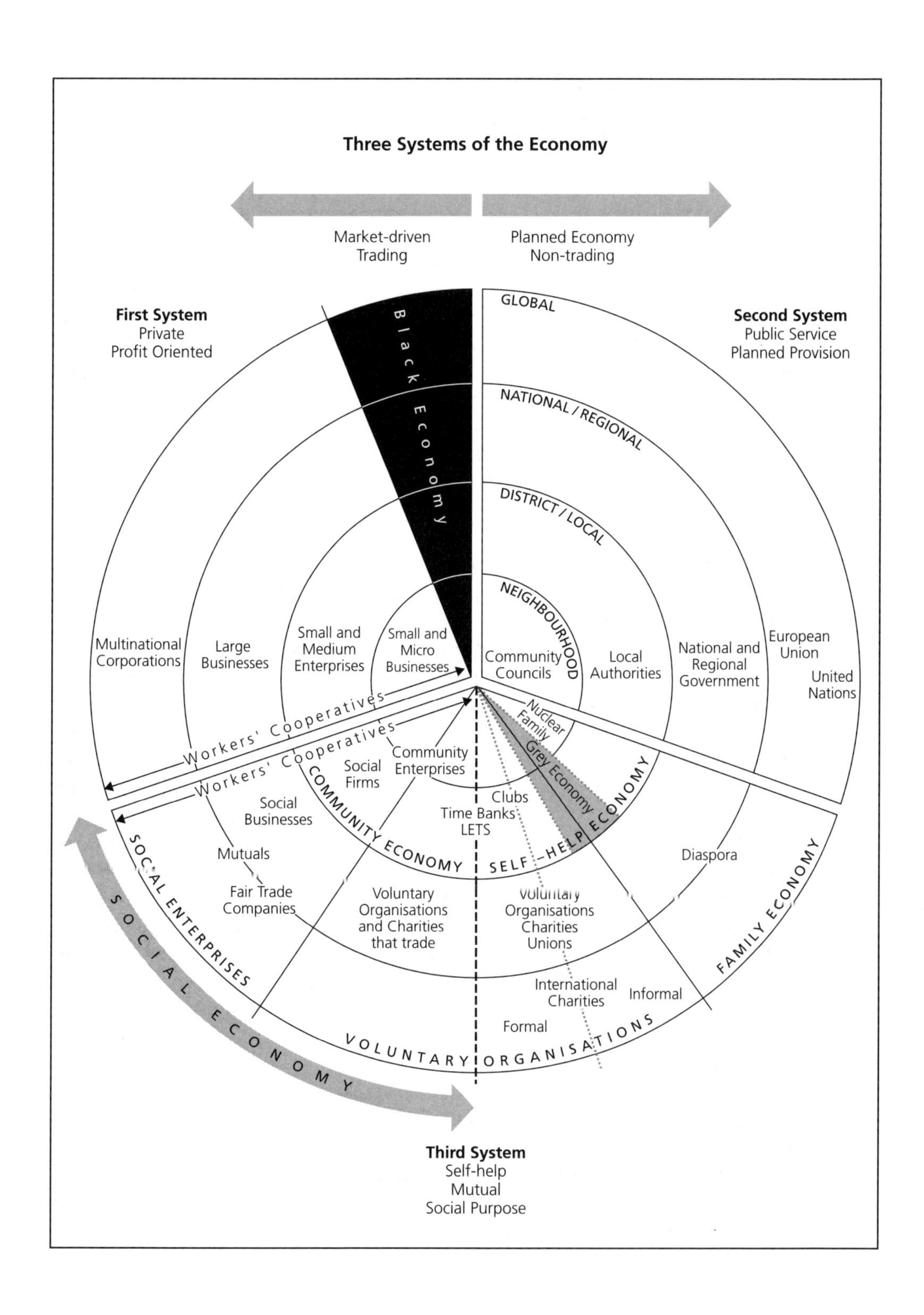

Three Systems of the Economy
Market-driven
Trading
Planned Economy
Non-trading
First System
Private
Profit Oriented
Second System
Public Service
Planned Provision
Black Economy
GLOBAL
NATIONAL / REGIONAL
DISTRICT / LOCAL
NEIGHBOURHOOD
Multinational Corporations
Large Businesses
Small and Medium Enterprises
Small and Micro Businesses
Community Councils
Local Authorities
National and Regional Government
European Union
United Nations
Workers' Cooperatives
Workers' Cooperatives
Nuclear Family
Grey Economy
Community Enterprises
Social Firms
Social Businesses
Mutuals
Fair Trade Companies
COMMUNITY ECONOMY
SELF-HELP ECONOMY
Clubs
Time Banks
LETS
Voluntary Organisations and Charities that trade
Organisations
Charities
Unions
Diaspora
FAMILY ECONOMY
SOCIAL ENTERPRISES
International Charities
Informal
Formal
VOLUNTARY ORGANISATIONS
SOCIAL ECONOMY
Third System
Self-help
Mutual
Social Purpose

The second system is about redistribution and planning, where the local district or the state takes the responsibility for providing services for the people and for managing aspects of the economy to that end. Conventionally referred to as the public sector, the second system is based on the principle of public service by democratically elected institutions. However the system has come to be seen as bureaucratic, paternalistic, centralised and inefficient, and in too many cases the democratic process has failed or been side-stepped. The nadir of the system was the failure of the centrally planned, totalitarian oligarchies of the former communist bloc. Beset by criticism and generally losing ground to the first, the second system nonetheless has played and continues to play a key role in the economy of all nations.

The third system is about citizens taking action to meet and satisfy needs themselves and working together in some collaborative way to do this. The third system embraces the domestic economy of the family and the informal economy of the neighbourhood through to the more formally structured institutions of the voluntary sector and those of the social economy. It is based on the principles of self-help and mutuality, of caring for others and of meeting social needs rather than maximising profit.

In all societies these three systems co-exist, with one or other of the first two in the ascendant. In contemporary western economies it is very much the first, private profit-oriented, system which has increasingly dominated in recent decades while the second, public service, system has been systematically diminished. Yet in wartime conditions and throughout the post-war reconstruction years the second system played a central role in many nations' affairs and fortunes.

The third system has rarely been accorded its due recognition. Indeed many commentators would argue that the social enterprise 'wedge' of the diagram should really be seen as a subset of the first system, leaving the remainder of the third system as a third sector with little or no recognised economic influence or importance. Such an argument fails to recognise the importance of the common value base which underpins the whole of the third system and which binds it together as another way of doing things. It also fails to see the crucial importance of all parts of the third system to the economy generally and notably to the smooth functioning of the first and second systems themselves. These depend entirely on the daily transactions within families and neighbourhoods: caring for the elderly and for children, preparing food and other domestic work, the mutual assistance of giving lifts and child-minding, running social clubs and the institutions of civic society – all work of unrecognised economic value but without which other parts of the economy would founder.

The three systems are fundamentally different ways of running the economy, but they should not be seen as mutually exclusive. Past experience of allowing one or other of the first and second systems to dominate has been unsuccessful. The centrally planned economies of the eastern bloc ultimately failed, leaving a heritage of run-down infrastructure, environmental degradation, collapsed industries and public services – to say nothing of decades of no democracy, no civil society and little scope for initiative and enterprise. However, the recent experience of the dominant first system, especially since the end of the cold war, has seen an increase in global problems such as poverty, ill-health and under-education. Disparities between rich and poor, both within nations and between nations, have grown, and the system has failed to address the serious environmental issues facing the planet as natural resources are depleted and toxic wastes and greenhouse gas emissions proliferate.

Nowhere, yet, has the third system been given the political and popular support to allow it to dominate, although chapter 1 attempted to envisage how things might be if that were to happen in one town. Were the third system to dominate it should not, however, be to the exclusion of the first and second systems. The third system would preside over a mixed economy of systems but third-system values would be expected to affect and influence the other systems and so constrain the excesses to which both, in different ways, are prone.

The diagram also distinguishes market-driven economic activity (the left side) from activity planned and managed largely by the state to provide services and goods (the right side). The left side can therefore be characterised as *trading* in the open marketplace whereas the right side is either *non-trading* or functioning in a managed or planned market. The first system is located wholly to the trading (market) side and includes within it the illegal or black economy while the second system is located on the non-trading (planned) side. It is perhaps an over-simplification which misses the grey areas where second-system agencies engage in trade and where first-system bodies work in partnership with the public sector. However it is a useful and important broad distinction to make, not least because the third system spreads over both sides of that trading/non-trading line.

Wedges of the third system

The third system is divided into a number of 'wedges'. To the right is what can be called the family or domestic economy – all that work within the nuclear and extended families (and even within the international diaspora) which makes society tick, the work which is seldom counted but which the other systems take for granted. To the right are also found the associations which people form so that they can organise how to do things for themselves, to help others, to campaign, or to represent the interests of certain groups. Sometimes these will be simple, informal associations with no legal structure: at neighbourhood level the baby-sitting circle, the reading group, the pub quiz team; at international level the e-mail network campaign group. Then there are more structured associations: sports clubs and teams, community and tenants' associations, allotment groups and over-60s clubs, right through to the voluntary organisations and charities which function at district, regional, national or international levels; trades unions and other solidarity associations and networks at all levels.

On the trading side we find those voluntary organisations which engage, to some extent, in commercial activity: selling a service or making a product for sale, often for fundraising purposes. The divide between trading and non-trading can be blurred: the pre-school playgroup can be seen as a neighbourhood enterprise, often employing a part-time leader and depending on parents paying for their children to attend, but most people will think of it not as an enterprise but as a community group. Similarly with the village hall association, as it maintains the hall and generates sufficient revenue from lets and other sources to pay the bills each year. The trading aspect of charity shops is seen as fundraising rather than business, and the idea of voluntary organisations running training courses under contract has yet to be properly recognised as trade.

Within the local neighbourhood segment of the third system we have located, opposite the illegal sector in the first system, what might best be described as the informal or grey sector. This includes the exchange of goods and services between individuals and groups where the value is not declared for tax or benefit purposes. It is thus strictly speaking illegal, but there are few people who do not from time to time take advantage of work done 'on the side' as a 'homer' or on a 'paperwork (i.e. – VAT)-free' basis. In the third system this grey local economic activity contributes to the survival of many and can evolve into legitimate enterprise endeavour as part of a Local Exchange Trading System (LETS) scheme, as a micro-enterprise or even as a community enterprise.

At neighbourhood level, also straddling the trading/non-trading divide, we find such organisations as LETS and time banks, formally organised institutions allowing members to provide and exchange goods and services, but on a barter or a time-credit system.

The social economy

The social economy is defined as all that part of the third system which is on the trading side. It includes therefore all those community and voluntary organisations which are involved in trading and all those in the social enterprise wedge of the diagram adjacent to the first system. This wedge comprises organisations which are *primarily* engaged in trading; their purpose is social but they achieve their purpose by being in business, by making products and providing services which are sold in the marketplace. At neighbourhood and local, district level these social enterprises are usually closely linked to their particular locality and so are more aptly known as community enterprises. Others, with a commitment to a membership or beneficiary constituency which is not geographically-based, are known as social enterprises. Thus community enterprises may be seen as a subset of social enterprises. The part of the trading wedge at neighbourhood and district levels, where there is a strong sense of local affiliation and identity, may be designated the 'community economy', while the adjacent non-trading wedge may be referred to as the 'self-help' sector.

This book is essentially about the social enterprise wedge although it also touches on the broader social economy including those voluntary organisations which carry out some trading. Nonetheless at all times it must be remembered that social enterprises are part of the wider third system. Throughout the book the term 'community enterprise' will be used for those enterprises located at neighbourhood or district level and rooted in the locality which they seek to benefit. All other enterprises will be referred to as social enterprises, including those which in the past have been described as community enterprises based on a community of interest. That has been a confusing concept. It is simpler to restrict the term 'community enterprise' to those with a definite local, geographical base and to use 'social enterprise' to include all those with a constituency which is not based on geography.

Within the social enterprise wedge is found a myriad of different designations for social enterprises. Each term has passionate adherents and each reflects a subtle shade of emphasis, intention or structure. The following table attempts to list all terms currently in use and to distinguish between those which may generally be considered to refer to community enterprises and those which are usually thought of as applying to social enterprises. It is not an exact science and some, of course, necessarily feature in both categories. For example, a social firm may be rooted in a neighbourhood or it may serve a constituency of people with a particular need over a district or a region. A credit union may be local community- or neighbourhood-based or it may have the common bond of a company or public-sector agency or of a much wider geographical area.

COMMUNITY ENTERPRISES	SOCIAL ENTERPRISES
Common ownership company	Building society
Community-based housing association	Charity trading arm
Community benefit corporation	Consumer retail society
Community business	Credit union
Community co-operative	Fair trade company
Community credit union	Housing association
Community development corporation	Intermediate labour market company
Community Development Finance Initiative	Marketing co-operative
Community housing trust	Mutual co-operative society
Community interest company	Public interest company
Community trading organisation	Social business
Community trust	Social firm
Employee-ownership business	Workers' co-operative
Housing co-operative	
(Local) Development trust	
Local Exchange Trading Scheme	
Neighbourhood co-operative	
Neighbourhood enterprise	
Social co-operative	
Social firm	
Time bank	
Voluntary enterprise	
Workers' co-operative	
NEIGHBOURHOOD • LOCAL • DISTRICT	REGIONAL • NATIONAL • INTERNATIONAL

There are other terms, not appearing in the table, which are more correctly forms of legal structure and these will be referred to later in that context (co-operative society, society for the benefit of the community, friendly society, company limited by guarantee.)

Some terms have developed rather precise meanings in recent years. A 'social firm' has come to mean an enterprise which specialises in employing people with some form of disability, physical or mental, and expects that at least 25% of its employees are drawn from that beneficiary constituency. A social firm is likely to be engaged in more than one trading activity. One which focuses on one activity and is structured as a workers' co-operative will more likely be called a 'social co-operative'.

In the 1980s the term 'community business' was the one most commonly used for all community-based enterprises, aiming to undertake a number of different activities, commercial and non-commercial. Today the generic term is 'social or community enterprise' and 'community business' tends to be reserved for locally based enterprises which focus on one specific trading activity. A 'social business', on the other hand, is taken to be an enterprise with a social purpose, which although often structured as a charitable trust, has little or no democratic accountability to a beneficiary group or community constituency.

Not all workers' co-operatives will necessarily be social enterprises and some may be considered (or will prefer to consider themselves) as part of the first system. The issue revolves around whether the workers' co-operative adopts the agreed defining characteristics of a social enterprise (see chapter 3). If the main purpose of the co-operative is to maximise profit for the working members, then it can easily be seen to be part of the first system, albeit with a commitment to operating to internal democratic standards. However, if the main purpose is understood more as social, for example the retention of jobs in a local community for present and future generations, or the allocation of (some) profits for community benefit, then the co-operative may be recognised as a social enterprise within the third system.

Unsurprisingly the world of social enterprise has developed its own jargon and a glossary of the main terms used in the writings and debates about the social economy can be found on pages 185–92.

As part of the third system social enterprises are predicated on certain values and key characteristics which distinguish them from organisations in the first and second systems. It is to those defining characteristics and values that make social enterprises 'another way of doing things' that we now turn.

NOTES

1. Karl Birkholzer *et al.*, *Key Values and Structures of Social Enterprises in Western Europe: Concepts and principles for new economy* (Technologie-Netzwerk Berlin with European Network for Economic Self-Help and Local Development, 1997); Birkholzer *et al.*, *The Employment Potential of Social Enterprises in Six EU Member States* (Interdisziplinäre Forschungsgruppe Lokale Ökonomie with European Network Berlin, 1999); and M.D. Evans *et al.*, *Key Concepts, Measures and Indicators* (Conscise Project, Middlesex University, 2000).

3 Defining social and community enterprise

In the previous chapter, we established that the phrase 'community enterprise' will be used specifically for those social enterprises which have a direct link to a geographical community. Thus community enterprises can be seen as a subset of social enterprises, which in turn form a part of the social economy, itself a part of the third system operating in the global economy. Now we turn to identifying the defining characteristics of social enterprises and then to the values on which they are founded.

While there is a considerable element of agreement on definitions of social enterprise (see the box on the following pages) there remain important areas of uncertainty and vagueness. Some even argue that social enterprises 'defy definition' or that definitions are unimportant as 'you know a social enterprise, like an elephant, when you see one' and 'it is best to get on with the job' rather than waste time in classification.

It is certainly true that considerable amounts of energy and passion have been devoted to the debate about definitions and that the process can sometimes be a distraction. However, a clear and unambiguous understanding of what social enterprises are and of the values on which they are based is essential, for two reasons.

First, it is important to differentiate social enterprise from the other systems, to establish its unique selling point. Some would prefer social enterprises simply to be a subset of the first, private, system and/or of the second, public, system. In this way social enterprises may be absorbed into the value and practice frameworks of the other systems and coupled to their purposes. If social enterprises are part of a third system which is 'another way of doing things', then it is essential that the values which distinguish social enterprises from private and from public enterprises are quite clear.

Second, it is important to know what is *not* a social enterprise, especially if certain fiscal and other benefits are to be offered to social enterprises to encourage their growth and to strengthen the third system in the UK economy.

Characteristics

There are six defining characteristics fundamental to social enterprise:

1. having a *social purpose or purposes*;
2. achieving the social purposes by, at least in part, *engaging in trade* in the marketplace;

3. *not distributing profits* to individuals;
4. holding assets and wealth *in trust for community benefit;*
5. *democratically* involving members of its constituency in the governance of the organisation; and
6. being independent organisations *accountable* to a defined constituency and to the wider community.

Definitions of social enterprise

'A social enterprise is a business with primarily social objectives whose surpluses are principally reinvested for that purpose in the business or in the community, rather than being driven by the need to maximise profits for shareholders and owners.' [1]

'Social enterprises

- Are not-for-profit organisations.
- Seek to meet social aims by engaging in economic and trading activities.
- Have legal structures which ensure that all assets and accumulated wealth are not in the ownership of individuals but are held in trust and for the benefit of those persons and/or areas that are the intended beneficiaries of the enterprise's social aims.
- Have organisational structures in which full participation of members is encouraged on a co-operative basis with equal rights accorded to all members.' [2]

'...organisations who are independent of the state and provide services, goods and trade for a social purpose and are non-profit-distributing.' [3]

'Social enterprises are competitive businesses, owned and trading for a social purpose. [They] have three common characteristics:

Enterprise orientation – [are] directly involved in producing goods or providing services to a market...seek to be viable trading concerns, making an operating surplus.

Have explicit social aims...have ethical values...are accountable to their members and the wider community for their social, environmental and economic impact.

Social ownership – are autonomous organisations with governance and ownership structures based on participation by stakeholder groups...profits are distributed as profit-sharing to stakeholders or used for the benefit of the community.' [4]

'Community enterprise organisations working for sustainable regeneration in their community through a mix of economic, environmental, cultural and social activities. They are independent, not-for-private-profit organisations, locally accountable and committed to involving local people in the process of regeneration.' [5]

'A community co-operative is a multifunctional business run for local benefit and directly owned and controlled by the community in which it operates. Some of its activities may be social in character, but it must make a profit overall.' [6]

'A community business is a sustainable commercial enterprise which is owned and controlled by the local community. It aims to create jobs and related training opportunities and to encourage local economic activity. Profits are used to create more jobs and businesses and to generate wealth for the benefit of the community.' [7]

'Social enterprises try to make a profit, but they operate on a not-for-personal-profit basis, applying any surplus they create to furthering their social objectives. They put people first and, through their economic activities, seek to deliver employment opportunities and other social, environmental, or community benefits.' [8]

'A community enterprise is a non-profit-making organisation which is controlled and run by local people in the community. It is sustainable in the sense that it manages to raise enough funds through its activities or through fundraising in order to make ends meet financially.' [9]

Social purpose

The primary purpose of a social enterprise is social: it aims to benefit the community or a specific beneficiary group. Commercial activity is secondary in the sense that it is the means to achieving the primary purpose.

For most social enterprises their social purpose is clear – although not always explicitly stated (see chapter 11 and Appendix ii on social accounting and audit): for example, creating employment for the long-term unemployed; providing training and work for people with a disability; providing a specific service to the community; selling fairly traded goods. Most social enterprises will have more than one objective. Indeed, one of the more exciting and creative aspects of social accounting for any organisation can be the process of exploring and agreeing all of its objectives, both internal and external.

The word 'social' must also be taken to include environmental factors and, indeed, for some social enterprises their primary purpose will be to achieve an environmental impact by, for example, recycling, organic food production or running a farmers' market. Any socially responsible organisation must be environmentally responsible. For social enterprises that should mean adopting practices which are environmentally non-injurious and moving towards reporting on their environmental as well as their social impacts. Social enterprises have not always had a good record so far as adopting environmental policies and practices is concerned and this remains an area for focused attention in the future.

For a small number of social enterprises, most likely community enterprises, their primary purpose is to benefit the local community by distributing profits as grants to community projects. They aim to maximise profits from trading in order to redistribute as much as possible to benefit the local community, and in that way are essentially a fundraising operation. However, it would be expected that even such profits-focused community enterprises would have subsidiary social purposes such as employing local people, resourcing supplies locally and, of course, adopting environmentally sound practices.

In the case of a workers' co-operative, if the sole purpose is maximising profit for the working group that would probably make it part of the first, private, system rather than a social enterprise. However, most workers' co-operatives do have social purposes such as safeguarding employment opportunities for future workers; being committed to a particular locality; retaining a percentage of profits for wider community benefit; and being proactive in promoting the third system. Such social objectives would qualify a workers' co-operative to be recognised as a social enterprise.

In the case of the larger mutual societies their purpose historically has been to provide a quality, good-value service for their members and this remains their primary purpose. However, they have also adopted additional social purposes which can be made explicit and reported on. Examples are the Co-operative Bank's pioneering ethical policies and the Co-operative Movement's recent recognition of its role as the largest player in the social economy and its commitment to benefit the wider community through its Co-operative Action Foundation. [10]

The purpose of social enterprises is to contribute to the common good, to benefit society and, more widely, the planet. Specific objectives will fit within this overarching sense of social purpose. Social enterprises are not primarily about running businesses.

Engaging in trade

It is a *sine qua non* that social enterprises engage to some degree in trade by providing goods and services for which customers pay. Engaging in such economic activity is how social enterprises achieve their social purpose.

This apparently simple proposition gives rise to a number of key questions:

- what counts as trading income?
- to what extent may a social enterprise be dependent on non-trading income?
- does 'trading' mean only the exchange of goods and services for money?

Most social enterprises generate a mix of income streams in order to pay their way:

1. cash trading receipts from the sale of goods and services;
2. contracts, including service level agreements, usually with the public (or quasi-public) sector to deliver services;

3. grants from the public sector;
4. grants from trusts and foundations;
5. revenue subsidies;
6. volunteer labour;
7. fundraising activities.

The growth of cash trading receipts from the open marketplace is clearly the most straightforward route to self-sufficiency and independence and so is for most social enterprises their holy grail. However, for many it remains just as elusive as the grail because of what they do and where they do it. Some social enterprises may always depend on other sources of income. It is a commonly held, but mistaken, assumption that self-sufficiency from trading receipts somehow makes one social enterprise 'better' than another.

Much of the work of social enterprises is contracted from public-sector bodies and these contracts can range from the straightforwardly commercial to the undoubtedly 'soft'. The move to contracts rather than grant-aid has generally been welcomed by social enterprises as it should clarify just what is expected of them: if they deliver, they get paid; if they do not deliver, they do not. The advent of 'Best Value' to replace the earlier Compulsory Competitive Tendering system has reintroduced the possibility of public agencies taking into consideration non-commercial aspects (and, therefore, desired benefits) when determining contracts. It appears, however, that significant numbers of authorities still remain reluctant to make use of the potential flexibility of Best Value and others struggle with determining just what non-commercial factors may be specified and how these intended benefits can be monitored and measured.

These are difficult, but not impossible, issues to resolve. The principles have now become clear. Best Value permits authorities to specify contracts in such a way that non-commercial factors can be considered. One important area of specification concerns limiting the size of contracts to ensure that smaller, local community-based social enterprises may be able to consider tendering. Social enterprises in return need to be clear about what added value they can offer and how they can demonstrate that such added value is being delivered.

It follows that grants in the traditional sense should be a dying species. On reflection, it is surprising that for so long the public agencies (and trusts and foundations) have given out substantial grants with often minimal requirements to report back. Social enterprises and the voluntary sector have been much criticised for being grant-dependent; seldom do we read any acknowledgement from the grant-givers that maybe their practices have been at fault. There is evidence to suggest that the grant-aid mentality, so roundly criticised, derives not from the community organisations and social enterprises themselves, but from the grant-givers.

There is much loose talk about reducing dependency on grants and shifting to an enterprising 'contract culture'. If social enterprises are expected to absorb the social costs inevitable in employing people with disadvantages and running businesses in low-income communities (as well as servicing the debt finance which comes with a shift from a grant to a loan culture) then they will be doomed to failure. Such social costs cannot usually be covered through ordinary trading but must be specified and paid for as part of any contract. It is heartening that the recently published Department of Trade and Industry strategy for social enterprises recognises 'that for some [social enterprises] the social cost of their businesses will always be too great to permit the business to generate sufficient surpluses unless that cost is paid for, at least in part, by some other means'.[11]

Grant-givers might also reflect on how their own rigid operating procedures sometimes militate against community organisations acting like social enterprises: grants being reduced (known as 'clawback') if the organisation manages to make savings or generate more than anticipated revenue, or budget allocations being so compartmentalised that under-spending may not be transferred to another purpose.

Revenue subsidies include such assistance as peppercorn rents for buildings, or use of machinery or other services free of charge, and other ways in which the costs of a social enterprise can be reduced, such as materials being donated by private businesses.

Unpaid labour is another significant way in which social enterprises can 'generate income'. Volunteers play a key role, not only when the enterprise is being planned, but often throughout its day-to-day life. Without such help many enterprises would not survive. One thinks of the island shop where volunteer directors help out at peak times and by so doing ensure that the shop remains viable and able to provide a service to the islanders. There is the community café, or the food co-operative, which runs entirely on volunteer labour and so is able to offer good-value food at affordable prices to local residents, or the multi-functional community centre which creates some paid jobs but which depends on volunteer input to survive.

It is fashionable to dismiss such social enterprises as 'not real businesses' but such criticism overlooks four important points. First, these enterprises can make an important contribution to a local economy by ensuring that certain services are available and affordable. Second, such enterprises may evolve over time into businesses better able to pay more staff and become more financially sustainable. Third, they serve as an enterprise training ground for individuals who may go on to start their own micro-business or other community enterprise. Fourth, pots should always be careful about calling kettles black. There are many small private businesses (farms and corner shops for example) which depend significantly on the unpaid effort of family members to survive. Why is it that they are acclaimed as hard-working examples of private enterprise while the social enterprise is written off as no more than an unviable community organisation dependent on volunteers?

Fundraising can be hard work and it may be for that reason that in the US funds which a community organisation raises are often counted as earned income rather than grants. Certainly it would be good to move away from judgemental criticism of organisations that have to engage in various forms of fundraising (much of it very enterprising) to survive. After all, if we think of it as raising investment, there is not such a huge distinction between fundraising and a share issue.

While social enterprises must trade in the marketplace they will also seek other sources of revenue to achieve sustainability. They should not be judged by whether they are businesses 'like any other' but by whether they are successful social enterprises, effectively meeting their objectives to benefit society, and be financially sustainable.

Non-profit distributing

The principle that social enterprises should not distribute profits to members or to directors (except as a reward for work done) is generally accepted. Essentially, social enterprises do not operate in order to increase the personal wealth of those involved in them and they do not allow external owners of capital to exert control because of their share-holding. Profits, after all costs have been met, including paying proper wages and paying for the cost of capital, are reserved for reinvestment in the enterprise (or new ventures), for the benefit of the defined community or constituency, and for bonus payments related to work done. In India such bonus payments are made through the device of paying a thirteenth month's salary in each year.

It is reasonable for a social enterprise to establish mechanisms which can reward its workers or its customers for their effort in achieving commercial survival and success. This can be arranged through some form of bonus payment scheme (or 'divi' or discount for customers) or through an accumulating savings account which the employee may access at some point in the future. These are rewards for work done or volume of purchases made and are not related to any capital contribution.

Similarly, any capital used by the social enterprise has to be paid for. If it is debt finance (e.g. a loan) then interest must be paid as well as the regular capital repayments. If it can be some form of equity then there will be a deferred payment which relates, like workers' bonuses, to performance.

Usually, a social enterprise will specify a maximum amount of profits which may be used for workforce bonuses and customer benefits, and a minimum amount which should be paid for community benefit.

Assets held 'in trust'

This is the common-ownership principle whereby the assets of a social enterprise may not be sold off and divided amongst the workers, directors, members or other group of stakeholders. The assets, including accumulated wealth, are held in trust for whatever constituency (or community in the case of community enterprises) the social enterprise exists to benefit. This is a key distinguishing feature and a generally accepted principle.

Nonetheless it is today being argued by some that a form of common ownership is not essential and that social enterprises may take the form of a private company limited by shares. 'The [Social Investment] Task Force takes the view that not all social and community enterprises need to have social ownership. Some are structured as traditional enterprises while still serving a social purpose and placing great emphasis on their accountability to the communities they serve.' [12] While it is undoubtedly true that some privately owned enterprises may deliver significant social benefit, they should not be recognised as social enterprises, for which the principle of common ownership should be reaffirmed as a non-negotiable defining characteristic.

Democracy

Having a democratic structure through which members can exercise control over the organisation is seemingly the most contentious of the defining characteristics and the one most likely to cause concerns to some people.

Community enterprises are established in order to benefit the residents of a particular geographical locality and it seems right as well as logical that the enterprise should be accountable to the people of that locality. Various other 'channels of accountability' may be established (see below) but the key one will be a democratic membership structure open to residents of the locality as well as to other stakeholders. That membership will elect at least a majority of the board of management.

In the case of social enterprises serving a separate community of interest such as a particular group of beneficiaries, it should be expected that they will also have some form of open membership through which their beneficiaries (or representatives of their beneficiaries) can legitimately be involved in governance and to whom the enterprise is expected to account for its performance.

There is a problem with those enterprises, usually calling themselves social businesses or social firms, which have been set up by one group of people in order to benefit another group. While the purpose may be entirely laudable and their performance extremely positive, it is hard to see how an enterprise which has no membership or denies a democratic voice to its constituency can be accepted as a genuine social enterprise. Then there are those enterprises which reject the idea of having any democracy in their structure – 'we are not a democratic experiment' – and those who argue that accountability may be achieved 'through market forces'.

Most legal structures adopted by social and community enterprises are based on the 'one member, one vote' principle. In a 'multistakeholder' model more than one membership constituency may be defined and each will have the right to elect representatives onto its board of directors or management committee.

The democracy issue goes much deeper. The third system essentially makes up what is often referred to as 'civil society', the institutions of the people through which the people organise themselves. And it is through organising in communities and in associations that the health of a society is maintained (see chapter 6 on social capital for a discussion of the importance of trust and effective networks to a community).

More than that, engaging in civil society is part of an engagement with the broader democratic process. Associations and clubs usually have democratic constitutions which permit all members an equal voting say in managing the affairs of the organisation. At a time when interest in elective democracy is waning and electoral turnouts are at an all-time low, any encouragement to people's participation in democratic processes should be welcomed. Social enterprises can play an important role by setting good examples of functioning democracy and encouraging people to participate in that process. It should be unthinkable that a genuine social enterprise can claim that democracy is unimportant or that encouraging democracy is 'not one of our objectives'.

Involving members in governance through an elective process does not imply that there is no place for engaging other, non-member stakeholders. Many social enterprises specify a mix of membership on their boards of management such that partner organisations, funding agencies, customer representatives and technical specialists can have a place and contribute to the way in which the social enterprise is managed. Where such 'partnership boards' are created, it should be axiomatic that the majority always rests with those elected from the recognised constituent membership on a one member, one vote basis. Within the Co-operative Movement, there is growing interest in multistakeholder co-operatives, recognising that different groups have an interest in the enterprise and, therefore, a legitimate claim to be involved in its governance. Typically, stakeholders will include workers, consumers/customers and the local community in which the enterprise operates.

Accountability

The sixth defining characteristic of social enterprises is accountability, to its membership (constituency) and also to the wider community. This issue of accountability is discussed in more detail in chapter 11 and a model process for social accounting and audit is also described in Appendix ii.

Accountability means accounting openly to stakeholders for what the organisation does – primarily to those people whom it affects. Practising accountability requires effective methods of gathering relevant information, consulting stakeholders, reporting on impacts and discussing the implications. It also requires the establishment of 'channels of accountability', the various ways through which an organisation engages with its stakeholders and reports on its performance.

Accounting should cover all that the organisation does to achieve its purpose and how it does it, as well as the values which underpin its work. Social enterprises should routinely recognise the need to report not just on social impact, but also on environmental impact, and not just on external impact, but also on how they function internally as an organisation. Accountability therefore goes beyond the immediate stakeholders affected by the social enterprise to the wider community, the general public. This idea of 'horizontal accountability' recognises that society has a legitimate right to know what benefits or dis-benefits an organisation is producing.

To date accountability practice by social enterprises has been patchy, although there is now a growing interest in social accounting and audit processes and a greater understanding of the need for more transparent methods for reporting on their performance, in ways which embrace the triple bottom line of social, environmental and financial performance. For a number of years some of the model constitutions available to social enterprises have included a social audit clause requiring the enterprise to report on social and environmental performance.[13] However, the inclusion of a clause in a constitution does not always translate into practice!

Thus we can identify six defining characteristics for a social enterprise which should be applied to all enterprises within the social enterprise wedge, from the smallest neighbourhood-based community enterprise through to the largest mutual society trading internationally. It should be possible to develop some form of 'social enterprise test' which establishes whether an organisation meets the six characteristics sufficiently to be recognised as a bona fide social enterprise. Chapter 8 considers how these defining characteristics might be tested and also how they can be embedded in social enterprise constitutions and into a process of regulation. We shall now continue by exploring the values which might be expected to underpin social enterprises and which, while not defined in constitutions, represent the ethical framework of the third system.

Values in the social economy

Certain defining characteristics distinguish social enterprises from first-system businesses and those characteristics should be enshrined in the legal structures they adopt. The third system is also predicated on values which make it quite distinct from the other two systems.

The European Network for Economic Self-Help and Local Development has defined 11 value statements in its paper *Key Values and Structure of Social Enterprises in Western Europe*.[14] These make up a form of charter to which all social economy organisations might be expected to subscribe. Some elements of the European Network's charter are covered by the defining characteristics already discussed, but there remain six further aspects of the value base.

Co-operation

People and organisations in the social economy should work together for mutual benefit. Many commentators point out that, while this may be an aspiration, in reality, it is often not the case. Organisations find themselves competing for limited funds and for a market share. Some believe that only their particular 'tendency' is the right path and that others are misguided if not actually wrong. Tempers and temperatures can rise over definitions and terminology. There has emerged a plethora of associations and support organisations, each with their own spin. Into this rather unco-operative mêlée the establishment in 2001 of the Coalition for Social Enterprise (and its Scottish and Welsh counterparts) is very much to be welcomed bringing, as it will do eventually, most of the hitherto dissenting tendencies together. Although it can inevitably set only a lowest common denominator of agreement, that is an important start. Channels of communication are being opened and strengthening trust will lead to closer agreements and the ability to speak with a louder common voice. That in turn will lead to more collaborative working.

The need for all parts of the social economy to work together and in close association with others in the third system cannot be over-emphasised. The system requires self-belief and confidence if it is to challenge the dominance of the other systems and it needs to generate the sense of trust and the social capital which will allow erstwhile competitors to work together. In this regard, the newly developing role of the Co-operative Group together with its Co-operative Union could prove significant as it positions itself to embrace and promote the social economy, bringing the financial and political resources to play a nation-wide role.

A further important area for developing co-operation among social enterprises is in the area of inter-trading. The third system taken as a whole represents a substantial market and there could be major advantages to social enterprises if all parts implemented a policy to shop within the system whenever possible.

Decentralisation

The third system is also about subsidiarity in action, allowing services to be organised at the lowest appropriate level. It has been described as 'reverse delegation', [15] that is, it rests on the assumption that local communities should be in charge of their own affairs and that what they can organise for themselves they should. But if there is discernible merit in delegating a function to some other, larger body then that should be done. The larger or higher body is always accountable to the smaller or lower body and that which has been delegated can always be taken away.

Decentralisation is what makes local democracy work because it vests power in people and in communities. It is about the people handing responsibility up to government and managing power within democratic structures. Third-system organisations, and especially social enterprises, should be at the heart of this process and at neighbourhood and district level may collaborate closely with those in the other two systems who share a common commitment and sense of belonging to the locality and so build local social capital.

Despite European rhetoric about subsidiarity the reality is generally quite different. The EU is perceived as a centralising bureaucracy and the UK is arguably one of the more centralised of the European states. The role and authority of local government has been rolled back. There are fears that devolution in Scotland and Wales is stopping in Edinburgh and Cardiff and not cascading powers and opportunities down to district and community levels. Regional devolution in

England seems set to repeat the pattern: strengthen the regional centres to the detriment of the component parts and ignore the legitimate historical and cultural claims of counties such as Cornwall for a greater say over their own affairs. Social enterprises should be at the forefront of persuading government to let go and allow local democracy to work, both in the lower tiers of elective government and in the citizens' organisations of the third system. The consequence may result in a patchwork of varied provision reflecting differing wishes and needs in different places. Untidy perhaps, but does that matter?

Decentralisation also involves focusing on the local economy and human-scale activity. Community enterprises in particular respond to local needs and are concerned about strengthening the local economy. This means looking at what can be done locally to 'plug the leaks' and use local labour to do local work.

A key challenge for the social economy will be to ensure that those social enterprises which function on a regional, national or international stage do in fact discharge their responsibilities downwards to local communities and adopt decentralist policies when these are appropriate. The recent determination of the Co-operative Group to strengthen its local membership and re-engage with local communities, despite continuing mergers in the consumer co-operative sector, is a good example of thinking small while growing big.

Inclusivity

Organisations within the social economy will ensure that all persons in their constituency have an equal right and equal opportunity to participate without discrimination as to race, gender, sexual orientation, ability, religion, political belief or social and/or economic disadvantage. Social economy organisations should be concerned also to respect and safeguard human diversity and recognise the fundamental basic rights of people to adequate food, shelter, health, education and work.

Good work

The concept of good work has two dimensions. First is the idea of undertaking work which is seen to be socially useful and which therefore enhances the quality of life either for people generally or for a particular group. Second is the idea of enjoyable work, good working conditions and acceptable, or fair, rewards for work done.

It is as a consequence of commitment to the first that the Co-operative Bank and Industrial Common Ownership Finance (ICOF) have developed ethical policies which avoid dealing with organisations engaged in activities which are considered to be socially harmful or dangerous (such as the manufacture of weapons and tobacco-related products).

It is not enough to assume that a social enterprise is doing good work simply because it is a social enterprise. Adopting the social accounting and audit process described later ensures that a social enterprise is clear about its objectives and therefore about the potential social impact it hopes to achieve. Sometimes social enterprises are not as clear about their social objectives as they might be, and occasionally they discover objectives they did not know they had. Articulating the social purpose clearly and overtly not only makes assessment of impact possible but ensures a focus on achieving some tangible social benefit or common good.

The second, internal, aspect of good work is also often assumed as a given, but that does not mean all social enterprises accord it the importance they might. In the social accounting process, social economy organisations are encouraged to declare an objective which is about 'being a good employer' or some other similar formulation. That not only points to an overt intention, but is also a commitment to report on performance and consult the relevant stakeholders, namely paid and unpaid workers.

Sustainability

This is another double concept, both in ensuring that work and practices are environmentally sound and preserve the resources of the planet for future generations, and in ensuring that the social enterprise itself is financially and organisationally sustainable. It should be axiomatic that an enterprise which has a social purpose will have a clear positive environmental policy, for to be environmentally irresponsible is to be socially irresponsible. Hence the concept of triple-bottom line reporting: understanding the social, environmental and financial impacts of an organisation as well as the way they interrelate.

Social enterprises have not, however, had a good record on environmental policies and practices. Many fail to recognise how the little they may do can make a difference and others simply see such considerations as getting in the way of achieving their social purpose. Although that situation is changing, awareness of the issues still needs to be raised, especially in exploring the practical ways which even the smallest social enterprise can adopt to reduce its environmental footprint. In this regard, an important first step could be the requirement that all social enterprises report on their environmental policies and impacts regularly as part of their social accounts.

The financial sustainability of any enterprise or organisation is, of course, an important determining factor, ensuring that there is sufficient commercial viability to sustain maximum social benefit. In this sense, achieving organisational sustainability becomes as important a social objective as any other and some social enterprises now routinely report on this in their social accounts and include insights into the impact that financial performance is having on social and environmental performance and organisational sustainability, as well as vice versa.

People-centred

The social economy adopts an integrated approach which embraces people and environment, culture and economy. The key focus is, however, on addressing the needs and wishes of people – always within a sustainable framework – rather than servicing the interest and demands of capital. So instead of being capitalist like the first system or statist like the second system, the third system is people-centred, in that performance will be measured in terms of impact on people and on society. The role of capital in social enterprises is to serve the interests of the people. The role of the state (national and local) is to provide the framework for people to create and manage their social economy organisations and so lead fulfilling lives.

'People before profit' is an engaging but all too easy catchphrase. Profit is necessary for sustainability. Meeting the needs of the people (and the planet) is the primary purpose and that purpose will be served by making profit, so long as that profit is not made at the expense of or to the detriment of the people whom the social enterprises set out to serve.

In the following chapter, we go on to explore in greater detail the nature of social enterprises.

NOTES

1. *Social Enterprise: A strategy for success* (London, Department of Trade and Industry, 2002).
2. M.D. Evans *et al., Key Concepts, Measures and Indicators* (Conscise Project, Middlesex University, 2000).
3. *Enterprise and Social Exclusion*, report of the National Strategy for Neighbourhood Renewal: Policy Action Team 3 (London, HM Treasury, 1999).
4. *Introducing Social Enterprise* (Social Enterprise London, 2001).
5. Development Trusts Association, London, *Annual Report 2000.*
6. *Community Co-operatives* (Highlands and Islands Development Board (HIDB), 1977).
7. *Definition of Community Business* (West Calder, Community Business Scotland, 1991).
8. *Opening the Gateway to Birmingham's Social Economy* (Birmingham Social Economy Consortium, 2001).
9. *All You Ever Wanted to Know about Community Enterprises* (Voluntary Action Lochaber, 2002).
10. 'The Social Economy and Co-operation' (chapter 6), in *The Co-operative Advantage: Creating a successful family of co-operative businesses*, report of the Co-operative Commission, 2001.
11. *Social Enterprise* (2002), see note 1.
12. *Enterprising Communities: Wealth beyond welfare* (Social Investment Task Force, 2000).
13. Co-operative Union (incorporating ICOM, the worker co-operative federation), enquiries.coopunion@co-op.co.uk; and Community Business Scotland Network, info@cbs-network.org.uk
14. Karl Birkholzer *et al., Key Values and Structures of Social Enterprises in Western Europe: Concepts and principles for new economy* (Technologie-Netzwerk Berlin with European Network for Economic Self-Help and Local Development, 1997).
15. Charles Handy, *The Empty Raincoat – Making sense of the future* (London, Hutchinson, 1994).

4 The nature of social enterprise

Within the framework of social enterprise there are, as we have seen, many types of organisation, having different legal structures and using different descriptions and terminology. The purpose of this chapter is to describe this disparate social enterprise family by defining nine dimensions or 'continua'. Each social enterprise sits somewhere on each continuum although over time it may move its position according to changing circumstances.

Nine dimensions of social enterprise

1. from very small to very large
2. from voluntary enterprise to social or community business
3. from dependence on grants and subsidies to financial independence
4. from people orientation to profit maximisation
5. from informal to formal economic activity
6. from mono- to multifunctional
7. from voluntary organisation to social enterprise
8. from radical to reformist
9. from individual to collective initiative

From very small to very large

First is the dimension which runs from very small to very large. 'Small' will include the smallest of enterprise endeavours in local communities which in some way generate income (or maybe reduce the cost of living) and/or provide a local service. These are the micro-level contributions to the local economy: examples might include local craft fairs or produce stalls; running a village or community hall association; the pre-school playgroup; the voluntary food co-operative or the local thrift shop. Some of these may be operating in – or developing out of – the 'grey economy'.

At the other end of the continuum, we find those remaining large mutual organisations such as building and insurance societies, the Co-operative Group (including the Co-operative Bank), companies like the John Lewis Partnership[1] and the Scott Bader Commonwealth,[2] and co-operatives such as Poptel[3] and Suma,[4] as well as the larger housing associations and credit unions. In between

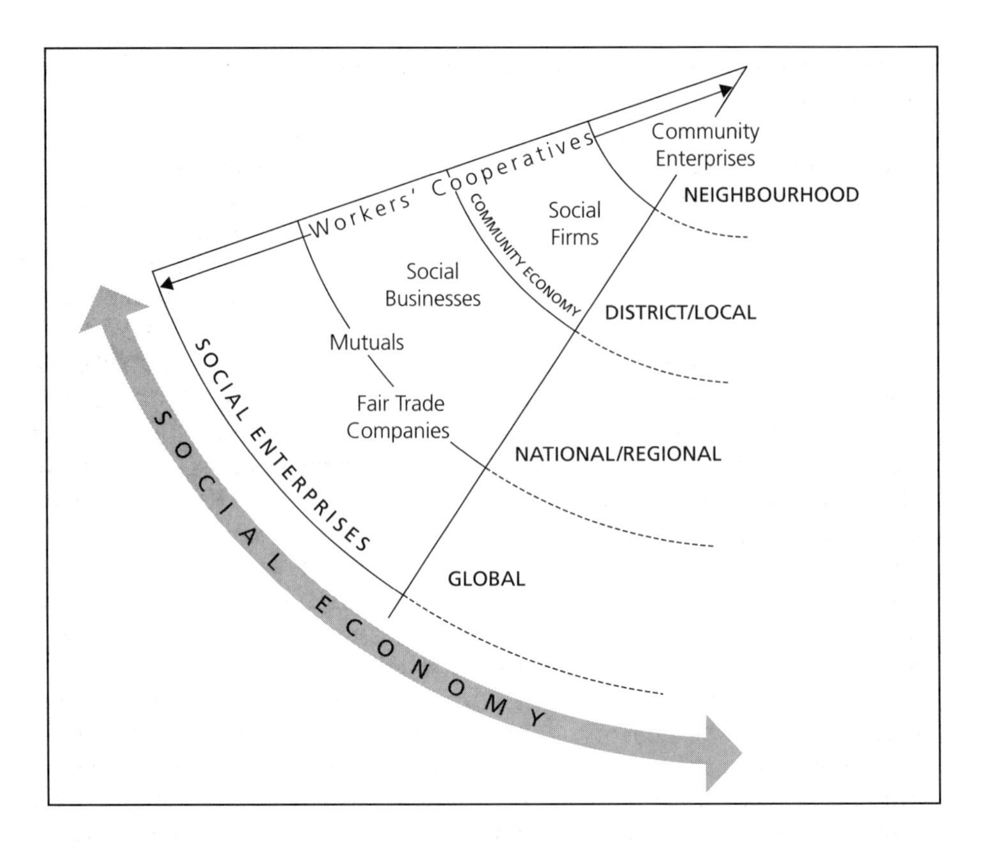

are all those community enterprises, development trusts, social firms, social businesses, fair trade companies and others which appear in the table on page 29.

What binds together these social enterprises should be the mutual acceptance of common values and the adoption of structures which enshrine the defining characteristics. Still lacking – but developing fast – is that sense of being part of one family, which can confidently publicise and promote the social economy.

It is important that attention is paid to generating new enterprises at all places in the wedge. Today's micro-community enterprise might evolve into tomorrow's large mutual. The Rochdale Pioneers started in 1844 as an evenings-only, volunteer-run, shop in an upper room, but from that modest beginning the world-wide Co-operative Movement grew.

Recent development strategies in some areas have been primarily targeted at enterprises with potential for growth, and for replication. While that makes some good sense, it should not be at the expense of encouraging the very local and very small new starts: they, after all, will represent the next generation not only of social enterprises but also of advocates for the third system.

From voluntary enterprise to social or community business

A voluntary enterprise depends almost entirely on volunteer labour while the independent business will be staffed mostly by paid employees. In between will be many different social and community enterprises, which depend to a greater or lesser extent on the input of volunteers.

At local, neighbourhood, level the use of volunteers in the enterprise may often be the trade-off for providing a service or goods at a cheap price. In other cases, it is members of the community contributing their 'sweat equity' to the survival of a local business which is important to the community in the same way as family members working unpaid and all hours to keep the family business alive. In yet other examples, volunteer labour may compensate for the lower productivity of certain disadvantaged members of the workforce and so permit an enterprise to survive in the marketplace. Almost all social enterprises will make use of volunteers in some way, if only as lay members of the board of directors.

The assumption is sometimes made that all social enterprises should move along this continuum, reducing dependence on volunteers and becoming more viable by employing paid staff. While this may be a mark of progress in some cases, it should never be assumed that the use of volunteers makes an enterprise any less of a business than one which pays all of its staff, nor that its contribution to the local economy is in any way lessened. Indeed, there may be movement in both directions along this continuum with some enterprises needing to rely more on volunteers when times are difficult.

The tendency must also be avoided to try and locate a start-up social enterprise in an unrealistic position on the continuum. It is unlikely that a thrift shop in a low-income area can ever be more than a voluntary enterprise. As such it can offer a valuable service and make an important contribution to the local economy. Try and set it up as a community business with paid staff and it is probably doomed to failure.

From dependence on grants and subsidies to full financial independence

At one end of this continuum are those organisations which remain dependent on grant aid or some other form of regular fundraising. At the other end are those which can be self-sustaining from their activities in the marketplace. Earlier we discussed the shades of grey along this particular continuum and the 'cocktail' of revenue income which may be generated in differing proportions to achieve viability (page 34).

Two points require emphasis. First, most social enterprises will shift their position in either direction on this continuum over time and, second, only a very few businesses (even in the first system) can honestly claim to be entirely free of all income other than which is earned through the marketplace.

From people-orientation to profit maximisation

The majority of social enterprises are people-centred in that their social purpose is not only about enhancing the quality of life for a target group. What they do, providing certain services, or producing certain goods employing a particular group of people, is itself directly achieving a more general social purpose. What they do commercially is of direct benefit to people.

For a minority of social enterprises, however, their main focus is on generating a financial profit which can be used to benefit people in their defined locality (or a defined target group of beneficiaries). For these social enterprises their trading activity is not itself directly part of the social purpose. However, even in such cases it would be expected that they adhere to the social economy values and in particular to 'good work'. No level of profits generated for use in the community could offset engagement in unethical work, or bad work practices.

From informal to formal economic activity

Local economy activities such as LETS (Local Exchange Trading Systems) and time banks are very much part of the social enterprise sector although they are based on barter and the multilateral exchange of services and goods either for a local currency or for time credits. Such schemes expand the range and potential of the community economy by allowing people to trade without ordinary money. Moreover they encourage people to go into 'debt' (known as commitment) because the greater the commitment, the greater the opportunities for others to trade.

Engaging in economic activity in this way, especially through LETS, can be an important first step for some people on the road to establishing their potential to do business and to set up some form of enterprise. It is part of a creative ferment where 'informal' meets 'grey' meets community enterprise. Encouraging informal economic activity should be an important part of any social enterprise strategy. It is also possible that a community enterprise which fails to make it as a formal business may be able to continue providing its service by operating wholly or partly through a LETS or time bank scheme.

From mono- to multifunctional

In the 1980s, the community business model which was being promoted from Scotland, based on the community co-operative scheme in the Highlands and Islands, envisaged an organisation which was part community enterprise holding company, running a variety of enterprises and projects locally, and part development agency, supporting the establishment of other local, community-based initiatives in the area.

Today, the phrase 'community business' is more usually associated with a community-owned enterprise operating in a defined locality and doing one particular thing. However, successful multifunctional community enterprises have survived throughout Scotland for more than a generation despite initial problems and a later tendency to favour mono-functional businesses. The principle behind the multifunctional idea is simply that the income generated by an assortment of trading activities and projects can sustain a stronger and more skilled central management capacity than any of the individual enterprises or projects alone. Equally, that central capacity can also offer development support to new enterprises and initiatives, some of which might be run as part of the multifunctional company itself while others are established as independent

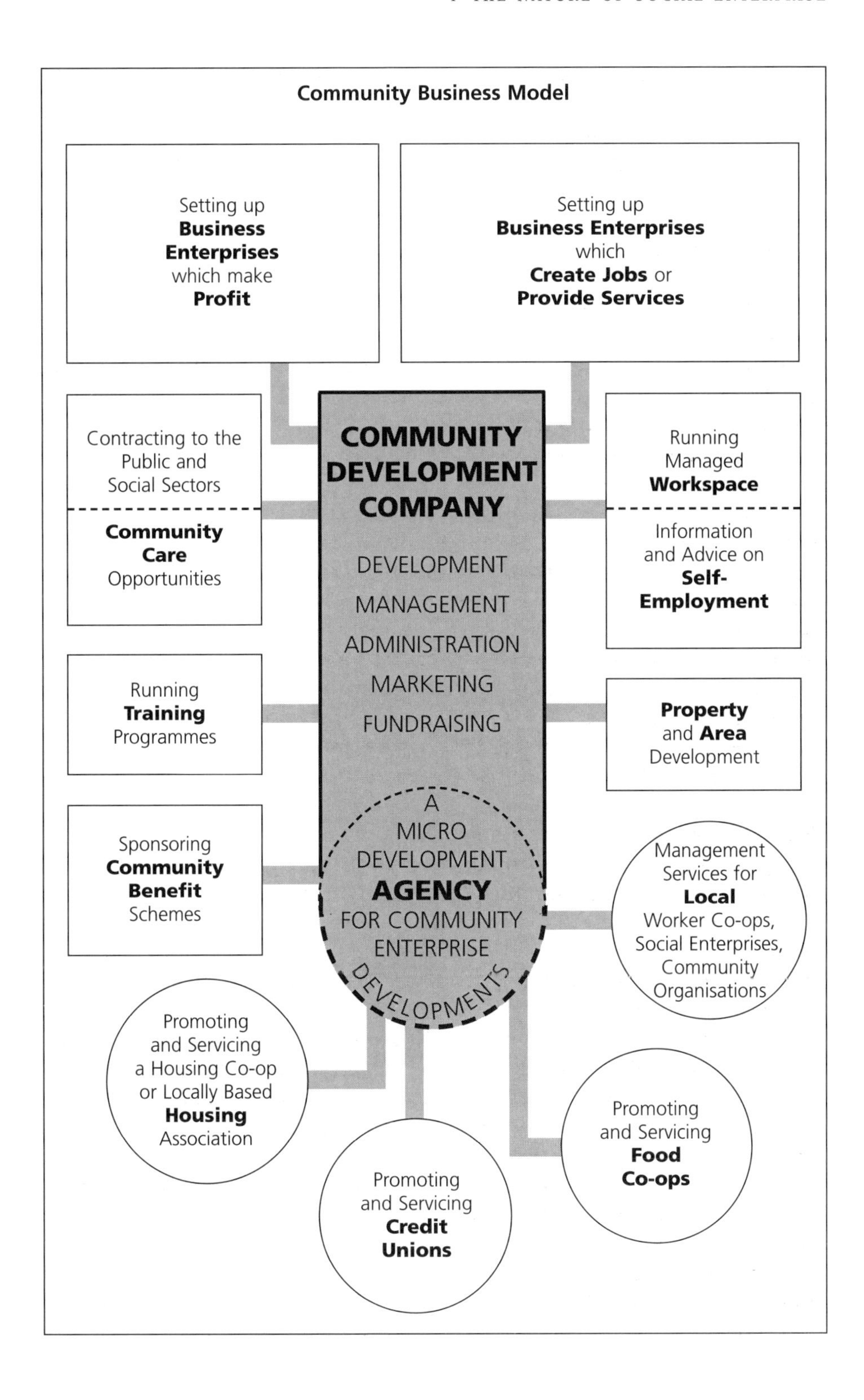
Community Business Model
Setting up Business Enterprises which make Profit
Setting up Business Enterprises which Create Jobs or Provide Services
Contracting to the Public and Social Sectors
Community Care Opportunities
COMMUNITY DEVELOPMENT COMPANY
DEVELOPMENT
MANAGEMENT
ADMINISTRATION
MARKETING
FUNDRAISING
Running Managed Workspace
Information and Advice on Self-Employment
Running Training Programmes
Property and Area Development
Sponsoring Community Benefit Schemes
A MICRO DEVELOPMENT AGENCY FOR COMMUNITY ENTERPRISE
DEVELOPMENTS
Management Services for Local Worker Co-ops, Social Enterprises, Community Organisations
Promoting and Servicing a Housing Co-op or Locally Based Housing Association
Promoting and Servicing Credit Unions
Promoting and Servicing Food Co-ops

community enterprises or projects. It was thought that while the management function would be self-funding this development agency role might attract external funding. The mantle of promoting multifunctionality has now been picked up by development trusts, community trusts (in Scotland) and by social firms, many of which are structured and operate on the multifunctional model.

At the other end of this continuum are those social and community enterprises which concentrate on one activity only, and in between are many which may engage in more than one line of trading, but do not aspire to be the complex multifunctional organisations depicted in the diagram.

From voluntary organisation to social enterprise

Increasingly, voluntary organisations are engaging in trading activities and are now estimated to earn as much as one-third of their income from the sales of goods or services. As the contract culture takes hold, so more of the work which in the past has been funded by grant is organised as a contract or service level agreement. Now that business thinking has infiltrated the third system, more voluntary organisations are looking to the possibility of securing their sustainability through trading activities.

Those voluntary organisations which trade in order to raise funds remain essentially voluntary organisations, while those for whom engaging in trade is the way in which they achieve their social purpose may redefine themselves as social enterprises. Some projects, such as the Bridge to the Social Economy of CBS Network in Scotland,[5] have been devised to assist voluntary organisations and community groups to begin to make that transition and move along the continuum from voluntary organisation to social enterprise. It will not however necessarily be one-way traffic along this particular continuum and some social enterprises may find themselves in circumstances which make them redefine themselves as voluntary organisations. The reality is that a large majority of social economy bodies will be in transit somewhere along this dimension.

From radical to reformist[6]

Whereas the reformist approach is about social enterprises serving as an extension to the first and second systems, largely engaged in activities from which the second system has withdrawn and from which the first system can make no profit, the radical approach analyses the situation from a much more political point of view. It sees social enterprise as part of a different way of doing things, as the stalking horse to introduce and evolve a political economy based on third-system values. At that end of the dimension social enterprise is about radical change, 'challenging capitalism on every front' as one person expressed it. These people and organisations will take every opportunity to publicise and promote social economy values and the social enterprise way of working. At the other end it is more about keeping the existing system going and often downplaying the fact of being a social enterprise while playing up the idea of being 'just a business like any other'.

The social economy is peopled with those who espouse one or other extreme view and there are many shades of opinion in between. But the resolution of this particular debate will be important because, ultimately, social enterprises probably cannot effect real and lasting change or introduce a new dominant system while at the same time collaborating with the existing order.

From individual to collective initiative

This dimension describes how a social enterprise comes into being: the initiative either of an energetic individual – a social or community entrepreneur – or of a community group or other body. In this dimension we would expect movement from both ends and some convergence in the middle. The individual social entrepreneur must establish roots in the community in which he or she is working and build the legitimacy of a community constituency which is eventually symbolised in the constitution adopted. An initiating group, on the other hand, will no doubt have its leaders who provide the initial drive and energy, but in time they too will need to find the right people with the right skills to manage and direct the enterprise which they bring into existence.

These nine dimensions are fluid and at all times social enterprises are shifting their position according to the changing community and commercial environment. No enterprise is static, but it is helpful for both enterprises and those who seek to support them to understand the dimensions and to recognise the need to craft appropriate support for all social enterprises along all continua.

Next, we explore the role of social enterprises and examine whether they are suited to some areas of activity more than others.

Four areas of work

Social enterprises are engaged in all aspects of the economy and represented in most commercial areas except those from which they would exclude themselves for ethical reasons as discussed in chapter 3. The four categories which follow suggest that there are underlying patterns to what social enterprises do, why they do it and what they are most successful at doing.

The categories described are not necessarily mutually exclusive and many, if not most, social enterprises would identify with more than one. They are:

1. Local development and regeneration
2. Working for the state
3. Providing services to the community
4. Market-driven business.

Local development and regeneration

A significant number of social enterprises engage in what may be termed local 'infrastructure work' providing services and facilities which support local economic activity. These include the provision of managed workspace or new-start 'incubator' workshops; enterprise training programmes; advice and support to local micro-enterprises. An interesting feature of this area of work is the role social enterprises adopt to help grow small-scale enterprises of the private system.

This demonstrates, especially at local neighbourhood and district level, a commitment to a mixed economy of social and private businesses, together with an understanding that small, private enterprises may be the most effective way of undertaking and developing certain business ideas. Equally, it shows that social enterprises can have the capacity to play an effective role in providing business support to small private businesses, an interesting role reversal which is generally overlooked in the debate about how mechanisms of the first system such as the Small Business Service can best provide business support in the social economy. Within local communities the links and reciprocal connections between organisations in all three systems can be close – and the closer and more effective they are, the greater the local social capital (see chapter 6).

As well as providing local economic infrastructure, social enterprises may take the lead in the physical redevelopment of an area, acting as a catalyst. Playing that role, often in partnership with organisations from the other systems, may lead also to the creation of joint ventures. Where this developmental role is played the benefits spread across the community, influencing the entire economic system. Thus a heritage centre established as a community enterprise can bring increased numbers of visitors to a town or village and so strengthen the business of other local traders. Coin Street Community Builders in London has created a mixed development of co-operative social housing, public open space, local workshops and market space as well as housing an exclusive restaurant in the Oxo Tower.[7] The physical redevelopment of a neighbourhood will provide opportunities for all three systems.

In Scotland several community trusts have been created in recent years which have acquired ownership of a former private estate or island and are now responsible for co-ordinating all aspects of local development: housing, physical infrastructure, welfare and social services, economic development and environmental conservation. In such contexts, the community trust virtually becomes a form of community government bringing all three systems together and ensuring that the first and second systems can play their parts effectively. One of the community leaders in Knoydart talks about the community trust 'stepping back into the background but providing the glue which holds us all together' and, by definition, getting things done.[8]

Elsewhere social and community enterprises have taken the lead in shaping local development or regeneration initiatives, thus putting the values of the third system at the front of that process, but recognising that it is a mixed, pluralistic economy which is being encouraged. In order to play this role the social enterprise has to engage in basic community development work (in its UK meaning – see chapter 5) and, therefore, requires to have the capacity to do that. For the past several years, the Development Trusts Association has reported that community development is the commonest task in which trusts engage, as revealed by their annual survey of members.[9]

Intermediary social enterprise organisations such as co-operative development agencies, community enterprise units, Community Development Finance Initiatives and the like play an important part in strengthening the local infrastructure and supporting the growth of social and community enterprises and are themselves part of the social economy. There are other support agencies which are not social enterprises (for example private consultancy organisations and sections of local authority departments) and in chapter 8 we examine both the support needs of social enterprises and the different structures through which those needs can best be met.

Working for the state

Increasingly, social enterprises are being regarded as agencies through which services may be delivered which were previously provided by the public sector. The Greenwich Leisure model where leisure and recreational services are transferred to an industrial and provident society, essentially a workers' co-operative with customer or community involvement, has been both successful and replicated by a growing number of local authorities. Childcare and domiciliary care are two other areas where social enterprises have established a strong track record, not least because many believe such care work is more appropriately undertaken through a local, mutual structure rather than through a private, profit-making enterprise. One of the biggest transfers into the social enterprise sector concerns housing, where substantial swathes of former council housing have now been transferred to housing associations as registered social landlords. Even schools are being considered for contracting out. The mutual ownership model has been adopted for Glas Cymru (Welsh Water) and although it was not chosen for Railtrack, the guarantee, not-for-profit, company structure adopted for its successor, Network Rail, does seem to represent a commitment to put quality of service before profit and to move the railways towards the third system.

Government support for the idea of social enterprises engaging in the provision of services has been clearly articulated. 'The Government believes social enterprises have the potential to play a far greater role in the delivery and reform of public services, and is currently considering a number of ways in which to increase the role of such organisations.'[10] There is here a sense of government beginning to see social enterprises as a mechanism through which some of its policy commitments can be delivered.

Social enterprise is also seen as a way of tackling social exclusion, poverty and disadvantage. 'Social enterprises provide disadvantaged and excluded groups with a mechanism for joining the labour market, support ongoing Government initiatives to "make work pay"; and can also play an active role in reducing crime and antisocial behaviour.'[11] A social enterprise or community enterprise dimension has become a *sine qua non* for most Single Regeneration Budget (SRB) projects and for many EU-funded programmes.

There are, however, very real problems with social enterprises being seen as an extension of the state. The independence of third-system organisations may be compromised and this could too easily lead to social enterprises being controlled by the public-sector agencies who engage them.

Related is the concern that social enterprises may be seen as the best-value option for delivering services only in the sense of 'lowest-cost'. There are legitimate concerns that where social enterprises are seen as a means of driving down costs, this may be achieved only by reducing wages (or quality of service) or by substituting free labour (volunteers or New Deal trainees) for properly paid labour.

It is these concerns which make some in the social economy uncertain about how far to engage with the delivery of government policies and the provision of former public services. Moreover, many in the wider labour movement suspiciously regard such moves as privatisation by the back door and rightly need to be convinced that quality of service and employment conditions will not be affected.

The idea of services being provided through mutual structures and social enterprises employing local people could be part of an exciting process of reinvigorating civil society and ushering in what the New Economics Foundation (NEF) has called 'the Mutual State'.[12] Under this model assets move from public ownership into common ownership, services are under community control rather than public-sector control, and the driving force will be quality delivered efficiently and not profits made at all cost. However, for this approach to work it has to gain enthusiastic support and acceptance, and in order for it to do that a number of key requirements must be met.

First, the model must be part of a wider political commitment to grow and strengthen the third system in general and the social enterprise wedge in particular. In other words, mutualisation should not just be about delivering services but about developing a genuinely different way of organising the wider economy, indeed a different 'mode of production'.

Second, the transfer of the provision of services to social enterprises should be backed up by the mechanisms necessary to encourage and facilitate social enterprises to take on service provision. One important aspect will be specifying contracts appropriately, so that smaller social and community enterprises are able realistically to go for them.

Third, the added value of social enterprises providing services should include the important value of local people doing local work, of profits not being distributed to shareholders, but being used for community benefit, and of growing assets still remaining in common ownership; and these factors should be included in contracts along with agreed, appropriate methods of monitoring performance and reporting to all relevant stakeholders.

Fourth, it will be important that the consent of existing workforces and their representatives is gained before embarking on such important changes. Contracts with social enterprises should specify both levels and quality of service and minimum standards of employment (e.g. wages, terms and conditions).

Providing services to the community

Quite separately from providing services which were once the province of the public sector, social enterprises are drawn into providing other services within their communities in response to local needs. Often these services are commercial, and ones from which the private sector has withdrawn because they are not sufficiently profitable. Thus the community enterprise runs the village shop, and maybe the petrol pumps too, as much as a community service as as a commercial enterprise. Viability may be achieved by the use of some volunteer labour to help out from time to time or through the community injecting other funds into the enterprise occasionally in order to safeguard and sustain its existence as a community asset.

In other contexts the services provided will seem to be more social than economic, such as managing the community centre as a multipurpose local facility or running a community café or second-hand shop. As ever, at neighbourhood level, the distinction between commercial and social is often very blurred. The distinguishing characteristic in the present context of discussion is that they are entirely independent of the public sector, sustaining their activities from their own resources and not providing a service on behalf of the state.

A further example of independent social enterprises providing a service are the doctors' co-operatives through which out-of-hours GP services are provided to the community. The point here is that a group of service providers is using the social enterprise model to provide the service for which they are contracted by the state.

Market-driven business

Our fourth category includes those elements of the social enterprise wedge that are simply out there in the market place, producing products, supplying services, independent and competing with businesses of the first system.

Indeed these social enterprises, often the workers' co-operatives, sometimes the community or social businesses, are indistinguishable from their first-system competitors until you examine their structure, their social purpose, their values and their adoption of the defining characteristics.

Some social enterprises in this category actually play down their social enterprise character for fear that it might disadvantage them in the marketplace. Others, more radical, ensure that the values by which they do business are widely known and understood and this forms their contribution to promoting the social economy. That some still believe they should keep their social enterprise character quiet is evidence of the distance yet to be covered in making social enterprises understood and recognised as a valid different system rather than an aberration from the norm.

All things to all people

One often hears inflated claims that social enterprises can do everything. It is not just government and other agencies who do this, for some elements of the sector itself fall into the same trap. We are told that social enterprises can make jobs for people with significant barriers to employment; that they can provide services to people in areas of the greatest need; that they can provide better-value (i.e. cheaper) services; that they can run a successful business in economically disadvantaged and low-income areas; that they can tackle social exclusion and crime, and encourage community participation; and that they can do all that effectively, be financially viable and self-sustaining, and probably make a profit along the way! Such claims are seductive and there are many who want to believe them. But they are also disingenuous and dangerous.

In the 1980s the community business movement in Scotland laid a similar trap for itself. Protagonists claimed that they would train and employ some of the longest-term unemployed people, in the poorest and most disadvantaged areas; that they would get people not only back into work but out into the wider labour market (thus having continually to recruit new labour); that they would undertake work appropriate to their largely unskilled workforce, generally low-added value, labour-intensive work; and that they would create profitable and therefore sustainable businesses within three years with no need of public-sector support. Unsurprisingly, those high hopes were not always realised and no matter how successful some businesses were in meeting their social goals they could barely manage to survive financially and several collapsed. They simply could not carry the social costs in difficult circumstances. Interestingly, research carried out in 1997 demonstrated that those early community businesses which had survived had been a very effective and good-value means of bringing the long-term unemployed back into employment, especially when compared to the more expensive Intermediate Labour Market schemes.[13]

Employing people with barriers to employment, whether those be disability or long-term unemployment or drug-related problems, incurs inevitable additional costs: in training, providing support, offering flexibility of working times, managing with lower productivity while people learn the job or, maybe, simply learn to work again. It is only rarely that such costs can be realistically paid for out of the trading profit. Profitability is bound to be challenged by slower rates of work and by the regular throughput of the labour force as workers move on and out into the wider labour market, moves seen by first- and second-system sponsors as desirable success. Such social costs have to be met from some public-sector subvention. It would be good practice to write that into contracts so that the nature of the social costs to be paid for are clearly described and a means of monitoring and reporting achievements agreed. But it is irresponsible not to recognise them and not to make arrangements to pay for them.

Similarly, the social enterprise which sustains a business which the private sector was unable to make pay will likely find that the business is at best marginal, and quite often that it returns a loss which has to be covered somehow. These are what have been referred to as 'deficient demand' enterprises, which will otherwise not be viable because people cannot afford to purchase the service (perhaps through poverty) or because there simply is not a large enough market (as in under-populated, remote areas). Yet without the service the quality of life for the population will be severely impaired. Expecting businesses to succeed which target low-income or remote populations will always throw up problems of sustainability.

Expectations from social enterprises must be realistic. It is dangerous to disguise, as some social enterprises and their paymasters do, the fact that a contract is 'soft' or that a special deal has been struck which implicitly recognises the social benefits to be gained but is fearful of making the deal explicit. That fear of making explicit the negotiations behind the figures can be attributed in large degree to the pressures on social enterprises to demonstrate that they are just as viable and market-driven as a business from the first system. The S-word is now as much a no-no as the P-word once was when organisations in the third system thought of profit as something only private business dirtied its hands with. Attitudes have substantially changed and throughout the third system there is now a business-like approach, a recognition that any organisation should adopt efficient practices and that to generate profit is to ensure long-term sustainability. What matters is how that profit is used. A colleague in Scotland expressed the point neatly by explaining how social enterprises 'make profits in order to provide services and deliver community benefit, while conventional businesses provide services to make profits'.[14]

Subsidy – the S-word – however, carries with it implications of propping up undeserving organisations and its reputation as a word has not been helped by its association and usage in the EU Common Agricultural Policy where the present subsidies now perpetuate inefficiencies in farming practice. Notwithstanding the tarnished image of subsidy, however, the concept is important: a mechanism whereby society can pay for something to be made or done which cannot be achieved through the mechanism of an entirely 'untouched' market.

'The market cannot deliver what social enterprises do' and for that reason social enterprises will need subsidies in order to do the things which society requires but which they cannot pay for from commercial earnings. We should not be afraid of acknowledging such subsidies and should avoid hiding them so as to make the enterprises appear commercially viable when in fact they are not.

Social enterprises should also be careful not to allow themselves to be boxed into the regeneration or anti-poverty corners. It is true that social enterprises, because of their ethos and values, have a commitment to a juster and fairer society and therefore naturally emerge to tackle social and economic issues in poorer localities. But they should not be seen as relevant only to poor people in low-income, under-invested communities. In the report of the Social Enterprise London conference in May 2001 at which the Secretary of State for Trade and Industry first articulated the Government's thoughts on working with social enterprises, that cautionary note was given rightful prominence: 'We need to establish the confidence to say that social enterprise, the social enterprise model, is not just for the poor and disadvantaged. We need to get out of that box, we need to be offering something which says that the social enterprise model can deliver for everybody and that it is in fact a more sustainable and healthier economic model for growth and development.'[15]

While the Co-operative Movement started in the nineteenth century from the self-help action of working people determined to improve the quality and opportunities of life for themselves and their fellow working people, it evolved a world-wide vision of a society run on mutual and self-help lines. That vision was inclusive across all sectors of society, applying Robert Owen's thinking and words to society generally: 'If there be one closet doctrine more contrary to truth than another, it is the notion that individual interest, as that term is now understood, is a more advantageous principle on which to found the social system, for the benefit of all, than the principle of union and mutual co-operation.'[16]

The social economy finds itself today at a crossroads, especially as it is being courted by government as a partner in the modernisation and delivery of public services. Will it build its vision for radical change and promote, argue, lobby and work for a social and economic system founded on third-system values, or will it settle for being no more than a reformist mechanism, helping to make the first and second systems work better by being 'an additional tool in the box' and 'an adjunct to the mainstream economy'?

Radical change will require something of a revolution in contemporary political and bureaucratic thinking, rejecting the capitalist model as the preferred dominant system and replacing it with the mutual model. Making mutual dominant does not imply that there is no role for the private or public but it would send out powerful messages about what is desired and therefore acceptable. The reformist approach will, some may argue, achieve the same end while avoiding confrontation. Maybe; but history shows us just how easily dominant systems can co-opt and stifle alternatives. It is hard to believe that the World Economic Forum invited representatives of the social economy to their meeting in New York for any other reason than to get them on-side and to promote 'brotherhood' between Forum members and upholders of the reformist approach. In itself that may be encouraging; social enterprise is now significant enough for the world's capitalist leaders to want to bend it to their purpose.

In the following chapter we explore some of the origins of social enterprise and the routes into it, and examine how language can imply and reflect important shifts in attitude towards social enterprise and its role in society.

NOTES

1. www.john-lewis-partnership.co.uk
2. www.scottbader.com
3. www.poptel.net
4. www.suma.co.uk
5. www.cbs-network.org.uk

6. See discussion in M.J. Gordon, *Voyages of Discovery: The contribution of the community co-operatives of the Highlands and Islands of Scotland to the development of the social economy* (Middlesex University, 2001).
7. www.coinstreet.org
8. Quoted by John Ross in 'This land is our land', *The Scotsman*, 6 July 2002.
9. Development Trusts Association, London, *Annual Membership Survey*, 2000, 2001, 2002.
10. *Social Enterprise: A strategy for success* (London, Department of Trade and Industry, 2002).
11. *Ibid.*
12. Ed Mayo and Henrietta Moore, *The Mutual State – How local communities can run public services* (London, New Economics Foundation, 2001).
13. Simon Clark and Alan McGregor, *Community Business and the Intermediate Labour Market: The West of Scotland experience* (Community Enterprise in Strathclyde, 1997).
14. Karen Maclean, working paper for Social Enterprise Scotland, August 2002.
15. Bob Grove in *Social Enterprise, Social Economy: Moving ahead*, conference report (Social Enterprise London, 2001).
16. Robert Owen, *A New View of Society and Other Writings* (London, Penguin, 1991).

5 The origins and changing language of social enterprise

So far we have looked at the role which social enterprise can play in the national and local economy. At this point it will be illuminating to examine the different, and varied, routes by which social enterprises have come about.

The traditional Co-op

The idea of social enterprise can trace its roots back to the medieval guilds of workers and through various political and social movements over the centuries which emphasised the idea of working together for a common social purpose. However, it is the Rochdale Pioneers, founders of an 'Equitable Society' in 1844, who are usually taken to be the immediate forerunners to what is now the Social Enterprise Movement.

The modern legacy of the Co-operative Movement in Britain is of course the 'Co-op' stores together with the Co-operative Bank and those building and insurance societies which have survived the demutualisation trend of the past decade and the agricultural and fishery co-operatives which have been formed over the years. Taken together these remain a very significant force in the British economy and have, through the Co-operative Commission, confirmed both their place as part of the social economy and their commitment to supporting the growth of social enterprises.

Although the number of these traditional co-operatives is likely to continue to decline, through mergers and the occasional further demutualisation, their role can be a powerful one in establishing new social enterprises in their areas of influence and moving into new fields of work. The West Midlands Society, for example, now runs care homes for the elderly while the Oxford, Swindon and Gloucester Society supports a growing network of children's nurseries.[1]

The radical 1970s

During the 1970s, which saw the formation of the Industrial Common Ownership Movement, there was a considerable wave of new co-operatives established by people with strong ideals and committed to alternative ways of living and of working. These 'lifestyle' co-operatives sought to challenge the political and economic status quo and to demonstrate that another, co-operative, way could work. Many of these co-operatives were organised as collectives, with decision-making shared amongst the members and with jobs often rotated.

Although these co-operatives engaged in a wide range of activities two in particular stand out: housing and wholefoods. The formation of housing co-operatives and co-ownership schemes allowed members to put their ideals into practice in daily life, and where workshops or a holding aimed at self-sufficiency were involved, on a daily working basis as well. Wholefood wholesaling, retailing and cafés were ways of living your values at the same time as promoting alternative lifestyles to others and earning a livelihood. Many of these businesses from the 1970s still exist, having established themselves and managed to adapt to a changing marketplace. Suma, the wholefood wholesalers based in Leeds, have, for example, just celebrated 25 years both 'as a co-operative and as a business' and have recently opened a new distribution centre on the M62.[2]

A generation on, in the new millennium, that radical buzz seems to be less apparent in new-start co-operatives and social enterprises, a consequence perhaps of the way in which being businesslike from the start has become engrained in all approaches to enterprise formation.

Job creation

A further trend was the use of social enterprises as a means to combat rising unemployment and to create jobs for the unemployed. During the 1970s the co-operatives at Kirkby and at Triumph Motorcycles in Coventry supported by the then Minister for Trade, Tony Benn, were short-lived and expensive attempts to use the worker co-operative model to save the jobs in enterprises that were ailing and failing in private hands.[3] They, and the equally short-lived *Scottish Daily News*, eventually bought up and closed by Robert Maxwell, did much to discredit the idea of the co-operative ideal as a workable organisational model.[4]

Nonetheless, local councils did promote workers' co-operatives and community enterprises as part of their strategies to create jobs for the increasing numbers of unemployed people in their areas, targeting especially the most disadvantaged people and the worst-hit neighbourhoods. The 1970s and 1980s saw the growth of a substantial network of co-operative development agencies (CDAs) and community enterprise support units, and the steady growth of co-operatives and of community enterprises. Many of these were inevitably struggling to be sustainable from the start, given that they were being established by people with little business experience, in areas of great disadvantage and in an economy where employment levels were collapsing. However, many did survive and 30 years later still contribute to their local economy.

Today, the job creation route to social enterprise comprises two distinct strands. First, the new-start strand where groups come together and are assisted to form a new social enterprise. The type of support structures required for a modern social economy are discussed in chapter 8. Second, the Intermediate Labour Market programmes (ILMs), a significant number of which are set up as or run by social enterprises. ILMs offer salaried training to unemployed people who learn both on the job and at day release college for periods up to one year during which time they are assisted to find a job within the wider labour market.

These schemes, which are relatively expensive (£15,000 per place is not uncommon) do not grow the social economy but 'through-put' labour into the first, private system.

Community development

The community development route to social enterprise is explored more fully in chapter 7. This is about people in communities determining their own priorities and using social enterprises as a means of turning visions into action. It is bottom-up development, addressing a raft of social, economic and environmental issues, often without distinction between one and the other.

Within the community development route, too, two strands may be distinguished. First, that based upon community planning as described in chapter 7 and second, that which derives from the 'passion of protest'. One of the foremost, and longest-established, examples of the latter is the North Kensington Amenity Trust which has developed the 23-acre site underneath the raised motorway in West London with a complex of social, economic and environmental initiatives, but which started as a community protest against the building of the motorway back in the mid-1960s.[5]

Social welfare

One particular route into social enterprise which is now gaining significant momentum involves the provision of services for groups of people with specific needs: those with disabilities, those suffering from mental ill-health, the elderly and those dependent on childcare. It is especially in this area of service provision by social enterprises that government is now showing interest, envisaging a substantial role for social enterprises in its drive to modernise the delivery of public services and likely to encourage such social enterprise activity in the future.

Social businesses

Social businesses, by contrast with most other social enterprises, are likely to have been created by an individual social entrepreneur who wishes to tackle a particular social problem and devotes his or her skills and energy to that end. Often such enterprises do not adopt the sort of democratic and accountable structure usually associated with social enterprises (see chapter 3). Programmes such as the School for Social Entrepreneurs have been promoting and encouraging the formation of social enterprises by social entrepreneurs.

Social housing

The provision of social housing has long been an area of activity for social enterprises although, curiously, it is only recently that housing providers have really been recognised as social enterprises – or indeed have begun to perceive themselves as such. Social housing provision has been seen as an acceptable activity for social organisations in a way that engagement in business has not.

In addition to the work of housing associations, there are growing numbers of housing co-operatives, self-build co-operative groups and tenant-management co-operatives, all functioning within the housing market as social enterprises. Also, organisations whose primary focus has in the past been housing are now engaging with other social and economic issues in their localities and either broadening their compass as social enterprises or supporting the formation of other, sometimes subsidiary, social enterprises.

The Eldonians in Liverpool for example, are a group which includes, alongside the original community-based housing association, a children's nursery, elderly persons' care home, a sports centre, and various training and community health initiatives as well as a development company through which they can undertake joint ventures with public and private partners.[6] As well as housing organisations extending their range of social enterprise activities, other social enterprises may begin to engage in the provision of housing. The Appin community co-operative in Scotland, which was set up to save the village store, petrol pump and post office, recognised the need to develop additional, affordable housing in the village in order to help sustain the community. Having acquired the necessary land, the community co-operative entered into partnership with a housing association to do just that.[7]

Financial services

Another important route comprises those social enterprises which provide financial services – the credit unions, either community-based or workplace-based. These bring a wide range of people into the social economy for personal financial reasons, but also open up the possibility for collective action to create social enterprises which are involved in trade. So far the regulations surrounding credit unions in the UK have not encouraged engagement in other forms of enterprise activity. This is not the case in Ireland where credit unions are often the driving force behind local enterprise initiatives.

More recently there has been a growth in second-tier, intermediary financial social enterprises known as Community Development Finance Initiatives (CDFIs), although the longest-established (Industrial Common Ownership Finance (ICOF)) dates from the early 1970s.[8] As well as being structured as social enterprises, some CDFIs target the lending of their resources at new-start and existing social enterprises. Radical Routes is a housing co-operative which has also established a social investment society, Rootstock, which makes loans to member co-operatives for the purchase of properties.[9]

Public-sector refugees

As government thinking about the delivery of public services has changed over the past two decades there has been a growth in social enterprises which take over the provision of services previously provided by local authorities. One of the best known is Greenwich Leisure.[10] It is clear that government policy is likely to encourage this trend and that the next decade will see a substantial growth in the number of social enterprises which were once part of the public sector. Increasing numbers of people once employed by public bodies will find themselves employed by social enterprises.

Voluntary sector refugees

It is now estimated that as much as one-third of the revenue income of voluntary organisations comes from the sale of goods and services. This trend is likely to speed up as more funding is offered in the form of contracts rather than grants and as more voluntary organisations begin to see themselves as social enterprises (see chapter 2 and the diagram on page 25).

Exit strategy enterprises

Where public, private or community partnerships are established for regeneration purposes the creation of a social enterprise, often in the form of a development trust, is considered as part of the exit strategy to ensure that the programmes initiated may be continued and, hopefully sustained. Such top-down creations bring with them their own particular problems relating to the sense of ownership and genuine involvement of the local community and the beneficiaries whom the enterprises have been set up to serve. Some seriously question whether such organisations can ever evolve into genuine, community-owned and -controlled social enterprises.

Succession enterprises

Probably the best known 'succession enterprise' in Britain is the Scott Bader Commonwealth, a chemicals company in Northamptonshire which was gifted by its founder to the employees as a common-ownership company in the 1960s and which played a key role in the formation of the Industrial Common Ownership Movement and the promotion of worker co-operation through the 1970s. Employee ownership or some other form of social enterprise represents a route for private companies to ensure their continuation after the retiral of the owner where there is no next generation to take on the business. Most co-operative development agencies devote a part of their efforts to promoting the idea of such conversions to private business people in their area and will facilitate the complex process of devising a suitable structure, transfer timetable and financing package. A recent – and growing – addition to the succession portfolio has been football clubs such as Lincoln City and Bournemouth which are turning themselves into mutual co-operative societies in order to safeguard their future and to engage the community and supporters as key stakeholders.

Piggy-backing

Following where others have led has always been a way of deciding what to do while learning from other people's mistakes. Most development agencies will include 'learning' visits and will provide and publish case studies of best practice – and lessons to be learned from things going wrong. Generally operators in the social economy have been generous in sharing their experiences and encouraging them to follow in their footsteps, but tailoring their plans to their local circumstances. However, recent talk about franchising suggests that within the social economy some people are beginning to recognise the commercial value of what they do and how they do it and are exploring to what extent they can sell their experience.

Sometimes a supply need of one social enterprise can be used to create, or sustain, a second social enterprise; or a new business idea evolves which the social enterprise 'spins off' as a new and independent project. In Liverpool, Dove Designs,[11] a social firm, manufactures frames for the nearby Furniture Resource Centre, a social business.[12]

Second-tier co-operatives

As the name suggests these are social enterprises which provide a service for a group of other social enterprises (such as marketing, selling or bulk-buying) or are a co-operative structure serving a group of self-employed individuals (such as taxi drivers or domiciliary care workers).

Intermediaries are another form of second-tier social enterprise, providing services for the social economy (and sometimes for other sectors also). Services might include running a managed workspace, small business information and advice, running training courses and so forth.

The changing language of social enterprise

While the routes into social enterprise have become ever more varied, the very language itself of social enterprise has been changing over the past 10 years. A decade ago the talk was of community and co-operative enterprise. The term 'social enterprise' was rarely used and, when it was, it implied a community enterprise which required some sort of public-sector subsidy to allow it to perform its particular service. Social enterprises then came somewhere between voluntary-run enterprises and independent, market-driven community businesses.

Those who worked in community development at that time engaged with communities, working with them to agree a vision, to develop a workable strategy, to take action to implement that strategy, and to create community-owned and -controlled organisations to act as vehicles for implementation. The work was often referred to as 'community economic development' although some resisted inserting the word 'economic' between community and development; all community development must engage with economic, social, environmental and cultural issues if it is to be relevant. To compartmentalise development into administratively convenient sectors runs contrary to how people in communities see the issues facing them: a complex weave of inter-related problems and possibilities.

The organisations which were set up were called community co-operatives, community development trusts, community businesses. Nowadays the new generic term 'social enterprise' is used instead. The people who initiate and make things happen – the community leaders and community activists – also have a new designation: 'social entrepreneur'.

In what might be called the 'community era' we talked of community action, community enterprise and community business. Today, in the contemporary 'social era', we are more likely to talk of social entrepreneurs, social enterprise and social business. Is there some serious significance in this shift in vocabulary from community to social? Does it matter?

Behind these vocabulary shifts it is possible to discern three strands of changing thought:

1. A shift from an emphasis on collective action to individual entrepreneurialism, albeit for social benefit;
2. A shift from emphasising the ownership and accountability structure of organisations to a focus on the social purpose, i.e. what they do;
3. A shift from a political perspective working for fundamental change to a more technical approach aimed at getting on with the job in hand.

From community to individual

In the community era the starting point was usually a group or a community coming together to arrive at a vision and agree what needed to be done, and then taking steps to implement that plan. There was a sense of collective endeavour. Of course all groups need leadership and there are always one or two people with the initiative to get something going and the drive and determination to push things forward. But they do that as a member of a group, accountable to the others and with support from the others.

The emphasis in the contemporary social era appears to be much more towards the individual and his or her capacity to make things happen to create change. The Ashoka Trust, for example, talks about 'outstanding individuals who are already building on their own ideas of what their societies need'[13] and that appears to encourage the notion of doing things *for* communities rather than *with* them.

The people now called social entrepreneurs have always been with us, as the long and rich history of co-operative and community enterprise testifies. The adoption of the new name is more a case of rebranding, emphasising the social purpose as well as the business role of the entrepreneur. The question remains, however: why was such rebranding needed?

Is it perhaps a legacy of a belief from the Thatcher years which has lingered on under New Labour, that business is the only way to run the affairs of humankind and that successful businesses are created only by individual entrepreneurs? In other words, is it part of the attempt to rub off onto social and community enterprises the ways of the marketplace and the first system? Is it a way to ensure that social enterprises are no more than an adjunct or a subset of the first system, rather than a truly alternative third system?

Or is it perhaps simply necessary, in this age of spin, to repackage old ideas as new concepts in order to make them politically acceptable and supportable? Maybe the older concepts of community and co-operative have become in some sense discredited.

Certainly there is hearsay evidence to suggest that the concept of community business became tarnished in the early 1990s when a small number of Scottish projects foundered, attracting undue publicity and political attention.[14] Failures there were, continue to be and always will be, but nothing on the scale of corruption to be found within the 'role models' of the contemporary corporate sector. Failures occur for many and varied reasons. It has been suggested elsewhere that we could perhaps learn more from a study of failures than from volumes of best practice but the challenge to undertake such a study remains unmet.[15]

In different ways the word 'co-operative' also became tarnished, associated as it was almost exclusively with the decaying and rather outmoded co-operative retail sector. However both the Co-op and the co-operative concept have fought back. The 'new co-operatives' have since the 1970s injected new life and ideas into the movement. Instead of simply rebranding itself, the co-operative idea has modernised and redefined its role in contemporary society, seeing itself as 'the largest player in the social economy' and the 'development of social enterprise as a balancing accompaniment to...globalisation'.[16]

In any discussion of social or community entrepreneurs it is important to recognise the difference between the person who is the innovator, who gets something going, and the person who can sustain an enterprise. We can all think of organisations which have had to face the crisis of how to accommodate or even get rid of the innovator. People who start things are often not the best people to sustain them. Sustaining and building-up an enterprise are likely to need different people, with different qualities and skills.

Those who support social enterprises need to help innovative social entrepreneurs understand when their role is completed and they should hand over to a 'sustainer'. And it is essential for social enterprises and community organisations to know when the innovator has done his or her job and to prepare for easing him or her out of the leading role. Such situations demonstrate the importance of a robust, workable organisational structure which provides a framework through which change may be managed and which ensures that the organisation is greater than any of the individuals who make it up.

From accountability structures to getting on with the job

In the community era great care was taken to ensure that the form of organisations reflected certain structural values: democracy based on membership, accountability to members and to the community, non-profit distribution, and assets owned in trust on behalf of and for the benefit of the community (see chapters 2 and 10). This approach has been criticised for creating bureaucratic and cumbersome structures and for trying to run enterprises by 'politically correct management committees'.

There is undoubtedly some validity in these critical comments and it can indeed be difficult to make the democratic, participatory structures of the community or co-operative enterprise work effectively and efficiently. But, the important point, which must not be lost sight of, is to ensure that the organisational form roots the enterprise in and renders it accountable to its community or recognised constituency.

Structures exist which allow efficient management to coexist with active participatory and democratic structures; they need not be mutually exclusive. It is important that social enterprises recognise the merit of separating the two functions, however, allowing management to manage, but always within the policy framework agreed by the board or management committee. Social enterprises such as the Queens Cross Group in Glasgow are both dynamic, working democracies with a substantial membership, and efficiently managed businesses.[17]

Making social enterprise structures work takes time and effort, in particular keeping in touch with the membership and other stakeholders and involving them in the operation. The structure itself, no matter how carefully the constitution is worded, cannot function effectively without that commitment of the organisation to make it work. Part of the Co-operative Group's success in re-establishing its membership roots has been through the work of its membership development officers. Where social and community enterprises adopt the social accounting process described in Appendix ii, channels of dialogue with stakeholders will be created, which in turn should serve to strengthen the organisation's effectiveness as well as to keep democracy alive.

For a true social enterprise, structure and social purpose are inextricably entwined. By contrast the social entrepreneur's focus is very specifically on the social purpose – getting on with the job to be done to benefit the community – and the organisational form is unimportant so long as the social purpose is met effectively: 'people not structures'. In this model, democratic structure and accountability are less important so long as the job is done and people benefit and, just as in the private sector, nothing gets in the way of managerial efficiency in the drive to meet targets of service or production. Indeed some would go so far as to argue that democratic structures and encouraging democracy are not necessarily what social enterprise is about, thus obviating the need to build into structures how the enterprise may be accountable and to which constituencies. Those who promote such an argument are essentially aligning themselves with top-down philanthropic agencies set up to benefit the people rather than with the bottom-up Social Enterprise Movement.

Some social enterprises, renowned for their valuable work, have been initially set up as private limited companies. In such a model any accountability to other stakeholders ultimately depends on the whim of the founding owner–directors. In one particular case the founders are conscientious about trying to be accountable and are now seeking how best to restructure their organisation so that the interests of workers and of beneficiaries may be safeguarded for the future. Most likely they will arrive at some form of community-/worker-owned and -controlled structure which balances accountability, democracy and competent management – the essence, in fact, of a good community or co-operative structure.

The emphasis on identifying and supporting individual social entrepreneurs and focusing on the social purpose independent of structures can be interpreted as demonstrating an elitist tendency, especially where it separates individuals from their community context. This emphasis could be the consequence of initiatives such as schools for social entrepreneurs and grant-making programmes like that of Unlimited, which are targeted at individuals.[18] Such programmes and other strategies need to find ways of empowering the many, to recognise that in all communities there are people with talents and skills and ideas who have the capacity to become community activists or social entrepreneurs, or, indeed, are already playing that role.

People who have worked in community development for any length of time are always struck by the many enterprising and innovative people in the most disadvantaged communities, developing projects, coming up with ideas, often succeeding against dreadful odds. Tony Gibson's book *The Power in our Hands* [19] or Richard Douthwaite's *Short Circuit* [20] both give a vivid sense of the amazing variety of initiatives around the world developed by ordinary people who have that spark of imagination and the determination 'to get on with it.' Empowering the many means fostering enterprise in the community setting rather than favouring the few, and fostering small as well as large social enterprises.

From political engagement to technocratic fixing

The political idea behind community economic development was that there must be a better way to run the affairs of communities, that economies should be predicated on concepts of common good rather than unlimited private gain. That was – and remains – a political framework, which holds a clear critique of the capitalist and corporatist structures which dominate the modern world. It is a critique which sought and continues to seek political changes which might rein in the liberated markets and bring them increasingly under social control. The community and co-operative organisations created at local level could be seen not just as projects tackling local problems but as part of the process of seeking and testing alternative economic and organisational forms based on democracy, mutuality and co-operation and on the restricted distribution and accumulation of wealth. That remains the position for those who advocate recognition of the third system as an alternative dominant system.

Much contemporary debate on social enterprise tends by contrast to be satisfied to identify sectors within the twenty-first century mainstream economy where it is considered appropriate for social enterprises to operate. That means taking on tasks which governments are insisting the public sector should no longer fulfil but in which the private sector has no interest because they are not really profitable. Social enterprises thus become the problem-fixers.

There is a danger here of social enterprises being boxed into that corner of the economy which deals only with the most disadvantaged in the poorest areas, mopping up the problems of society as cheaply as possible by using voluntary and work-for-the-dole labour. In this scenario the social economy would continue to be no more than the prop which underpins the 'real' economy – very much the third sector, subservient to the public and to the private, pre-eminent, sector. Not a third system and no longer an agent for change.

Community development and community development

The term 'community development' has been generally used in the UK to describe that process of working with groups of people and communities to define needs, agree strategies and plans for tackling them, and take action to carry through those plans using local organisations controlled by and accountable to the community.

In the US the term has become increasingly associated with applying an economic edge to the development of poor communities, focusing on business-led development, and more generally with the physical regeneration of property and neighbourhoods. While some of that development may be controlled by community organisations, much will be through individual entrepreneurs and businesses and by outside companies being persuaded to invest in the under-served or under-invested area.

This North American interpretation has in recent years been introduced to the British vocabulary through the term 'Community Development Finance Initiative' (CDFI), mechanisms for delivering loans and other finance primarily for business development in poor communities. CDFIs are not about community development in the traditional British sense, although those that do support social enterprise initiatives rather than individual entrepreneurs may recognise the importance of the community development process which is generally the essential forerunner to the establishment of a community enterprise.

Other people's language

Social enterprises are generally ill-served by the language used to characterise them – as grant-dependent, managerially inefficient, slow-moving, unviable – always in contrast to the private business sector which we are told is profitable, lean and mean, efficient and sharp. Even the Government in its recent Social Enterprise Strategy continues this criticism when it says: 'Social enterprises must see themselves as businesses, seek to become more professional and continuously raise their standards of performance and their ambitions',[21] implying that social enterprises are at present none of those things. The Social Investment Task Force's report referred to a 'culture of begging and benevolence' working against 'practising entrepreneurship'.[22]

Even people working within the social economy surprisingly perpetuate such mythologies: 'There are some brilliant examples of social enterprises which are real businesses achieving significant social value. But they are few and far between. Most community-based social enterprises are very fragile and would immediately collapse if the grants underpinning them were removed.'[23] Such observations tarnish the image of social enterprise.

There is scant evidence, mostly allegation, that social enterprises are not well managed. Social enterprise managers have to contend with a much more complex situation than the average private-sector manager. They have to juggle social and commercial considerations, help make a democratic structure work, ensure that working and other conditions are of a high standard, cope with bureaucratic public-sector contracting or funding bodies, are usually dealing with undercapitalisation and a hostile banking world, and trying to survive by employing some of the most difficult people or by offering a marginal service in a poor area. The fact is that social enterprise managers are highly skilled and capable and the surprise surely is that so many enterprises survive, succeed and even expand. The rapid expansion and growth of social enterprises over the past 10 years is testimony to capability, not incompetence.

The special range of qualities and skills required by social enterprise management make the sector's demands quite different from those of the private sector. There are not a few examples of private-sector people coming to the social economy and being quite unable to cope with the complex demands made of them.

And is there any real evidence that the private sector is more managerially competent? In the year that has seen the dramatic events in companies such as Enron, WorldCom, or even Railtrack, the blanket claims of competence and ability in the private sector can hardly be sustained. In all systems there are examples of good and bad management. The issue surely is to ensure that there is appropriate management with the right skills and qualities for organisations in each system. The assumption that only the private sector knows how to manage, and therefore knows how to manage social (and public) enterprises should be laughable. Maybe in the wake of Enron and WorldCom, that wisdom will have been shaken.

Our society seems to be risk averse when it comes to social enterprise, but not so much when it comes to small business generally. The failure of a social enterprise is likely to lead to comments such as 'told-you-so – poor management' while the significant failure rates for small- and medium-sized businesses will be buried amongst the statistics showing the continued growth of business start-ups. Small businesses fail all the time: they may have problems of cash flow, they fail to read the market, deliver on time or modernise; there are difficulties with worker relations, hands in the till – in two words 'poor management'.

The phrase 'begging and benevolence' also requires a little attention. Elsewhere we saw how the so-called 'grant mentality' comes from the grant-givers just as much as from the grant-receivers (chapter 3). Yet much industrial development policy is predicated on persuading employers to relocate to where they can obtain rent- and rate-reduced premises, housing for key workers, grants for new employees and the like. Employers shop around for the best deals, not 'begging or seeking benevolence' but 'driving a hard bargain'. Social enterprises and their managers are also skilled and adept at making full use of the funding regimes on offer, but why does this have to be denigrated?

Another term which has recently swept into the language is 'social capital'. The following chapter explores this elusive concept and its relevance to social enterprise.

NOTES

1. John Cunningham, 'Goodwill hunting', in *The Guardian*, 27 February 2002.
2. Bob Cannell, 'Still trying to change the world after 25 years', in *New Sector*, September 2002.
3. Ken Coates, ed., *The New Worker Co-operatives* (Nottingham, Spokesman Books, 1976).
4. Ron McKay and Brian Barr, *The Story of the Scottish Daily News* (Edinburgh, Canongate, 1976).
5. Andrew Duncan, *Taking on the Motorway* (Kensington and Chelsea Community History Group, 1992).
6. www.eldonians.org.uk
7. Appin Community Co-operative, Appin, Argyll, PA38 4BN, Tel: 01631 730 235.
8. www.icof.co.uk
9. www.radicalroutes.org.uk
10. www.gll.org
11. www.dovedesigns.org.uk
12. www.furnitureresourcecentre.com
13. *Backing the Changemakers* (London, Ashoka Trust, 1998).
14. Ed Mayo, 'The dream and the reality', in *New Statesman*, June 2002.
15. John Pearce, *At the Heart of the Community Economy: Community enterprise in a changing world* (London, Calouste Gulbenkian Foundation, 1993).
16. 'The Social Economy and Co-operation' (chapter 6), in *The Co-operative Advantage: Creating a successful family of co-operative businesses*, report of the Co-operative Commission, 2001.
17. www.qcgroup.co.uk
18. www.unltd.org.uk
19. Tony Gibson, *The Power in our Hands* (Charlbury, Oxon., Jon Carpenter, 1996).
20. Richard Douthwaite, *Short Circuit – Strengthening local economies for security in an unstable world* (Totnes, Resurgence, 1996).
21. *Social Enterprise: A strategy for success* (London, Department of Trade and Industry, 2002).
22. *Enterprising Communities: Wealth beyond welfare* (Social Investment Task Force, 2000).
23. Liam Black, 'Passing the not-for-profit acid test', in *New Start*, 14 September 2001.

6 Social capital in building the social economy

by Alan Kay

The term 'social capital' has come to be found everywhere and there is hardly an article on the social economy which does not use the term. But what is it? Can we measure it and, more importantly, is it useful to organisations and to individuals working in the social economy? In this chapter we shall define social capital and show its importance in developing social enterprises and hence the social economy.

Social capital – the context

There is a large amount of academic literature on social capital, reflecting the struggle which commentators have had in trying to define the concept and extract from it some useful and practical ideas.

The term 'social capital' was first used in 1961 by Jane Jacobs,[1] although the concept has been recognised by writers since the nineteenth century. More recently, thinking around social capital has been greatly influenced by James Coleman,[2] an American sociologist writing in the 1980s, and Robert Putnam[3] – also an American, and a political scientist writing in the 1990s; and to a lesser extent by Bourdieu[4] and Hirschmann.[5]

It is impossible in this short chapter to detail the mountain of literature on social capital. However, to summarise:

- *Putnam* recognised that 'good governance was closely related to civic engagement'[6] and that social cohesion in communities depends on social networks, norms and trust. He affirms that these components make up social capital in communities and that this is necessary for improving the quality of life and for community development.
- *Coleman's* wider definition of social capital was used to construct a social theory which stated that the 'closure' of social networks can produce closer connections between people and that this in itself can generate obligations and sanctions on the community.
- *Bourdieu* shows how social capital exists alongside economic and cultural capital and can be part of a strategy for individuals and groups to produce more social capital and/or convert it into other forms of capital.
- *Hirschman* uses the term 'social energy' and suggests that it is made up of three components: 'friendship' emphasising the personal impact of social

capital; 'ideals' which may lead to a shared vision based on values; and 'ideas' which enable groups and individuals to present new solutions to their problems.

Clearly, there are different approaches to social capital leading to varying hypotheses. But there is general consensus that it is something that exists between individuals and organisations. This 'something' emerges from connections between entities and is further developed through trust, mutual understanding and reciprocal actions based on shared norms and values.

Defining social capital

Social capital has been defined in a number of different ways (see box).

> 'Social capital is defined by its function. It is not a single entity, like other forms of capital, social capital is productive, making possible the achievement of certain ends that would not be attainable in its absence...Social capital is embodied in the relations among persons....(a) group whose members manifest trustworthiness and place extensive trust in one another will be able to accomplish more than a comparable group lacking that trustworthiness and trust.'[7]
>
> 'Social capital...refers to features of social organisation, such as trust, norms and networks, that can improve the efficiency of society by facilitating co-ordinated actions.'[8]
>
> '...(social capital is) the sum of resources, actual and virtual, that accrue to an individual or group by virtue of possessing a durable network of more or less institutionalised relationships of mutual acquaintance and recognition.'[9]
>
> 'Social capital consists of features of social organisations such as networks, norms and social trust that facilitate co-ordination and co-operation for mutual benefit.'[10]

A more recent definition from the Conscise Project has tried to encapsulate the key parts of the previous definitions under six headings, as follows:[11]

'Social capital consists of resources within communities which are created through the presence of high levels of...

1. trust,
2. reciprocity and mutuality,
3. shared norms of behaviour,

4. shared commitment and belonging,
5. both formal and informal social networks; and
6. effective information channels,

...which may be used productively by individuals and groups to facilitate actions to benefit individuals, groups and the community more generally.'

Social capital is defined as a resource. There is a strong argument that the word 'capital' in the term is confusing and that it may be more helpful to adopt 'resource' – that is, something that enables development.

Therefore, social capital is that intangible 'something' that exists between individuals and organisations within a community; the connections and trusting contacts that people make while going about their daily business. These contacts can then be used on a mutual and reciprocal basis both to further their own ends and/or for the development of the community. Like other forms of capital, it is productive and represents a 'stock' or 'fund' or 'resource' that can be used. However, it differs from other forms of capital in that the more social capital is used, the more social capital is generated. That is, the more organisations or individuals trust and develop relationships between themselves and others, the more those relationships, and thus social capital, are strengthened.

The six elements of social capital as specified in the Conscise Project definition above are interlinked. It is very difficult to separate one element of social capital from another in real life and together they generate a sense of community which is 'a web of relationships defined by a significant level of mutual care and commitment'.[12] An example might be that one person makes friendly contact with another which leads to mutual trust developing between them, resulting, in turn, in mutual understanding and some reciprocal actions and that may lead on to further social contacts and so on.

Recent work by the Conscise Project indicates that the six elements themselves fall into three categories:

- *Trust, social networks* and *reciprocity/mutuality* are about relationships between individuals and organisations.
- *Shared norms of behaviour* and *shared commitment and belonging* are about more than one individual and/or organisation sharing values, sharing a way of thinking.
- Effective *information channels* permit individuals and organisations to access information from outside and within their community.

The measurement of social capital is not easy. This is because the definition remains rather woolly and because each of the elements is qualitative and open to subjective interpretation. The Conscise Project made an attempt to measure the level of social capital in communities using a questionnaire with 'proxy indicators' which provided some insight into local people's attitudes regarding trust, social networks, etc. (see box). Although this experiment into measurement was inconclusive due to the small size of the sample and other biases, it did demonstrate that the measurement of social capital may not be impossible.

What are proxy indicators?

The proxy indicators used in the Conscise Project were in the form of statements; local people were asked to decide how much they agreed with the statements.

Two examples of the statements on trust:

- *When everything is taken into account, this locality is a safe place to live.*
- *If I were looking after a child and in an emergency I needed to go out for a while, I would trust my neighbours to look after the child.*

Two examples of the statements on reciprocity and mutuality:

- *By helping other people you help yourself in the long run.*
- *If I see litter in the neighbourhood, I normally pick it up even if I have not dropped it there.*

Ten findings about social capital

The Conscise Project has identified certain key findings about social capital from its action research with eight social enterprises in four European states.

1. The research suggests that there is a hierarchy of the six elements listed above, with trust being the most important.[13] For example, social contacts are made through networks; people then tend to work with others and organisations who share the same values (norms of behaviour and sense of belonging/ commitment); this may then lead on to working together. But without trust none of this may develop, and certainly not reciprocity. For the maintenance of social capital, trust is therefore overridingly important. When it breaks down social capital is noticeably depleted. But trust itself comes about only if people meet and talk; hence the crucial importance also of social networks. Trust, therefore, needs a context in which to develop and grow.
2. It is also recognised that people tend to work best with those people and organisations who *share the same values*. Two such individuals are more likely to form a trusting relationship faster. Therefore, shared values and norms can significantly speed up the establishment and development of social capital.
3. The Conscise Project has shown that *social capital is strong between individuals* but not always so evident between organisations.[14] To put this another way, the social capital between organisations may depend on individuals. Thus, if

a key person leaves an organisation, social capital in relation to other organisations is likely to decline, but not necessarily disappear.

4. Social capital itself is *value-free*. It can be used to include, support, develop and create, thus helping the development of a community and of society as a whole. Equally, it can be used to exclude, undermine, destroy and suppress. This is similar to other forms of capital, which may be used to benefit society or to subvert. Criminal organisations such as the Mafia, for example, have strong social capital but are intent on criminal and antisocial activity.
5. It is generally held that there are two dimensions to social capital,[15] depending on how it is used:

   - *Bonding* social capital which develops within a group and binds individuals, groups and organisations together; and
   - *Bridging* social capital which allows a group to reach out, involve and network creatively with other individuals, groups and organisations.

   It would appear that organisations use differing proportions of bonding and bridging social capital depending on the stage they have reached in their organisational development. Other recent work has suggested that there may be a third dimension, *linking* social capital, which forms connections between different levels of power or social status.[16] The difference between this and bridging social capital is not entirely clear, however, except that the concept of 'linking' appears to accept hierarchies of class and political power as givens, and therefore as not challengeable.
6. In understanding social capital, history is crucially important. The level of social capital, within a community is often determined by its historical development which has set the pattern of what is normal for that community. For example, close communities in Fife which were originally based on the mining industry have developed a strong sense of mutual trust, manifest in a robust trades union tradition and many social and sports clubs. Traces of this social capital are still evident despite the fact that the mines have all closed and the area has recently suffered economic and social decline.
7. Social capital is linked to, and affected by, the context in which it operates and the prevailing attitudes of local authorities and other powerful local influences. This is especially important as regards the development of the social economy. The political and statutory climate may be more conducive to the development of the social economy in one area than in another.
8. Social capital is sometimes defined as the glue that binds a community together and enables collective action to be taken for the benefit of that community. It has also been referred to as the grease that enables things to happen smoothly. It has been suggested that the 'glue' part of social capital works in the interests of community development and the third system, while the 'grease' aspect is emphasised by the first system as a means of getting things done.

9. Trust is fragile and can be destroyed in a moment while taking a very long time to develop and establish.[17] This especially affects social enterprises and there are examples where mistrust between organisations and individuals has hampered co-operation and opportunities for mutual development or where the failure of one enterprise has damaged trust in the whole sector locally.
10. There has been other useful research into the links between people's health and social capital which shows that a breakdown in social capital within communities has an adverse effect on the level of health of those communities.[18] This suggests that working on ways to increase social capital by getting people to engage with each other – making contacts, building trust and so on – can lead to improved health.

Social capital is not a precise concept but when people start talking about its component elements they quickly recognise its existence and its relevance to their day-to-day lives. Although intangible, it is part of an accepted way of working together and this, arguably, is how people and communities have always functioned. In this sense, social capital is no more than a modern academic tag given to age-old processes which permit healthy communities to function. The question is whether or not social capital can be used to generate the social economy and if so, how it does this.

Social capital and the social economy

Paradoxically, social capital is most noticeable when it is absent from local communities. When there are few social networks, a lack of trust, little effective mutuality, no shared norms and no commitment to the area, community cohesiveness declines and social under-development is likely to occur. That shows itself in an increase in crime, a desire to leave the area, mutual suspicion, lack of information, few social facilities, lower health standards, a degraded physical environment – in short, all the hallmarks of a disadvantaged neighbourhood. By recognising the existence of social capital our understanding of the way communities operate and how they function is enhanced and directs our community development strategies towards interventions that will help build, or rebuild, social capital.

Social enterprises generate social capital in their area, mostly by using social capital. Explicit, shared values create solidarity between like-minded social enterprises. Trust and reciprocity build up into co-operation and collaboration. Informal and formal social networks are actively built upon – bonding the social enterprises together and also bridging to other social enterprise organisations outside the immediate group. It has been noticeable that where there is an energetic co-operative or community enterprise development agency, a cluster of social enterprises is likely to develop.

Some social enterprises possess an inherent structure likely to create more social capital than others. For example, a LETS scheme with its network of members exchanging goods and services both uses and builds social capital all the time. The Conscise research indicated that rural communities tended to rely on and therefore generate more social capital than those that were predominantly urban.[19]

However, there are limitations to what social capital can do. It cannot build the social economy alone, but has to be used in conjunction with the other forms of capital – financial, human, environmental and cultural. Adding to social capital within a local area is not a substitute for other forms of capital and will not of itself grow the social economy.

Supporting organisations in the third system that actively create, use and generate social capital can make an area a better place to live. It can help establish a more vibrant social economy where the welfare and the quality of life of residents are more important than a drive towards a more efficient capitalist economy. This reinforces the need to take a community development approach rather than a business development approach in supporting social enterprises (see chapter 8).

Local social capital

Within a local community there are people, organisations and companies from all three systems operating alongside each other. Post offices and corner shops (of the first system) provide services to the local communities and employ local people; community councils and local authority offices (of the second system) do the same. Voluntary and community organisations (of the third system) provide a web of social networks and also create paid and unpaid jobs. All this activity by the systems and between the systems adds to the overall development of the community, to the community economy and to a better quality of life for residents. Together they generate and maintain local social capital. Many individuals are actively involved in all three systems. At a neighbourhood level (the inner circle of the diagram on page 25) the three systems tend to be closer and operate in a more integrated way than in the outer circles.

At this local level social capital plays a significant role in the development of the local economy across the systems. For example, it can reduce transaction costs to the point where there can be unwritten agreements and mutual understanding instead of formal contracts. The role of social enterprises running managed workspaces and offering training and advice to the self-employed on behalf of a local authority is a good example of the three systems working together and building local social capital for the benefit of the community. Similarly it is noticeable how much of the work in which social enterprises are engaged is based on trust: childcare, domiciliary care, estate security. The quality of this work is enhanced also by local knowledge and a sense of belonging to the community: local people doing local work.

Social capital is of course also apparent at regional/district, national and global levels. It manifests itself wherever there are networks and relationships between individuals and organisations. Social capital currently thrives within the seemingly close relationships between multinational companies and government ministers and officials just as much as it can be enthusiastically used by the manager of a social enterprise or the local shopkeeper and the local librarian. The importance is in the relationship and how that is used to develop trust which may lead on to reciprocal assistance.

Some cautionary remarks

Having established that social capital is more difficult to define than, for example, financial capital, it is also necessary to understand that it is open to different interpretations: 'What looks like a strong sense of social solidarity from one perspective can be seen as atomisation, divisiveness and stratification from another.'[20]

Local social capital that concentrates too much on binding the community into a cohesive unit can make a community more isolated and less tolerant of strangers and outsiders. Both bonding and bridging social capital are required to ensure there is a healthy balance within the local community.

In its publication *Prove It!* the New Economics Foundation (NEF) noted that '...many of the elements of human and social capital are beneficial up to a point, but harmful beyond it. Self-esteem can turn into vanity, sanctions into oppression and close-kindness into corruption.'[21]

Social capital is not always 'a good thing'. The development of social capital can, for example, have an adverse effect on equal opportunities when jobs are filled through the network or on the grapevine rather than through public advertisement. Networks and connections are usually formed and trusting relationships developed between people who share the same values. This can actively exclude others and not allow new and different people to become part of a network. This cannot be healthy or desirable. However, we all have the potential to be exclusive and by recognising social capital as a real concept we can begin to counter some of its negative aspects and at the same time use the more positive elements for the development of our local communities.

Social capital has always existed. It flourished and still does in the 'old boy' networks; the wearing of the old school tie to interviews; the way you shake hands; dressing in a particular way to reflect internally held values; the connections made in clubs; the social networks developed through meeting people at parties, Rotary Clubs and Round Tables; membership of secret societies. Throughout the ages people have used social capital to further their own personal ends. In the social economy, because of shared values, social capital is more likely to be used to generate public good. But there may be a danger of encouraging it among the poor in order to justify its use by the powerful to sustain their positions through their exclusive, elitist networks.

Social capital is not a new concept. But there is value in articulating and analysing it so that it may be recognised and thus help in the diagnosis of what may be wrong in certain communities. Once the absence of social capital in dysfunctional communities is recognised, strategies can be put in place to encourage its development.

Implications for social economy policy

The recognition and understanding of social capital has implications for governments and local authorities who wish to create policies to strengthen the social economy. The creation and generation of social capital seems to depend on the context in which an organisation operates. Conversely, it may be possible to encourage the generation of social capital by altering the context in which the social economy operates.

At a local level, policies could be developed that encourage local people to get together and form social networks. The formation of community and voluntary organisations along with LETS and volunteer schemes will contribute directly to the building of local social capital. Institutions and programmes that foster a sense of community and help articulate shared values can be encouraged. Local social capital may be strengthened by encouraging community ownership and management of assets such as community centres and village halls.[22]

The public sector might adopt new approaches to urban planning which bring people together more easily and so help build social capital. Restricting vehicle access to small neighbourhoods and building cul-de-sacs encourages residents and children to interact more on the street. The creation of semi-public space where people can meet and form relationships creates the links from which trust may build. At regional or national level support to third-system organisations and the encouragement of joint working through coalitions and forums will serve to strengthen social capital. Further research into new structures that support the development of social capital such as time banks, LETS systems and others might suggest other ways of rebuilding social capital at community level.

Although the third system is a distinct entity, as illustrated in the diagram on page 25, it is rather fragmented. Awareness of social capital could help to unify it. First, there has to be clarity and agreement on the specific values attributed to the system, which should connect the smallest neighbourhood enterprise to the largest mutual organisation. Second, providing support to national forums and networking organisations will improve networking and help build trust such that organisations which at present emphasise their differences can start to see, and to build on, the common ground which unites them. Once trust develops, then mutual help and working together will follow. Third, further research is required to look at ways in which social capital may be measured, perhaps through an extension of social accounting and audit. Fourth, the level of social capital within society generally requires to be monitored. If it begins to reduce or if it is used to exclude, steps must to be taken to counter this, to ensure that it is used to create a healthy, balanced and equitable society. A high level of social capital will of itself achieve nothing. It has to be *used*, by people working through their organisations and structures: in short, through civil society.

Social capital is important to the development of the third system. As our understanding of how things work and do not work within communities becomes clearer, we can recognise that society is made up of connections just as much as it is made up of money, material resources and human resources. That connective social capital is what can help to realise the vision of the social economy.

From social capital we turn to the importance of process and in the following chapter explore the role of community development in stimulating the formation of community enterprises.

NOTES

1. Jane Jacobs, *The Death and Life of Great American Cities* (New York, Random House, 1961).
2. J. Coleman, *Foundation of Social Theory* (Cambridge, Harvard University Press, 1990).
3. Robert Putnam, 'The Prosperous Community – Social capital and public life', in *The American Prospect,* 13 , 1993.
4. Pierre Bourdieu, 'The Forms of Capital', in J. Richardson, ed., *Handbook of Theory and Research for the Sociology of Education* (Westport, CT, Greenwood Press, 1986).
5. Perry Walker *et al.*, New Economics Foundation, *Prove It! Measuring the effect of neighbourhood renewal on local people* (London, Groundwork and New Economics Foundation, 2001).
6. *Ibid.*
7. Coleman (1990), see note 2 .
8. Putnam (1993), see note 3.
9. Bourdieu (1986), see note 4.
10. M.D. Evans *et al.*, *Key Concepts, Measures and Indicators* (Conscise Project, Middlesex University, 2000).
11. *Ibid.*
12. Walker *et al.* (2001), see note 5.
13. www.conscise.mdx.ac.uk
14. *Ibid.*
15. R. Gittel and A. Vidal, *Community Organising: Building social capital as a development strategy* (London, Sage Publications, 1998).
16. Performance and Innovation Unit, *Social Capital: A discussion paper* (Cabinet Office, UK Government, April 2002).
17. Walker *et al.* (2001), see note 5.
18. M. Kelly, 'Social Capital – Making the links with community health', in *Healthlines,* June 1999.
19. www.conscise.mdx.ac.uk
20. Francis Fukuyama, *Trust: The social virtues and creation of prosperity* (New York, Free Press, 1995).
21. Walker *et al.* (2001), see note 5.
22. PIU (2002), see note 16.

7 Taking the initiative – community development and community enterprise

The best-laid schemes o' mice and men
Gang aft agley,
An' lea'e us nought but grief an' pain
For promis'd joy! [1]

Sometimes the establishment of a community enterprise appears to have been a spontaneous event. Local people get together, talk, plan and organise. More usually someone, from within the community or from outside, feels that 'something' ought to be done but is unsure about how to start taking the initiative. This chapter is about how the community development approach can be used to 'kick-start' an initiative, to allow an agency or a group of people to intervene in a community, often with the result that a community enterprise is formed. It examines briefly the recent history of community development in the UK and its relation to local economic development, and considers some of the important chance factors without which success can prove elusive. The chapter goes on to outline one particular community development process which has been devised and used, with some success, by the present writer.

History of community economic development

The modern history of community economic development may be traced, first, to the impact of the 1970s Labour Governments' Job Creation Programme (JCP). This gave voluntary and community organisations a first taste of setting up and running projects which not only created jobs but which allowed some trading in the marketplace. Second was the simultaneous growth in interest in workers' co-operatives as a means of creating work by and for the increasing numbers of long-term unemployed. Third, in Scotland, was the launch in 1976 of the seminal community co-operative programme in the Highlands and Islands by the then Highlands and Islands Development Board (HIDB) (see chapter 8).

Other pioneering work soon followed in Scotland's central belt: in Edinburgh (where Craigmillar Festival Enterprises was established), by Glasgow Council of Voluntary Services (which initiated Goodwill Incorporated) and Strathclyde Region's Local Enterprise Advisory Project (LEAP) – based at Paisley College. Although there were some links with traditional community development at that time (for example, LEAP was rooted in Strathclyde's anti-poverty social strategy and described itself as taking a 'community development approach to local economic development')[2] for the most part these local, community-based economic development initiatives developed separately from the mainstream community development tradition.

Much community development was then, in the 1970s (and still is), locked into managing community facilities on behalf of local authorities or into delivering council services. Within local government, community development has been more usually located within housing, education or leisure and recreation departments and only occasionally in the economic development or planning departments. Historically, community development in Britain has been linked to social welfare, education and recreation and *not* to the economy, reflecting that social–economic divide which the very term 'social economy' seeks to break down.

Perhaps the most significant contribution of the Community Development Projects (CDPs) of the 1970s was to focus attention on the role of the economy, of industrial history and of contemporary change in creating and sustaining poverty and disadvantage in the society of today.[3] The human and social ills in the handful of neighbourhoods covered by the CDP were shown to be the consequence not of social pathology but of structural changes and historical practices over which local people had little, if any, influence. In the face of this increasingly powerful analysis, community development responded in one of three ways. First, by working with people's and labour organisations to empower them to challenge, fight against and publicise and politicise the causes of poverty and disempowerment. Second, by simply retreating further into service provision and facilities management. Third, by adopting community development techniques to work with local people to create local, independent, alternative structures and organisations which engaged in the local economy, creating some jobs, providing some services and giving some element of control over limited parts of the local economy. The growth of social and community enterprise derives from this third approach.

During the concluding decade of the last century, however, there were signs that the three tendencies were beginning to come together, not least perhaps because the more strident and sectional claims of the first and third approaches had become modified in the light of practical experience in the UK political climate and shifts in world affairs. In particular, adherents of the first approach are more likely to recognise that, in the pluralistic society of the twenty-first century, the fight to change the nature and direction of the world's political and economic systems cannot ignore the need for people to have their own institutions, through which they can provide and control goods and services and which may become one of the key means of challenging the existing order. At the same time the third approach has come to realise that the creation of alternative, community-controlled mechanisms at the local level is of itself inadequate to challenge the macro-institutions which must themselves change, and so its radical proponents have come to seek wider, political alliances. Meanwhile the world of the middle approach has been turned upside-down by the onslaught on the role and powers of local government, the separation of procuring and providing, and the trend towards contracting-out and the consequent search for partners and for 'arms-length' ways of managing facilities which is increasingly pushing local government practitioners into the third approach.

Almost overnight, the voluntary and community sectors began to be counted as part of the economy and are now required to operate more as businesses. Income rarely comes as a grant and will probably be a service level agreement or some other form of contract. Organisations depend on a mix of funding sources to make the books balance: earned income from sales is mixed with various styles of contract, with free labour (volunteers) and with fund-raised income. The National Council for Voluntary Organisations (NCVO) reports that as much as one-third of voluntary sector income now comes from some form of trade.[4] This should not be seen as community and voluntary organisations becoming businesses, but rather about their adopting more business-like approaches to the management of their affairs.

The distinction between community organisation and community enterprise has become increasingly blurred and within the concept of the third system we can expect movement in both directions – from right to left and left to right of the diagram on page 25 – as some voluntary organisations evolve into social enterprises while some social enterprises reposition themselves as voluntary organisations. Whereas in the 1970s and 1980s it was common practice to set up separate specialist development agencies for the development of co-operatives, community enterprises and credit unions, now those agencies which remain are likely to be offering a support and development service across the spectrum of community and social enterprises.

There has been a steady and inevitable merging of community development, community economic development and co-operative development. Always the starting point is with groups of people, with a neighbourhood or a geographical focus, or with some other common bond. Ideally we should be able to use the term 'community development' as the generic expression to cover all aspects of development at local level. The term 'community economic development' is no longer useful, perpetuating, as it does, the separation of economic from social. There is economic advantage in social activity and social advantage in economic activity. The role of community development will be to support all forms of activity within the third system and to do away with false and unhelpful distinctions.

Development starts with the community as it is and how the people perceive their situation, their needs and the problems they face. For them 'development' is what they want to see happen and what accords with their perceptions of what should and can be done. That is a holistic approach which will always defy the convenient categorisation or pigeon-hole approach beloved of official agencies and bureaucrats. It makes planning in an abstract sense more problematic.

The happenstance factor in local development

Then there is happenstance, or as one person put it 'accidents of person and place'.

In 2001 I revisited, for the first time in over two years, a remote community in the Scottish Highlands where I had had the good fortune to work with the local community some years before on projects which formed part of a local community development plan. The plan had been agreed through a process of fairly extensive community consultation which had led to a vision for the future and to an agend a for action – perhaps, with the benefit of hindsight, a more apt term than 'plan'. The occasion of my visit was Regatta day and the formal inauguration of the waterfront improvements, which had just been completed. They comprise an extended jetty, complete with sheltering wall to wind- and sea-ward; a renovated bothy on the shore now serving as the store for the Regatta and the Jetty Associations; and a second and erstwhile tumbledown bothy opposite the jetty converted to provide showers and toilets for visiting yachtspeople and others.

The new community centre, one of the first funded through the Millennium Commission's programme in Scotland for village hall improvements, is now a thriving community enterprise. It provides a tourist information centre, tea-shop and wet-weather games facilities for visitors; accommodates the local doctor's surgery; hosts the weekly senior citizens' lunch club plus a wide range of regular local social events and meetings, including serving as the village primary school's gym. Three people are employed, and many others give a great deal of voluntary effort to make the centre a success.

The lighthouse visitor centre, also run as an independent community trust and supported by the council, has been open for a number of years and was enjoying its busiest season ever (foot and mouth notwithstanding) for day visitors and for bookings for its two holiday cottages. New workshops built beside the community centre by the local enterprise company house the outreach IT training programme of the FE college 80 miles away. One workshop was then empty – available and waiting for someone else to start up a new business. For the past few years the local community has raised the money to maintain and manage a winter ferry service to the neighbouring island, giving access to the high school and to the shopping and banking services there.

I noticed other things had happened. The petrol station had been tidied up and landscaped with two new benches. The district housing association had bought back two former council houses. The school roll had increased by half, such that a second teacher was to be appointed. The younger generation of some longstanding residents had returned, with children. A new public service employee had arrived, also with children. New houses were being built.

All in all there was a sense of improvement and steady development impressive for a small community which in winter numbers no more than 150 people.

From outside it is possible to see how different parts of the development puzzle begin to fit together, each successive piece in place making it easier for the next to be fitted. But it is not possible to claim that here is a grand development plan which is unfolding exactly as laid down some years ago. Then, there was a vision about what might happen and some concrete ideas, some of which have now come about. But so much of what has happened and is happening depends on two crucial, but largely unplannable, factors.

First, it takes an enormous amount of energy and hard work on the part of the local people in small remote communities (and indeed in communities anywhere) just to keep them going, let alone undertake new plans and projects. As elsewhere, not everybody joins in actively, so those who do have an even greater task. It is hard to find an evening free – or half an evening – for a meeting in this community, such is the pressure on the activists' time. One couple who were moving away to a small town a 25-minute launch ride distant had to resign from no fewer than 13 committees when they left!

The second factor is happenstance, the chance that brings the young generation home wanting to revive the family business and bringing children, new skills and new energy. The chance of man meeting woman and deciding to stay on and run a business using modern communication technology from the remote location. The chance of noticing an advertisement for a job when on holiday in the area and deciding to come and live there. The chance of a house coming onto the market at the right time. The chance that brings the right cocktail of people and energies together to get things done. The chance that makes it possible for so many people from different backgrounds to work together. The chance that there is sufficient energy and bloody-mindedness to see things through.

Energy and happenstance: crucial to the development process and the factors which account for why something works in one place but not in another. The factors which bureaucracies and bureaucrats find difficult to cope with because they mean people and local circumstances can cause the best-laid plans to 'gang aft agley'. These are the factors which keep those of us working in local development in touch with the real world and which mock any efforts to come up with plans of the 'one size fits all' variety.

Community Futures Workshops

Community Futures Workshops (CFW) were devised as a means of attempting to initiate a development process within a community which may lead to the decision to form a community enterprise or indeed more than one. It recognises that the initiative to do something may come from within the community (the local councillor, a community organisation, a group of people talking in the pub) or it may come from outside (typically, the local council or other agency which equally thinks 'something' should be done). Whatever the starting point, there needs to be a process which determines what that something might be and establishes whether there is support for doing it.

Although the hope clearly is that 'something will be done', those promoting the process should recognise from the start that the time or other happenstance factors may not be right for something to gel and develop. In other words, coming to the conclusion that it is *not* possible to proceed with preparing and implementing a development plan should be accepted as a possible outcome.

CFW was devised so that people taking part should know clearly what it was they were being asked to engage in and that it would be for a finite period, at the end of which decisions would be taken about whether and how to proceed. In this way, no person or agency would be locked into an open-ended commitment which was going nowhere but which was difficult to get out of. The process was devised so as to be affordable. The workshops described below and in Appendix i could easily be embellished and extended, although each extra feature adds costs.

Community Futures is a community development process designed to identify a common vision which leads to economic and social action in a community. The process is based on a series of five Community Futures Workshops which aim to initiate and focus local development.

The workshop process is based on the following key principles:

- That local development should be community-led;
- That it should involve all community stakeholders: residents, local business and industry, the public sector, and church and voluntary organisations;
- That developing a common understanding of the nature of a community and its problems will lead to a common vision which in turn will lead to a common purpose;
- That community development should be based on an equality of partnership between stakeholders;
- That discussion about local development should lead to practical plans for *action*;
- That development should embrace, connect with and tackle social, economic and environmental issues.

The process is designed to enable a lead local group or an agency to initiate development in the community; it is a step-by-step process where all taking part can understand what will happen; it is time-limited, in that there is an end-point to the initial process, at which time decisions have to be made about whether and how to continue; and it restrains the cost. The five-workshops process has been extensively used in Merseyside and on Teesside, but it is by no means a unique method. There are other similar ones, created by other development workers and agencies, in use around the country. Most are based on participatory consultative principles and in describing the present method the intention is to highlight those principles and to demonstrate how such a development process could be crucial to the expansion of social enterprise throughout local communities.

The CFW process recognises that, while the residents of a community may be the most important stakeholder group as their quality of life will be affected by a development process (or lack of it), other stakeholders are involved, who depend on or have a responsibility for the community but who do not live there. These representatives of the three systems include public-sector agencies, voluntary and church organisations, local businesses, employers of local labour and so forth. The development planning process should seek to engage those stakeholders from the beginning so that they, as well as residents, have some sense of ownership of whatever plans may emerge and, by being involved in the process, have a better understanding of how and why certain choices may have been made. It is a common mistake for residents to develop their own vision and plan alone and then spend frustrating years knocking at the doors of other bodies trying to persuade them to give support and backing.

The process is therefore based on the concept of building up an agreed vision for the community based on a common understanding of the issues involved. It is that sense of common purpose which is crucial: community-led, but in partnership with the other stakeholders who have their own commitments and responsibilities to the community.

A further key principle is to adopt a holistic approach which responds to and embraces all aspects: social, economic, environmental and cultural. The process is not about 'developing the local economy', it is about developing the community in the belief that all aspects interconnect and have an impact one on the other. Tackling what is perceived as an environmental problem or an issue of personal security may well have unexpected effects on the local economy. That means not falling into the popular trap of talking from the outset only about 'economic development'.

Finally, the process is designed to lead to an agenda for action: clear proposals for projects which form pieces of the jigsaw and which in turn may stimulate people to pick up other pieces. All this is as much about stimulating and generating impetus as about implementation.

A detailed description of how the five workshops may be run and what they each seek to achieve can be found in Appendix i.

The CFW process is about unleashing the chemistry of collective action and forging a community-led enterprise to work in partnership with different shareholders. This will not always happen. Where the process succeeds, a sound foundation can be laid in a relatively short time and at reasonable cost. Where it fails, other approaches must be employed to make it possible for a future development process to take root. Maybe there are some communities where it just cannot happen. We should not fear failure, but we should celebrate and support success.

In the next chapter we examine the specific support needed for growing social enterprises in the UK and emphasise the importance of support structures which are of the social economy and belong to the third system itself.

NOTES

1. Robert Burns, *The Complete Illustrated Poems, Songs and Ballads* (London, Lomond Books, 1990).
2. Local Enterprise Advisory Project, *Annual Report 1979–80* (Local Government Unit, Paisley College).
3. See, for example, H. Butcher, J. Pearce, I Cole and A. Glen, *Community Participation and Poverty: Final report of the Cumbria Community Development Project* (University of York, 1979), and other local and national CDP publications of that era.
4. www.ncvo-vol.org.uk

8 Supporting social enterprise

The striking development of the last five years has been the growth of avowed political and administrative support for social enterprise, especially since the 1997 general election. At Westminster, responsibility for social enterprise has been specifically given to the Department of Trade and Industry (DTI), and a junior minister appointed. There has been a Social Investment Task Force[1] and the government's Social Exclusion Unit Policy Action Team 3 (PAT3), focused on social enterprise,[2] has made recommendations which have been carried through by the Small Business Service (SBS) and the Regional Development Agencies (RDAs). Although support for social enterprise is largely a devolved matter, potential support for it will always rest to some extent with the London government and so it is encouraging that Westminster has taken the lead. And it is a substantial lead.

Whereas in the 1980s the community enterprise movement was led from Scotland and the other parts of the Celtic fringe, learning from and building on the Irish examples of community co-operatives in the West of Ireland, the current drive to develop a role for social enterprise is coming from England. For activists in Scotland it is an especially difficult time as the Scottish Executive's commitment to social enterprise seems to have got lost in the personnel changes within the Executive and seems unlikely to re-emerge until after the 2003 elections.

Government support has been translated into the establishment of a small Social Enterprise Unit within the DTI with the remit to:

- act as a focal point and co-ordinator for policy-making affecting social enterprise;
- promote and champion social enterprise;
- take action needed to address the barriers to the growth of social enterprise;
- identify and spread good practice.[3]

Written and spoken support has come from the Prime Minister himself: 'Government seeks to do all it can to help the future development of social enterprise'[4] and comes regularly from the present Secretary of State for Trade and Industry, Patricia Hewitt: 'I believe we now have a real opportunity to create a much larger mainstream social enterprise sector in Britain.'[5]

Around the country the SBS has been required to make an explicit commitment to support social enterprise. The RDAs are expected likewise to have strategies for supporting social enterprise and these are now emerging.[6] The national Phoenix Fund announced in 1999 to encourage entrepreneurship in disadvantaged areas has been used extensively to support social enterprise (except in Scotland). RDAs and local authorities have commissioned various mapping exercises of their local social economy (leading some to feel the sector is being 'mapped to death') and local councils continue to prepare social economy strategies. The bidding guidelines for Single Regeneration Budget (SRB) 6 explicitly featured social enterprise. European programmes have also targeted resources at the social economy; for example the current EQUAL Programme theme D is 'Strengthening the Social Economy'.

Social economy war talk

Outside government and the public sector there has been a widening involvement in and support for the social economy. Banks, notably NatWest and The Royal Bank of Scotland, have supported Community Development Finance Initiatives (CDFIs) including Social Investment Scotland. National Award Schemes have been established for the Social Enterprise of the Year. *New Start* magazine profiles a 'Social Entrepreneur of the Month' and a week in March 2002 was designated 'Social Economy Week'. University courses in social and community enterprise have appeared. The Co-operative Movement, after many years keeping rather aloof from modern community enterprise trends, has now clearly aligned itself as part of the social economy and, through the Co-operative Union (now merged with the Industrial Common Ownership Movement) is playing an increasingly active part in offering support. National organisations such as the New Economics Foundation, Development Trusts Association and Community Action Network, with Social Enterprise London and others, have built a higher profile for social enterprises through their research, publications, lobbying and publicity work. This growth in talk (as well as action) about social enterprise is significant and important. As one source pointed out, Churchill's most important role as wartime leader was allegedly to talk about the war and make people believe it could be won, at times in the face of what seemed impossible odds.

In the social economy war talk the government position seems increasingly to be about using social enterprises to deliver government policies; 'modernising and reforming' public services. It is as if Government is saying, not 'How can we help social enterprises?' but 'How can social enterprises help us?' This of course begs the bigger question, which has been discussed earlier, about whether social enterprises are about substantial change in society or about making the current system work better. Opinions are sharply divided, from 'The death of share capitalism was not in the government's manifesto' to present policies being no more than 'There's a wee sweetie – go away and play.'

Although it is tempting to forget the bigger issue in order to get on with the job, it does inevitably impinge on how support is delivered to the social economy.

Reformers will be happy to seek support from the existing public and private-sector systems while radicals will be more likely to advocate letting go and building new mechanisms which belong to the third system.

Bespoke support services

While it is good that Business Links (Small Business Gateways in Scotland) is required to understand what social enterprises are, it should not necessarily be seen as the primary support mechanism for social enterprises. The SBS and the Local Enterprise Companies, in Scotland, were established primarily to grow first-system businesses, and their competence is in dealing with first-system business. It is from that system that most business advisers are recruited and they derive their service ethos from it.

While it has become fashionable to argue that social enterprises are not really any different from first-system businesses, in truth they are radically different and require a support mechanism which derives from the third system itself. It all comes down to the fundamental issue of whether social enterprises should be an 'integral and dynamic' part of the 'real' economy or whether they should be in the forefront of developing a more dominant and distinctive third system. One commentator has estimated that social enterprises are 80% like other businesses, while another has explained that 'social enterprises should be served like other enterprises and, subject to their social goals, they should act like other businesses'.[7] It is however the difference which is important and which drives both social enterprise and its need for separate, bespoke support services. For example, while a first-system business may manage with a business plan, a social enterprise must have a *social enterprise plan* demonstrating not only that its commercial plan is viable and achievable but also that its social aims are compatible with the business plan and also achievable. A social enterprise plan will have social performance targets as well as business performance targets.

With political commitment to developing the social economy, public-sector support for social enterprise will be crucial for providing a support framework and ensuring that the necessary mechanisms exist. But rather than take the lead, the public sector should let go to enable the social economy itself to take the lead. 'Let the sector use the tools' as one person expressed it. That supportive framework should create the necessary legal frameworks, encourage and facilitate the requisite financial and investment mechanisms, require public-sector agencies to have policies which reflect the political intent to build the social economy, and provide the funds needed to support a network of independent social enterprise development agencies.

At present there is a maze of support arrangements for the social economy. A recent review in London revealed no fewer than 83 different support bodies.[8] A similar Scottish review in 2001 discovered more than 35 non-statutory bodies.[9] In addition to these identifiable bodies there are in all areas increasing numbers of private consultancy agencies specialising in social economy support work, and of course there are those social enterprises themselves which take on a development role working with social enterprises, often through a subsidiary consultancy company.

This growth of support mechanisms is to be welcomed, although it does bring with it questions of competence and quality. In all areas there should be different styles of support and delivery arrangements to reflect local circumstances. Partnerships may be developed which involve third-, second- and first-system people working together. Such is already the case in areas such as Lochaber in Scotland where the Local Enterprise Company, Highland Council and Voluntary Action Lochaber have co-ordinated to create Community Enterprise Lochaber as a local social economy support agency – small as yet but starting in an existing, supportive environment where 25% of the enterprises on the small business database of Lochaber Enterprise are recognised to be community enterprises.[10] In other areas, notably Devon and Birmingham, arrangements have been made for the public-sector agencies to sub-contract their support role for social enterprises to agencies which belong to the sector itself.[11]

Accountable to the social economy

Such trends follow what should surely be the key principle guiding the main provision of support services for the social economy – that they come from the social economy and are accountable to the social economy. This support may be delivered at three distinct levels.

At local level existing successful social enterprises can provide a support service especially for new-start community enterprises in their locality. This is the local development role which was envisaged in the original Community Business model (see page 49) and was described as the function of a 'core community business' in *At the Heart of the Community Economy*.[12] Many development trusts now play this role and some local authorities, Liverpool and Fife for example, have specifically contracted with local social enterprises to provide a support and development service. In Liverpool these were designated 'enabling bodies' – enabling community-based economic development to take place.[13]

A second tier of support should be available through intermediary support organisations that are established themselves as social enterprises, accountable to a social and community enterprise membership in their area (and to other appropriate stakeholders such as public-sector agencies or national funding bodies). Such bodies will be similar to the co-operative development agencies and the community enterprise support units of the past, where these were independent and accountable to their own sector. It has been fairly well established that where there is an active and competent local development body, a growing cluster of social enterprises is likely to emerge, not dependent on the unit, but supporting each other, networking and inter-trading. Such development bodies are fundamentally different, however, from those support agencies established as arms-length bodies by the public sector, and effectively controlled by it. It should also be clear that this second level of support is specific to the social economy – that part of the third system which engages in trade. It is not about general support to voluntary organisations, except where they are seeking to develop into social enterprises. Voluntary organisations are well served by a national network of Councils of Voluntary Service (CVSs).

Some would include all voluntary organisations in the sweep of the social economy and argue that CVSs can be the appropriate bodies to offer support across the whole sector. This is unlikely to be a successful strategy. It is better to recognise the distinction between trading and non-trading (as expressed in the diagram on page 25) and to see the CVS network focus on the voluntary organisation sector while social enterprise support bodies concentrate on social economy organisations. Linkages and collaboration should exist at all levels, but the enterprise focus of social enterprises calls for dedicated support structures.

The presumption should not be that the second-tier support bodies would themselves provide all the support services directly. In practice they would co-ordinate and facilitate, and procure by sub-contracting to the first tier and to the private consultancies operating in this field. They will therefore need to develop some form of quality control in respect of their sub-contractors. Already most regional and local networks have built up databases of consultants and expert practitioners. The London Social Economy Task Force has proposed a system of approving contractors and of issuing vouchers. First, the London Social Economy Agency would approve those persons they considered competent to offer services to social enterprises, services such as business planning, project development, legal structures, financial management and advice, market research, preparing feasibility studies, staff recruitment and staff training, and so build up a register of approved contractors. Second, when offering financial support for a social enterprise, say for help with preparing a social enterprise plan or with training directors about their roles and responsibilities, they would offer a voucher which could be used to engage only a practitioner from the approved list. In this way the social economy would keep control of the delivery of the support services even when using non-sector contractors and would ensure that only effective practitioners were used.[14]

A third tier of support will come from the various national networks, (such as the Co-operative Union, Industrial Common Ownership Movement (ICOM), Development Trusts Association (DTA), or Community Business Scotland Network (CBSN)) which are themselves modelled on social enterprise structures, with members to whom they are accountable. The national bodies will be able to provide those services which are better organised or financed at national level, a good example being the Social Enterprise Partnership established to deliver in Great Britain an EQUAL Programme: Strengthening the Social Economy.[15]

Also part of this third tier will be specialist networks (such as the Community Recycling Network)[16] or trade associations (such as the recently formed Association of Community Development Finance Initiatives (CDFIs))[17]. Such networks and associations will offer the capability to function rather like the consortia of social co-operatives in Italy, working together to bulk-purchase materials, lever financial support and tender for contracts as well as share their specialist information and experience. Social Enterprise London has similarly been developing such consortia.

The goal should be to build the support capacity within the social economy and deliver it through agencies that are of the social economy. While some specialist and technical expertise will always be accessed from outside the social economy, increasingly support will be sought from within, from people and agencies who understand how it works. This calls for a substantial shift in thinking. At present, policy tends to be geared to the premise that social enterprises may need some specialist help to get going, but can then 'graduate' to the support systems of the first system like other businesses. New thinking argues that social enterprises require appropriate social economy support, all the way along.

Specialist support, mutually provided

Support structures must target enterprises at all stages and locations within the social enterprise wedge. At very local level that means working with those individuals, groups and organisations who are feeling their way towards setting up a social or community enterprise, sometimes referred to as 'pre-start-up' development. This is the community development approach rather than a business development approach and is about 'creating community enterprises' not just 'starting up businesses in poor communities'.

Setting up a social enterprise is very different from setting up a first-system business. Its business ideas must tie in with a clear social purpose, based on a consensus vision of the host community or constituency. Social enterprise development must focus on how groups work together, on how social enterprise structures function, on training lay directors to understand the business and financial aspects, on making democracy work, on calculating how the social costs will be met, on managing unpaid along with paid staff – as well as on the standard nuts and bolts of running a business. The diagram on Community Enterprise Planning and Monitoring, which was first developed for *At the Heart of the Community Economy*, attempts to show how at all stages of social enterprise development the social and the business aspects must be planned and monitored in tandem, with an understanding of how each influences the other. A social enterprise which adopts the practice of social accounting and audit will have social management accounts to consider as well as financial.

At all stages of a social enterprise's development its support needs are different from those of first-system businesses and require customised input. Raising finance requires appropriate models. Legal structures require specialist advice and guidance, not least for the larger mutuals on how to avoid carpet-bagging and demutualisation. A serious task which confronts the social economy generally, and its existing national bodies specifically, is to strengthen its own capacity to mutually provide such expert help. Here there is an important role for the large mutuals, for the Co-operative Group, including the Co-operative Bank, and for the other well-established social enterprises like the housing associations to take a lead and make their combined experience and expertise more readily

Community Enterprise Planning and Monitoring
Commercial
Community Benefit
What product or service? What market gap?
Market Research
What community needs? Which to tackle?
Confirm business objective(s)
Objectives
Define social and environmental objective(s)
What will the business do? By whom? With what?
Description
What will be done? By whom? How? When?
Materials, labour, overheads: turnover, margins, price
Costings
Time, use of facilities, materials
Agree targets: sales, turnover, profit
Targets
Confirm realistic social performance targets
Set up systems: cash flow, P&L, balance sheet, time management, job sheets, etc.
Management & Financial Information
Set up social book-keeping and accounting systems
Monthly management accounts
Monitor
Monthly/quarterly report on social performance and cost
Adjust in light of reality
Adjustments
Adjust in light of reality
Assets/liabilities, liquidity, performance, net worth
Annual Audit
Performance verified showing cost to company and contribution to society
PROFIT/LOSS

available. That lead could result in secondments to national networks or regional social enterprise development bodies, in making experts available through the national networks, in offering mentors to work alongside smaller or newly forming social enterprises, in building opportunities for procurement from within the social economy and in encouraging greater inter-trading. This surely must be the practical implication of the Co-operative Movement's assertion that it must 'be seen as part of the wider family of businesses that trade profitably and for a social purpose'.[18] Now is the moment to show that family relationships matter, and for social enterprises and the social economy to take greater responsibility themselves for growing their own movement and translating the principle of mutual help into positive action.

Learning from the past

Even if an independent social economy support network is developed based on the three levels described, there will also be programmes or regimes of support coming from government (or from the national and regional authorities) and from Europe. Historically, one of the most imaginative – and successful – was the original community co-operative programme of the Highlands and Islands Development Board (HIDB) in 1976. It provided for the appointment of development workers to promote the idea of forming a co-operative and to help communities come to the decision to set one up and to support the planning and development process. Later this development function was taken over by the Association of Community Enterprises in the Highlands and Islands (ACEHI), an autonomous and democratic federation of the co-operatives themselves.

The programme provided a capital fund which matched pound for pound the money raised by the communities. Since they were formed as co-operatives those funds raised locally (and from the Highland diaspora) were in the form of co-operative shares (one member, one vote; not in relation to the size of shareholding) and there are people in the Highlands today still proud of their £25 share in the remaining, successful community co-operatives. The aim of the programme was to encourage the formation of multifunctional co-operatives and management grants were available, typically for three years, to subsidise the appointment of managers at an early stage to steer the developments, long before they might be financially able to sustain the costs of professional management. And finally, all the community co-operatives could access the other financial and technical support programmes for small businesses in the Highlands and Islands.

The HIDB scheme was emulated in the central belt of Scotland, in particular in Strathclyde, with two important differences. First, pound for pound matching grants were not included as it was considered unlikely that disadvantaged urban communities would be able to raise funds to be matched; community businesses qualified for start-up and management grants without raising their own funds. Second, community businesses also had difficulty accessing other support available for small business on the grounds that they were already being supported as community businesses with public funds.

The idea of matching grants worked well with the community co-operatives, generating both money and widespread community support and involvement, and giving people a tangible stake in their community enterprise. Although it is argued that the matching grant idea can work only in relatively small and homogeneous communities, it has in fact seldom been tried or applied elsewhere. It is likely that similar levels of involvement and commitment might be developed in some urban communities, bringing the same sense of having a tangible stake in the project. Certainly that was the case with the Galliagh Community Enterprise in Derry in the 1980s, where residents collected funds door-to-door to raise the money needed to buy the local supermarket into community ownership.[19]

The Strathclyde model of financial support was based around maximum grants of £30,000 which led to a proliferation of '£30,000 companies', claiming this amount irrespective of what they may have been aiming to do. As can too easily happen, the funding regime available drove the development process rather than responding to it.[20] Although these models of grant-aiding social enterprises are becoming unfashionable through the wish to avoid grant dependency they can nonetheless be an effective way of injecting public investment into the creation of social enterprise provided certain lessons are learned. First, it is vital that the grants are paid immediately and in full rather than drip-fed quarterly in arrears, and second, that they are seen as investments in an enterprise rather than as grants for specific, individually auditable purposes. The Irish government still uses a comprehensive grant scheme for community enterprise which, as well as covering a wage grant for a manager, includes a capital grant per employee, a wage grant per employee equivalent to the national minimum wage and a contribution to training and general overheads. Grants may be paid for up to three years. New Zealand's Community Employment Organisation Programme also has comparable features.

Another model from 1980s Scotland, the 'Tayside' model, applied a business development approach to the creation of social enterprise, rather than a community development approach. This entailed establishing a city-wide 'community business' as the ownership vehicle for businesses which would be researched and then set up in the town, either located in a disadvantaged neighbourhood or taking most of their workforce from such an area. This top-down, business-led model, also used in Middlesbrough, was not generally successful. Where businesses were set up and traded they were in no real sense connected to a community and were without sustainable roots. The top-down approach is being repeated in contemporary moves to franchise or replicate successful social enterprises in other areas. While there has been some success with this approach, notably by the Aspire Group,[21] care must be taken not simply to try and 'parachute' enterprise into a new area. Initial community development work will always be required, to build interest and support and to put down the roots which will allow the enterprise to become 'of' the community rather than 'for' the community.

It is also salutary to remember that all successful social enterprises, like the Co-op, started small and built up slowly. There is a danger in showcasing examples of successful social enterprises as they are in the glory days, without emphasising the low-key, hard-work start.

Community Land Unit

An excellent contemporary example of a public-sector support regime is the Community Land Unit (CLU) of Highlands and Islands Enterprise.[22] Its remit is to facilitate and support Highland communities who wish to try and purchase the island or estate on which they live and work and manage their affairs as a community enterprise. Operating with clear political support from the Scottish Executive and with access to finance the CLU has been able to co-ordinate – along with many other agencies and community players – the successful acquisition into community ownership of such islands as Eigg and Gigha and such estates as Knoydart and Assynt.[23]

In microcosm, the CLU is a good example of what can happen when the political vision and will are there. What has sometimes been lacking, however, is ground-level support for communities wishing to explore the possibility of a community buy-out. ACEHI closed down in 1996 having failed to become financially self-sustaining, and since that time the availability of support in remote parts of Scotland has been patchy and *ad hoc.*

The experience of ACEHI was not unique. Throughout Great Britain independent co-operative and community enterprise units have closed down because of reductions in funding from the public sector. Those which have survived have often been transformed into consultancy organisations chasing contracts to sustain themselves or into delivery agencies for EU and government programmes. Either way they become funding-driven and lose their capacity to engage in grass-roots development work using the crucial community development approach to create social enterprise. Such work cannot be financially self-sustaining; it has to be paid for through public-sector finance and must be a well-resourced element of the proposed network of independent social enterprise support bodies.

The original programme of the London-based School for Social Entrepreneurs (SSE), founded by the late Michael Young in 1997, seemed to take something of an elitist approach to training individual social entrepreneurs.[24] However, a newer generation of locally based 'schools' often connected to social enterprises has begun to emerge to support the idea of practitioner-to-practitioner learning. The Regen School in Sheffield[25] and the School for Social Entrepreneurs run by BRAG Enterprises in Fife[26] are in the forefront of this very practical approach to intra-social economy learning and support.

The new university courses offering a range of postgraduate qualifications are evidence that the social economy is infiltrating ever more corners of public life and thinking. Developing a stronger academic capacity within the social economy and offering a theoretical framework for the social economy will be important benefits to come from engagement with academic institutions.

Asset transfer

Two specific aspects of essential public-sector support for social enterprise focus on the transfer of assets to social enterprises and public-sector procurement practice.

The acquisition of assets – usually property – can transform the balance sheet of a social enterprise and help it generate revenue. Use of assets in this way can contribute significantly to the financial viability of a social enterprise. Recently government has indicated its intention to tackle perceived barriers to the transfer of assets to social enterprises. The Social Enterprise Strategy states: 'We will explore how best to address any real and perceived barriers to the transfer of assets to social enterprises.'[27] Such moves are very much to be welcomed coming, as they do, after a lengthy period characterised by the reluctance of the public sector, and local authorities in particular, to consider the transfer of assets.

Too often councils appear to hide behind central government rules, but problems experienced by social enterprises suggest that this often masks a more deep-seated resistance to 'letting go'. That resistance may stem from a number of factors. First, there has been a real sense of frustration and anger within local government about the way its role and importance was diminished during the years of Conservative government. That has been exacerbated since 1997 by the continuing verbal and actual attacks by the New Labour government. Understandably, this can make local councillors and officials less than enthusiastic about passing assets to newly created and independent social enterprise bodies. Second, and related to the first, there is the issue of power and control. Traditionally, councils have provided services for the people and it is difficult for them to change this approach to allow the people to do things for themselves. Government, despite its rhetoric, shares that problem also and sometimes lacks confidence in the ability of social and community enterprises to deliver. Third, and perversely, local and central government has acquired a misguided belief that only the private sector really knows how to run things.

One of the most notorious examples of reluctance to part with assets concerns Govan Workspace's dealings with the former Strathclyde Regional Council. One of Scotland's first community businesses and one of the most successful, Govan Workspace Limited (GWL) now runs three properties in Glasgow. The tale of frustration and anger spanning a decade over acquiring the former primary school which was their first workspace was told by Pat Cassidy in GWL's twentieth birthday celebration booklet: 'The final victory was achieved in August 1991 when Six Harmony Row was sold to Govan Workspace for £200,000, a figure arrived at as a commercial valuation of the property. But it was by no means a perfect outcome and pushed the company into unnecessary debt. In essence, what it meant was that, having taken over a valueless property in 1981 and invested several thousand pounds in refurbishment, Govan Workspace would have to pay for it all over again.'[28]

The Govan Workspace story has been repeated in all its key features around the country; yet the transfer of assets to social and community enterprises can be an effective way of keeping them in community ownership, ensuring that they continue to be used for the common good and retaining any appreciation in value for use by society.

Procurement

Public procurement policies also can be used more effectively to allow social enterprises to bid for and win contracts for the delivery of public services. Although councils often argue that they are constrained by government and EU regulations, the government has stated its belief that 'within the existing regulatory framework, local authorities have opportunities to open up the procurement process to social enterprises'.[29]

Part of the problem, as with asset transfer, is to make public-sector agencies more willing to consider contracting with social enterprises and prepared to consider specifying contracts in such a way as to make it easier for social enterprises to tender. Part of that specification should include being absolutely clear what non-commercial benefits are expected to be delivered and how they may be monitored, measured and reported.

In the North-East of England, Uniun Enterprise Trust has a negotiated contract with its local council to carry out the repair and maintenance work on all council houses in the village of Pegswood. The council agreed the contract as being 'Best Value' and has been willing to specify a separate contract for the relatively small number of houses in the village.[30] In Ealing, the borough council has developed a tendering assistance programme to help social enterprises through the complicated paperwork associated with submitting bids. Government is proposing to prepare a tendering 'tool kit' to advise social enterprises on winning public-sector business.[31] For their part social enterprises can consider forming consortia in order to be better able to bid for larger contracts, along the lines of the model successfully used by the Italian social co-operatives and currently being developed by Social Enterprise London in respect of childcare and other social enterprise activities in London.[32]

National networking

The social economy has a plethora of networks which reflect the many different approaches to and interpretations of what social economy and social enterprise are. The establishment of the UK Social Enterprise Coalition in 2001 was a most significant step, bringing together the full range of protagonists in the social economy.[33] It symbolises the unification of the traditional co-operative faction with the new community and social enterprise factions. Once similar coalitions exist in all the nations and the regions there will be a comprehensive geographical spread within the Coalition. It is also encouraging that government, at least in England, is willing both to support the Coalition financially, in partnership with the Co-operative Group, and to recognise it as a 'strong voice' and a 'focal point' for the sector. The remit of the Coalition is to:

- be a voice for social enterprise;
- develop capacity and raise quality within the sector;
- develop targeted initiatives; and
- work for a legal and financial framework that will encourage the growth and development of social enterprises.

The UK social enterprise charter

'We believe that the UK needs an expansion of all forms of social enterprise to support sustainable economic and social regeneration and provide for a diverse national economy.

'Social enterprise is an umbrella term for organisations that achieve a variety of social aims predominantly, but not necessarily exclusively, by trading in goods and services. They are competitive businesses, which often will have invented innovative ways of meeting local needs. Across the UK, they have proved to be a very effective way of developing, then channelling, the skills and talents of diverse groups into producing the services and products – from new technologies to housing management, and from manufacturing to credit unions.

'We believe that national, regional and local governments and agencies should integrate the support and promotion of social enterprises into their policies and plans and funding programmes.

'The support provided to businesses should encourage and assist their formation and all social investment strategies should include provision for social enterprise development.'

The aim must be for the Coalition to act as the 'peak' body for the social economy, but be accountable to its members in the nations and the regions. That will require it to adopt a robust democratic structure and to ensure that the structure works effectively. Its inception was perceived as a London-based initiative involving a predominance of south-east agencies and people. However, the opportunity is now presenting itself to develop a national consensus of what the social economy is, and, more importantly, what it could be. Building contacts, building strength and, especially, building trust will allow the Coalition to speak with authority, representing the combined might of the sector.

It is also to be hoped that over time the number of different 'tendencies' might reduce as well as the number of different networks, representative bodies and support agencies. A hint of what could happen can be perceived in the GB Social Enterprise Partnership. That Partnership brings together the New Economics Foundation, the Development Trust Association, the Co-operative Union, Social Firms UK and Social Enterprise London. Similar partnership working is being replicated in some of the regions and the nations. In Scotland, for example, the delivery partnership Social Enterprise Scotland has brought together the Scottish Co-operative and Mutual Forum, CBS Network, Social Firms Scotland, Employee Ownership Scotland, Unlimited Scotland and Community Action Network (Highlands and Islands), and a Scottish Forum for Social Enterprise is being launched. It is to be hoped that the experience of working together will lead to more permanent collaborations.

Kitemark

There have been suggestions that the social economy should adopt some form of social enterprise kitemark.[34] This would be rather like the fair trade mark, allowing the public to know when they are dealing with a social enterprise. This would certainly serve to strengthen public awareness of what social enterprises are and could form part of a wider public education campaign to show that there is an alternative and viable option to the first-system way of doing business. A social enterprise label, backed by the regulatory system proposed in chapter 10, would give the public the confidence to know that if they bought from or invested in a registered social enterprise they would be contributing to the common good and not to shareholder dividends and 'fat-cat' directors' remuneration. A social enterprise label could also encourage and facilitate inter-trading and mutual help within the social economy.

A major task for the Coalition, and indeed for all involved, is to promote the concept and wider knowledge about the social economy and the significant role it already plays in the affairs of the nation. The daunting scale of this particular challenge is epitomised by a comment from the incoming chair of Business in the Community in an interview with *Social Enterprise* magazine: 'I do not think we have got many good examples yet of not-for-profit companies, but we should keep trying.'[35] Not only is the comment wide of the mark but it typifies the willingness of some people to talk down the social economy.

NOTES

1. *Enterprising Communities: Wealth beyond welfare* (Social Investment Task Force, 2000).
2. *Enterprise and Social Exclusion*, report of the National Strategy for Neighbourhood Renewal: Policy Action Team 3 (London, HM Treasury, 1999).
3. *Social Enterprise: A strategy for success* (London, Department of Trade and Industry, 2002).
4. *Ibid.*
5. Bob Grove in *Social Enterprise, Social Economy: Moving ahead*, conference report (Social Enterprise London, 2001).

6. *Social Enterprise* (2002), see note 3.
7. *Enterprise and Social Exclusion* (1999), see note 2.
8. *Time to Deliver: A social enterprise business support strategy for London*, consultation draft (London Development Agency Social Economy Task Force, July 2002).
9. Alan Kay, Sue Sadler, Ian Hunter and John Pearce, *The Role of Intermediary Support Structures in promoting Third System Employment Activities at Local Level* (West Calder, Community Business Scotland Network and Berlin, European Network for Economic Self-help and Local Development, 2001).
10. See John Pearce, 'Social economy as important as tourism', in *New Sector*, February 2002.
11. www.co-active.org.uk; www.coenterprise.co.uk
12. John Pearce, *At the Heart of the Community Economy: Community enterprise in a changing world* (London, Calouste Gulbenkian Foundation, 1993).
13. Economic Initiatives Unit, *Community-based Economic Development Strategy* (Liverpool City Council, 1994).
14. *Time to Deliver* (2002), see note 8.
15. shines@cqm.co.uk
16. www.crn.org.uk
17. www.cdfa.org.uk
18. 'The Social Economy and Co-operation' (chapter 6), in *The Co-operative Advantage: Creating a successful family of co-operative businesses*, report of the Co-operative Commission, 2001.
19. Kay Caldwell, 'Where are they now?', in *New Sector*, April 1996.
20. Pearce (1993), see note 12.
21. Paul@aspire-group.com
22. www.hie.co.uk (click on 'Strengthening Communities for Community Land Unit').
23. John Ross, 'This land is our land', in *The Scotsman*, 6 July 2002.
24. www.sse.org.uk
25. www.regenschool.com
26. www.brag.uk
27. *Social Enterprise* (2002), see note 3.
28. Pat Cassidy, *Nothing without Work* (Glasgow, Govan Workspace Limited, 2001).
29. *Social Enterprise* (2002), see note 3.
30. Uniuntrust@hotmail.com
31. *Social Enterprise* (2002), see note 3.
32. www.sel.org.uk
33. www.socialenterprise.org.uk
34. *Social Enterprise* (2002), see 3; *Enterprise and Social Exclusion* (1999), see note 2.
35. Quoted by Tim West in 'High ideals', *Social Enterprise*, July 2002.

9 Financing social enterprises

In chapter 3 we described the variety of sources of income which contribute to the viability of social enterprises. This chapter examines the different ways in which funds are or might be invested in social enterprises.

Grants and loans

Not all who work in the social economy agree that finding finance is one of the main problems facing a social enterprise. They argue that the finance is there if you have a sound proposal and if you know how to set about finding it. They describe intricate packages of finance which they have raised for particular projects: grants from UK and EU sources, 'clean' money which can be 'matched' (and 'unclean' which cannot), grants from the Community Fund and from trusts and foundations. They may also have obtained finance from private companies, loans from specialist social enterprise funds or even loans from the bank. They will explain that those specialist social enterprise loan funds which do exist are generally so small that they can only part-finance any substantial proposal.

Although many social enterprises have successfully accessed substantial funding, consummate skill is needed amongst social economy activists to use the ever-changing grant regimes to the advantage of their enterprises. It can be hard and tortuous work, completing complex application forms, learning the language the funders wish to hear, often with short deadlines followed by slow and protracted decision-making. But significant investment is then won for social enterprises. And if grants are available, why bother with loans? After all, loans have to be repaid, but a grant is forever.

It is curious how the contemporary mantra that social enterprises must be 'weaned off' grants somehow implies that it is the fault of the social enterprises that they are 'dependent' on grants. A social pathology is relied on rather than a structural analysis which would reveal the fact that the grant culture and the grant dependence (if such they are) have been created by the agencies who offer grants. Grant-funding is what has been on offer. Grant regimes make odder and odder rules, and construct stranger and stranger application procedures, and applicants have to jump through the hoops. Any system which says that you cannot use a grant to run 'training sessions' for business advisers, but if you change the wording to 'awareness-raising' that will be fine, is clearly laughable.[1] But social enterprises have learned that it is worth playing the game because that is where the serious money is. It is not yet available through the banking system or through any of the social investment mechanisms.

The rhetoric about shifting from a grant to a loan culture betrays a too simplistic analysis. It overlooks the dangers of any organisation being totally debt-financed, dependent on loans. It overlooks too the need for society to invest in social enterprises in some long-term, more constructive way which recognises and pays for the inevitable social costs incurred in achieving social benefits.

An investment culture

More recently the talk has wisely shifted to advocating an 'investment culture': seeing grants not as a gift, but as an investment by society which will bring certain specific dividends. These dividends will therefore need to be spelled out so that they may be monitored, measured and reported on. Sometimes those dividends may be financial: paying for the capital invested and replacing it so that it can be used again. Mostly the dividends will be social and environmental, making a contribution to the common good. Social and financial dividends to society are not necessarily mutually exclusive and it could be expected that some social enterprises might produce the social dividends expected of them and, in the longer term, also produce some financial dividend by repaying some of the initial public-sector investment.

For grant-givers a step-shift to an investment culture implies several important changes in the way they manage their programmes:

First, investment should be negotiated and agreed which relates to the *total* needs of the enterprise or project being proposed. In other words, investment which is only for the salary of a manager, and may not be used for any other purpose, such as working capital, is unhelpful.

Second, investment should not be so narrowly related to financial years that if it has not been spent by 31 March it must be repaid. What sort of lesson in financial management is it that encourages people to spend unused grant, maybe unnecessarily, before the financial year-end for fear of having to pay it back, rather than holding it in reserve for when it is needed?

Third, as well as agreeing financial investment, clear 'social dividends' should be negotiated and agreed which the investors are seeking to achieve, for the community or for specific beneficiaries.

Fourth, accounting for the use of the investment should only be through the overall accounts of the enterprise, avoiding any requirement to account specifically for isolated budget items.

Recoverable grants

An investment culture, as it relates to public funds in particular, should introduce the concept of 'recoverable' grants and recognise that social enterprises need 'patient' capital. That means taking a long-term view, much longer than is usual in the public sector. The extent of investment recovery (grant repayment) must be linked to the financial profitability of a social enterprise after all its social costs have been met and its social benefits paid for. That implies that social enterprises will pay less than the market rate by way of financial return on investment. A reverse precedent has in a sense usefully been established with Public Finance Initiatives (PFIs) – and Public–Private Partnerships (PPPs). Here it is accepted that private investors are taking a higher risk and are therefore entitled to take a higher rate of return in order to compensate for that risk. Turn that on its head and in the case of Public–Community Partnerships the public sector should accept a lower rate of return in recognition of the social and environmental benefits being delivered by the social enterprise. Better a lower financial return in exchange for demonstrable community benefit than permitting higher levels of profit in exchange for questionable public benefit. PFIs are also long-term arrangements, 20 years being not untypical, and the time-scales adopted for public-sector investment in social enterprises should be similar.

Social enterprises which meet the defining characteristics (chapter 3) accept that surplus will be used in three ways: a) as reserves for reinvestment and growth; b) as bonus payments for workers (and sometimes customers); c) as community benefit. This three-way allocation was endorsed by the Co-operative Commission.[2] Where public-sector investment is to be recovered it would be appropriate to add that as a fourth use of surplus, but to make it subject to a reasonable maximum percentage of the total surplus. Investment recovery might for example operate only for a given number of years, say 15 of 20. Thus, a certain percentage of surplus would be paid as investment (grant) recovery, starting five years after the investment was first agreed. After 15 years' payments recovery would end, irrespective of the amount of initial investment which had actually been recovered.

Cumbersome though this may seem, it would provide a mechanism for recovering public-sector investment from those social enterprises that are sufficiently financially profitable to be able to pay. The system would depend entirely on an effective regulatory mechanism as described in chapter 10 as any mechanisms that aid social enterprises should rightly be accompanied by mechanisms to monitor them and ensure that only bona fide social enterprises benefit and that the social dividends are achieved. Recovered grant would return to a revolving investment fund for re-use.

In the 1980s, Strathclyde Community Business (SCB) managed block grants of urban aid funds from the Scottish Office and Strathclyde Regional Council and attempted to adopt more of an investment approach. Because the funds were held by SCB it was possible to process applications reasonably quickly (usually within six to eight weeks). The block grant could be used to pay for capital investment in a community business and could be released either as grant or as loan (or as a mix of both). Management grants could also be awarded. The specific condition set down by the Scottish Office was that public-sector investment in the community businesses should not be used by them to charge unrealistically low rates for their work or to pay wages above the industry norm. In other words, public funds should not be used to encourage unfair, subsidised competition in the marketplace. The capital grants and loans were up-front payments made as any other investment would be. The management grants, however, were paid only quarterly and although administrative flexibility allowed them to contribute to cash flow and working capital, they did not have the sort of investment impact that was needed. Most community businesses of that era were under-capitalised and therefore tended to go into low-added value, labour-intensive work. One can only speculate about the difference which might have been achieved had those three-year management grants also been paid up-front, as real capital investment.

Public-sector investment

In the interests of adopting an investment approach the public sector can ring-fence funds within certain budgets (such as the Phoenix Fund, or Regional Development Agencies' budgets) for investment in social enterprises. In addition there will always be specific grants which social enterprises, like other bodies, should be able to access where government has set up a specific programme (New Deal, for example).

Elsewhere we have discussed the importance of public-sector procurement practices to social enterprises in opening up new markets for them. Such contracts should recognise the social costs incurred by social enterprises when they employ certain groups of people or work in certain areas, and build in appropriate payments to meet these social costs. These payments are not subsidies but proper recompense for delivering additional services.

We have already discussed the importance of asset transfer to the capitalisation and financial stability of social enterprises. Building an asset base, usually property, can be a straightforward means of building a strong balance sheet and securing a regular revenue stream. Once the barriers to asset transfer are dismantled (or disappear) there may be a danger of liabilities rather than assets being off-loaded onto social enterprises. Any transfer has to be effectively thought through and the use of the asset must be a potentially viable operation.[3]

Investment mechanisms for the social economy

One of the proposals of the Social Investment Task Force which reported in 2000 was to build support for Community Development Finance Initiatives (CDFIs). These are essentially about bringing investment into small businesses in poor, under-invested areas. CDFIs are not specifically about supporting social enterprise, but are targeted at micro-enterprises, defined as having 10 or fewer employees and accounting for 89% of all British business. It is hard to suppress the passing thought that the banks' apparent enthusiasm for supporting the CDFI movement may be for them a neat opt-out from having to deal in the normal way with small businesses in disadvantaged areas.

Other proposals of the Task Force which are being put into effect include a Community Investment Tax Credit and a Community Development Ventu
Fund. The tax credit was introduced in the 2002 Budget and is an incenti

individuals, businesses, banks and investment organisations to invest in accredited CDFIs, these being known, somewhat confusingly, as 'wholesale CDFIs'. It is hoped to raise up to £1bn in this way for business development in deprived areas with up to 50% of the funds raised being available for the development of non-residential property by non-profit-distributing enterprises. The Bridges Community Development Venture Fund was launched in May 2002, as a joint venture between government and the venture capital industry to supply venture capital to firms operating in disadvantaged areas. Concerns have been expressed that this fund may be (mis)used by outside companies relocating to one of the 25% poorest, most 'under-invested' areas and meeting the criterion of employing 35% of their workforce from the area. Real community development should be about building indigenous business, not about inward investment.[4]

All these initiatives, and some CDFIs in particular, can be relevant to social enterprises. Some are themselves structured as social enterprises and form, therefore, part of the social enterprise wedge. Rather like managed workspaces, they are part of the infrastructure support for the local economy which is provided by social enterprises. Others are both structured as social enterprises and offer loans exclusively to social enterprises. One such is Industrial Common Ownership Finance (ICOF), with a 30-year history of successfully raising capital and lending to social enterprises and now finding itself called a CDFI rather than a revolving loan fund, as it had been since 1973. ICOF's mission neatly highlights the importance of taking risk: 'to lend at risk in order to create opportunity'.

CDFIs have received a considerable 'fair wind' of encouragement and in June 2002 launched their trade association at a UK conference held in Glasgow. The implication seems to be that there may be a proliferation of these small-scale loan funds operating in disadvantaged areas across the nation. That would appear to contradict the known difficulties of running small loan funds where, in order to keep transaction costs and therefore the cost of borrowing at a reasonable level, procedures and monitoring have in the past been minimal. In order to be sustainable in the long term, local CDFIs will surely require some form of ongoing support for administration.

Consideration is also being given to whether CDFIs which serve social enterprises could also undertake a developmental role. That in turn flies in the face of past experience from the 1980s which argued that it is better to separate the process of development support from financial appraisal and the monitoring of investment. Certainly lending bodies, such as ICOF, can and do advise and assist with putting together financial packages, but that part of the deal comes only when the enterprise is ready to come to the lender. Before that is a lengthy process of development and training which leads up to the point when the lending agency becomes involved. That development work should be seen as a separate task and be undertaken by the three-tier support structure described in chapter 8.

ICOF has managed over the years to keep its transaction costs (and therefore interest rates) relatively low by running a 'lean' operation and by taking on the management of several loan funds. This achieves economies of scale and builds on hard-won experience, yet retains the sense of a local fund serving local social enterprises. Such a model might be a preferred way of proliferating local loan funds.

Bankability

By comparison to bank loans, loans from CDFIs are often expensive. But they are available and are targeted at enterprises described as 'viable but not bankable', which means that banks will not lend to them. The implicit aim is to make social enterprises bankable, overcoming the prejudices of the banks and demonstrating that the enterprise is after all no greater a risk than any other and that it is safe for the bank to take it on. The concept is one of making social enterprises suit the banks rather than getting the banks to suit social enterprises. This approach sees the social enterprises as being at fault, not the banking system with its entrenched prejudice against micro-businesses and disadvantaged areas in general, and to social enterprises in particular.

ICOF has a long record of persuading banks and other lenders to join a funding package, usually by taking the first decision to lend, by accepting a second or third call on any security behind other lenders, and by lending its weight to the probable viability and profitability of the proposal. The irony is of course that it is the small CDFI which takes the greatest risk in order to persuade the highly profitable banks to join in. Of course, social enterprises do successfully obtain loans from banks (Govan Workspace borrowed £750,000 from the Clydesdale Bank to develop its second property back in 1985) and there are always individuals within the banks who are sympathetic and inclined to lend to social enterprises. The community development banking section within NatWest and The Royal Bank of Scotland has a remit to promote a better understanding of the emerging social enterprise market across the banking group. Nonetheless the general attitude in the banking system is caution and scepticism and a knee-jerk rejection of any structure they do not understand or values which challenge their own world view.

Despite the growth of funds specialising in the social economy the amount of money at its disposal remains relatively small. The London Rebuilding Society is hoping to raise £500,000 from a share issue later in 2002,[5] but that is less than Govan Workspace needed in 1985. Four banks have contributed a total of £5m to Social Investment Scotland, established in 2002, to focus on 'near-bankable' social enterprises. In order to extract that money (which is loaned, not gifted) from the banks, however, the public-sector agency Scottish Enterprise had to underwrite it by 50%! Not only does that underline the reluctance of the banks to engage seriously with social enterprises, but the amounts being made available are actually derisorily small. Coin Street Community Builders on London's South Bank required £11m in 1993 to finance their proposed development alone. Set against that sort of requirement even the recent failed attempt by Fsquared to raise £20m in the City as a capital fund for social enterprises would have been relatively small beer.[6]

'Patient' equity is essential, investment which is repaid over a long timeframe and which is invested not just to obtain a financial return but also to achieve a social dividend. Equity for social enterprises has to be equity which does not seek to wrest control from the democratic ownership and control structures. That means it may not be equity in the true sense of ownership shares. It will of necessity be shares which do not give control (such as preference shares or co-operative shares); it will be quasi-equity (such as loan stock); it will be in ways which provide for buy-back by the social enterprise; it will be through joint ventures in subsidiary enterprises in which the social enterprise retains a controlling interest. All these models – and others – exist and have been tried and tested. The central issue is to find the investors who want to invest in social enterprises because of what these are and what they do. It does not make sense to go chasing equity which is only interested in maximising investor income and capital gain.

The scale of investment available is the other impediment to the growth of the sector. Existing funds are small, and small funds will give rise to small enterprises. If we wish to see larger social enterprises evolve then there must be access to substantial investment finance. Much already goes into social enterprises from the public sector. Take Intermediate Labour Market (ILM) projects for example. The average cost per trainee per year is estimated at £15,000 and a conservative estimate would suggest that there are at least 5,000 ILM places in the UK each year. That amounts to £75m annually, much of it spent through social enterprises to train labour for first-system enterprises. Similar-scale funds invested year on year in social enterprises to fund the acquisition of assets and to capitalise bigger projects would go some way towards building a social economy which can have a serious impact on our society.

'Mutualist financing within the social economy'

However, while it is appropriate and necessary for the public sector to take a lead there is also a key role for the social economy itself and the third system generally. The substantial investment funds which are required should not only be managed from within the social economy but they should begin to come through self-help and mutuality. We need to build a social economy finance sector which is founded on social economy values.

Rather than social enterprises becoming 'bankable', the aim should be to make banks become 'social enterprisable' and contribute to and work with social economy investment institutions. Mechanisms such as the community investment tax credit may be developed as 'sweeteners' but what is needed is social investment, because investors want to buy into the social benefit as well as into some financial return.

Clearly small funds such as ICOF and the Aston Reinvestment Trust, which are rooted in the social economy, already fit the description of a social economy finance institution, unlike for example Social Investment Scotland which has been created by the Scottish Executive and the banks. By contrast the Scottish

Community Enterprise Investment Fund (SCEIF), which was established in 1990 and is now absorbed into the Charity Bank, belonged to the community business movement itself. Likewise the Triodos Bank and the Ecology Building Society, both of which demonstrate that there is money out there in the community to be invested in institutions which have clear ethical, social and environmental purposes, and so can be seen as institutions which belong to the social economy.

The recently created Charity Bank[7] points to another important step forward by creating a vehicle through which people may choose to invest in social enterprises which are charities, adding to what Malcolm Hayday has called the 'social capital marketplace'.[8] In the future, if social enterprises and charity law are disentangled and social enterprises regulated in the manner described in chapter 10, it would be hoped that the Charity Bank's remit would extend to include all registered social enterprises as well as charities.

Reference has been made elsewhere (in chapter 8) to the pound for pound matching grants which formed a key part of the Highlands and Islands Development Board Community Co-operative Scheme in the 1970s. Such a programme should be revived as a means of encouraging social enterprises to raise some of their capital needs themselves.

The social economy already has within it financial institutions such as the Co-operative Bank, Unity Trust and other remaining mutuals such as Standard Life. If the Co-operative Movement is to take seriously its stated intention to be part of the wider social economy family, then we should expect a stronger lead to be taken by these bodies, far greater than just the establishment of the Co-operative Action Foundation[9] and a revenue grant to the Coalition for Social Enterprise. Ironically, it has been investment in community development banking by NatWest and The Royal Bank of Scotland which have so far taken the lead which might have been expected of the Co-operative Movement's own institutions.

Social enterprises need their own financing mechanisms. Through CDFIs there are growing facilities for small-scale loans. What is lacking is the bank which can assist with serious funding and the investment fund which is set up to offer patient capital to social enterprises. The capacity is surely there for the co-operative financial institutions to build mechanisms for receiving social investment and for making investment in social enterprises. A useful start would be to persuade all social enterprises (and other third-system organisations) to bank with the Co-operative Bank or Unity Trust on the understanding that social enterprise money is used to the benefit of the third system.

The example of Community Sector Banking (CSB) in Australia could be an alternative model. Formed as a joint venture between Bendigo Bank and a wide-ranging consortium of third-system organisations (Community 21 Ltd), CSB aims to offer a full banking service especially tailored to social enterprises and voluntary organisations by garnering the substantial funds belonging to the third system which are otherwise lost in the first-system banks.[10]

The principle is clear: build on self-help and mutuality, and create financial and investment institutions which belong to the third system and which build funds and seek social as well as financial returns. The capacity is there. The opportunity is there. Will it be seized?

From matters of finance we turn to questions of legal structures and the case for establishing a regulatory system for social enterprises.

NOTES

1. This is a real example of a hoop through which an EU-funded programme was asked to jump.
2. 'Re-establishing the Co-operative Advantage' (chapter 1), in *The Co-operative Advantage: Creating a successful family of co-operative businesses*, report of the Co-operative Commission, 2001.
3. See Lorraine Hart and Deborah Bell, *Developing an Asset-base* (London, Development Trusts Association, 2001).
4. Henry Palmer, 'A bridge too far?', in *Social Enterprise*, June 2002.
5. www.londonrebuilding.com
6. Henry Palmer, 'Flotation fails but Big Issue duo don't sink', in *Social Enterprise*, July 2002.
7. www.charitybank.org
8. Malcolm Hayday, *The Social Capital of the Future*, paper for 7th European Conference on Social Economy, Gävle, Sweden, June 2001.
9. www.co-operativeaction.coop
10. www.csbanking.com.au

10 Legal frameworks for social enterprise

The social enterprise test

In chapter 3 we defined the six characteristics (see box) which distinguish social enterprises from other businesses and which can therefore form the basis of a 'social enterprise test'. These characteristics should be fixed and therefore non-negotiable. Any enterprise which displays the six characteristics will be recognised as a social enterprise. We shall consider the benefits of some form of compliance or regulatory system later, but first it is necessary to consider how a social enterprise test may be developed.

Defining characteristics

1. social purpose
2. trading
3. no distribution for private profit
4. common ownership
5. democratic structure
6. accountability

For each defining characteristic there would be a number of key questions:

Social purpose

- Does the enterprise have a primary social purpose?
- What are its social and environmental objectives?
- Are they adequately expressed in the constitution?

It will be necessary to develop some agreement about what is acceptable as a social purpose, and what would not be acceptable. There will need to be some flexibility built into whatever compliance or regulatory process is developed to ensure that what is acceptable as social purpose is regularly reviewed. It will also be vital to monitor not just what an organisation says it intends to do but also what it actually does, and in this regard the social accounting and audit process will be particularly important (see chapter 11).

Trading

- Does the enterprise engage in trade? and to what extent?

It will be necessary to agree what constitutes trading income and to consider if a percentage threshold of trading income should be established, defined as selling goods or services in the marketplace, including contracts and service level agreements with public-sector agencies. It has been suggested that the qualifying threshold might be 50%. This arrangement would be similar to that of the social firms movement which states that a genuine social firm should a) recruit at least 25% of its workforce from people unable, by reason of disability, to hold down a job in the open labour market and b) earn at least 50% of its income from trading.

It may be easier to agree maximum percentages of revenue income which may be received as grants or as fundraising activities not connected to the main social purpose of the organisation. In particular it will be necessary to decide how to deal with unpaid labour (volunteers) and with sweat equity contributed by members and others.

No distribution for private profit

- Does the constitution of the enterprise have a clause which precludes distribution of profits to members for personal gain?
- Is it clear that profits are to be reserved for reinvestment, for community (constituency) benefit or for bonus payments to workers, related to work done?
- Are there acceptable minimum/maximum stipulations regarding the three uses of profit?

Agreement will have to be reached on what might be acceptable percentage allocations of profits to the three uses.

Common ownership

- Does the constitution of the enterprise have a clause which ensures that assets and wealth are held 'in trust' for the community (or its defined constituency) and may not be sold for the personal benefit of members, workers or directors?

Dissolution clauses will be needed which clearly specify how assets may be distributed in that event. Provision will also require to be made for realising assets in order to benefit the community or beneficiary group. Workable models already exist whereby equity capital may be introduced into a social enterprise without compromising the principle of common ownership.

Democratic structure

- Does the constitution provide for a democratic structure whereby its constituents may join as members and elect a majority of the board/management committee?

There will need to be some mechanism for monitoring that the democratic structure is not only theoretically in place but is actually being implemented.

Accountability

- Does the constitution include a clause committing it to undertake a regular social audit?
- Does the enterprise produce accounts regularly which report on its social and environmental performance and impacts?
- Are these accounts independently verified? (see chapter 11 and Appendix ii.)

It will be difficult, but it should not be impossible, to develop agreed criteria for each element of the 'social enterprise test'. All six elements will be covered in the constitution of social enterprises, so the first, basic part of the test will be to check that constitutions include the necessary and appropriately worded clauses. Models already exist on which to build these provisions, using both the Companies Acts and the Industrial and Provident Societies Acts.

The characteristics of social purpose, use of profits, democracy and accountability should be covered through a competent social accounting and audit process which includes both external objectives (what the social enterprise does to benefit other people) and internal objectives (how the social enterprise manages itself as an organisation). The second part of the test will therefore be to ensure that social enterprises prepare competent social accounts for regular verification.

The characteristics regarding extent of trading and the use of profits will be reported in the audited financial accounts which are already a legal requirement. It will be necessary to specify the detail of additional information which should be reported on trading and use of profits.

A Regulator for social enterprise

A national system of regulation for social enterprises would:

1. ensure that a satisfactory constitution had been adopted.
2. ensure that all social enterprises prepared social accounts, and that they reported competently on compliance with the defining characteristics. Verified social accounts would be filed with the Regulator.
3. require social enterprises to file their financial accounts with the Regulator, and ensure that they reported adequately on defining characteristics 2 and 3 within their audited financial accounts, to a prescribed format.

The regulatory process would therefore consist of initially confirming that an organisation may call itself a registered social enterprise and then renewing that registration annually on the basis of receiving (and approving) the audited social and financial accounts. This proposed procedure puts considerable emphasis on the social accounting process and especially on the independent verification. This, in turn, has implications for developing a national register of approved social auditors which is considered in chapter 11.

There has been a precedent for such regulation already in the social economy. Following the passage of the Industrial Common Ownership Act (ICO Act) in 1976 there was a process through which co-operatives could be registered as bona fide common ownership companies. Only registered co-operatives and common-ownership companies were able to apply for loans from the fund which was created through that legislation. As industry regulation is something with which we have become increasingly familiar in recent years, it is not difficult to envisage a Regulator for Social Enterprises (OffSEnt perhaps, complete with yellow and red cards for those found not to be complying?) whose role and performance would be closely monitored both by government and by the Social Enterprise Movement, probably through the Social Enterprise Coalition.

Establishing a regulatory process also gives the opportunity for a kitemark. The very establishment of a kitemark and the formal registration process would send out a signal that social enterprises are important and that government and society wish to encourage them, to support them and to know who they are. At the time of the ICO Act it was interesting that some longstanding co-operative companies, including as the first applicant the Scott Bader Commonwealth, applied for their certificate, not because they wanted to apply for a loan, but because they wanted their existence as a bona fide, and therefore certificated, common-ownership company to be publicly known and more widely recognised.

Regulation would serve to determine which organisations are *not* social enterprises, as well as those that are. Those which did not meet the criteria would have the option of either changing their constitutions or practices (or both) in order to comply, or of not doing so and thus remaining unregistered. Undoubtedly, some enterprises would choose not to go for registration: social entrepreneurs who preferred not to submit themselves to some element of control from a democratic structure or who wished to retain personal ownership of their organisation's assets; workers' co-operatives which wished to retain the option of distributing all profits to working members; small voluntary enterprises who decided it was not worth the bother.

The fact of registration would make it easier for government and others to discriminate in favour of social enterprises. If, as a society, we wish our government to support and encourage social enterprises then we will want to ensure that any favourable treatment goes only to bona fide social enterprises. Thus as well as giving a sense of public recognition, registration would be the key for social enterprises to access certain financial, fiscal and other support which could be made available.

Furthermore, it is likely that private businesses would also welcome a process of registration. First, it would reduce some sensitivities about unfair competition if they understand that the other body is a registered social enterprise, working for the common good rather than for private profit. Second, it would make it easier for private businesses to distinguish between those social organisations they may wish to support and those they do not. It may also make it easier for some private companies, perhaps especially when considering what to do about succession, to opt for the social enterprise model in order to secure the future of the enterprise for a particular locality and group of workers. A private business which is marginal but providing an important local service could more easily be transformed into a social enterprise, access some of the fiscal and other advantages and so secure its position in the local economy. This would be especially relevant in underpopulated rural areas.

A further benefit from regulation is that there would be an automatic annual census of social enterprises, updating the national and regional maps and giving accurate information about the growth and development of that part of the national economy.

Fiscal and other benefits

There are a number of fiscal and other benefits which government could arrange to make available to registered social enterprises as part of an overarching policy to expand the social economy:

Company taxation: many social enterprises register as charities and adopt cumbersome structures involving a holding company and subsidiaries in order to gain the benefit of not paying corporation tax on their trading activities. Charitable status is really inappropriate for social enterprises and although charity law is under review and will shortly be revised and updated (the basic statute dates, after all, from 1601) it would be far preferable for social enterprises to be granted a special rate of corporation tax in their own right. That rate could be 0% so that social enterprises were in the same situation as charities, or it could be a discounted rate of, say, 10%. This would disentangle social enterprises from charity law and would permit them to adopt simpler legal structures. There is a precedent for granting a lower rate of corporation tax to social enterprises: historically, co-operatives were able to opt for a rate of 30% when the standard rate was higher.

National Insurance: consideration could be given to either exempting social enterprises from NI payments or introducing a lower rate, especially when particular groups of people with defined barriers to employment are employed. There are precedents for such positive discrimination in other European states.

VAT: consideration could be given to exempting social enterprises from VAT or substantially raising the VAT threshold for them. Such a move would assist the smaller social and community enterprises in particular. One of the reasons the Greenwich Leisure model of social enterprise has been so successful is because the provision of sport and leisure services attracts a lower rate of VAT. It should be possible to see if there are other services often provided by social enterprises (for example, childcare, domiciliary care) which could be treated in the same way.

Rates Relief: social enterprises could qualify for the same level of rates relief as is accorded to charities.

Welfare benefits: a number of issues to do with people in receipt of welfare benefits could be reviewed. These include allowing certain categories of people working for social enterprises to have their earnings disregarded for an agreed period; ensuring that volunteers' involvement does not jeopardise their entitlement to benefits; adapting the Enterprise Rehearsal arrangement so that it can be used for social enterprises in formation, possibly through some scheme of 'capitalising' the benefits that would be received over, say, a six-month period. In Spain such capitalisation of benefits has been used to good effect.

Asset Transfer: this has been discussed more fully in chapter 8, but it will be easier to relax rules on the transfer of assets to registered social enterprises once that process of regulation and registration is introduced.

Public procurement: similarly, it will be easier to relax rules on public procurement in respect of registered social enterprises because any relaxation will benefit only those enterprises which properly meet the defining characteristics of social enterprise and deliver an agreed and measurable public benefit.

A further advantage of charitable status is being able to receive funds from another charity or benefit from gift aid. Some arrangements would be required to ensure that these benefits were also available to social enterprises, either by according them similar status to charities (as has been done for Local Enterprise Companies in the past) or by establishing regional and national Social Enterprise Funds with the appropriate status through which such financial support could be channelled.

Additional fiscal and other benefits could, and no doubt will, be offered. Together they would form a strong policy discriminating in favour of social enterprises. Such a policy can only be adopted, however, if there is, first, the prior political determination to grow the social enterprise sector as a distinctive and important other way in the economy. Second, it can work only if we are quite clear what we mean by social enterprises and what we expect them to do for society. That can be achieved only by effective regulation, and social accounting and audit.

Legislative recognition

A decade ago some elements in the community enterprise movement argued for a system of registration and regulation similar to that described above. The aim was to gain legislative and then public recognition for a distinctive form of enterprise and at the same time establish a means by which government could target support to genuine community enterprises in return for demonstrable community benefits. At that time the term 'community benefit corporation' was proposed.[1]

The more recent terms to have been adopted are those of 'community interest company' and 'public interest company'. While the sense and the intent are the same, contemporary debate is recognising the relevance of such structures not only at neighbourhood level in the 'community economy' but right through to the ownership and management of national public utilities. But, perhaps most importantly, they begin to 'fix' an alternative model into the public and political consciousness. 'Public interest companies could give recognition to social enterprises as a new sector of the economy without having to resort to charitable status. The credibility associated with a distinctive legal form would bolster the attempts of social enterprises to gain funding from financial institutions, grant-making bodies and the public. Funders would be sure that monies lent or donated would remain in the public sphere in perpetuity.'[2]

Between 1865 and 1914 there was a phenomenal rate of formation of mutual, friendly and co-operative societies, in part certainly due to the existence of the Industrial and Provident Societies legislation which not only made the formation of such societies easy (and safe with limited liability) but meant that they were an accepted part of society. Similarly, in Italy the legislative recognition of social co-operatives not only provided a framework of political and fiscal support but led to a rapid growth in the formation of new social co-operatives because they had become a recognised element of the economy and of the provision of certain services.

In fact, establishing a system to regulate social enterprises and to recognise them as community benefit corporations or public interest companies does not require any primary legislation. Existing law for incorporating companies and co-operatives can readily accommodate the needs of social enterprises – indeed it has already done so. Since the resurgence of social and community enterprises in the late 1970s, the Companies Acts, particularly in the case of the company limited by guarantee, have generally been favoured over the Industrial and Provident Societies Acts (I and PS Acts) to provide the legal structures. This has been because the former are generally more flexible and models can be easily customised to suit specific local requirements. Furthermore the costs of registration and the filing of annual returns have been cheaper than under the I and PS Acts.

A number of organisations have developed over the years a range of model constitutions to provide for virtually any eventuality, including associating a workers' co-operative with a community enterprise, subsidiary share companies for the introduction of equity, combinations of companies with an I and PS to introduce equity but retain control with the co-operative/social enterprise members and so on.[3] With regard to the introduction of equity into social enterprises the issue is not one of how to do so by legal structure, but what sort of equity and on what conditions. Poptel, the co-operative internet service provider, is a recent example of a co-operative which has successfully introduced outside equity without losing either mutual status or control by the co-operative members. Other models have included employee share ownership plans (ESOPs) as a mechanism to allow worker–owners to hold equity along with external investors, and employee common-ownership plans (ECOPs) which allow equity to be held by workers, the community and external investors.

One of the advantages of the Companies Acts has been that the memorandum and articles of association can be changed relatively readily by agreement of the members. Usually in social enterprise constitutions this requires a 75% majority vote. While it is helpful and desirable to be able to make necessary changes in response to the evolution and growth of a social enterprise, it is also essential to ensure that the clauses which set down the defining characteristics may not be changed without certain safeguards.

In the 1980s Community Business Scotland (CBS) introduced the notion of the 'golden share' into its model constitution for community business. The golden share was held by a nominated body (maybe CBS itself, or the Scottish Office or a regional council) and the holder of the golden share had to agree any proposed changes to the key defining clauses in the memorandum and articles of association. Traidcraft Exchange[4] has introduced a similar 'guardianship share' in the community businesses they establish overseas, an altogether preferable term introducing the notion of care over the spirit of the enterprise.

Were a social enterprise regulatory system established, it would be appropriate for the Regulator (or his or her national or regional representatives) to hold the guardianship share. On an annual basis, of course, the Regulator would be informed of any other changes which a social enterprise might have made to its constitution, in much the same way as the Community Fund now requires of the organisations it supports.

Mutuals

Whereas company law reflects the values and needs of the first, capitalist system, I and PS law reflects the values of the third system. 'Under a mutual system, investor ownership is replaced by community ownership, with those running companies obliged to act in the best interests of the community, not the corporation.'[5] In many ways the I and PS Acts are the most appropriate legislation for social enterprises, deriving as they do from the need to develop structures for the nineteenth-century growth in mutual associations, the forerunners and historical spirit of the modern social economy.

In recent years, I and PS structures have not been favoured because they have been more expensive than Companies Act structures, less flexible and administered in slow-moving bureaucratic fashion. The recent change of management from the Register of Friendly Societies to the Financial Services Authority (FSA) does not seem to have changed matters, especially with regard to the cost of filing annual returns. In this particular situation, though, the FSA has backed down in the face of representations from the co-operative and mutual sectors.

Over the years many and varied sets of model rules have been devised for use by social enterprises which demonstrate how the legislation can easily accommodate changing needs. Examples include the society for the benefit of the community (sometimes referred to as a 'bencom'), the mutual model used for Glas Cymru (Welsh Water), and the model used for raising capital for investing in social and fair trade organisations such as ICOF's Community Capital Ltd and the Shared Interest Society.[6] The mutual model has also, interestingly, been adopted by two football clubs, Lincoln City and Bournemouth AFC, where: 'The supporters have acquired ownership of their clubs in a form of common ownership. Fans are represented on the board, the assets cannot be flogged off for profit, but at the same time managers have to perform to targets and have incentives to be as efficient as the best of the private sector.'[7] Recently, a private member's bill introduced by Gareth Thomas MP has provided an important amendment to the legislation to make it more difficult for mutual societies to be 'carpet-bagged' and demutualised.

An opportunity exists to ensure that co-operative law is interpreted and, more especially, administered in such a way as to encourage the use of these models rather than company models which were, after all, devised for the quite different needs of private capital. If a Social Enterprise Regulator were appointed, that same office could take over the regulation of the I and PS Acts. Such a move would confirm co-operative law as the appropriate law for social enterprises and shift its monitoring out of the first system and into the third.

The preparation of social accounts by social enterprises may be a key method of ensuring that they continue to meet the requirements of a bona fide social enterprise. In addition, social accounting allows the enterprise to better plan and manage its work and account effectively to its stakeholders. The next chapter (and Appendix ii) introduce the social accounting model which is now being adopted by growing numbers of social enterprises.

NOTES

1. As these pages were being finalised for publication the Government's Strategy Unit released its report on charity law, *Private Action, Public Benefit* (2002), which includes proposals to establish a new legal form for social enterprises, the 'Community Interest Company', with protection against demutualisation and provisions to lock in assets and profits for social purposes.
2. Stephen Lloyd and Abbie Rumbold, 'Ready for take off?', in *Social Enterprise*, April 2002.
3. www.co-opunion.coop (click on ICOM); www.cbs-network.org.uk
4. www.traidcraft.co.uk
5. Larry Elliott, 'Kick-off for mutuality fightback', in *The Guardian*, 13 November 2000.
6. www.shared-interest.com
7. Felicity Lawrence, 'A goal to aim for', in *The Guardian*, 18 February 2002.

11 Social accounting for social enterprises

'Forty-two!' yelled Loonquawl, 'Is that all you've got to show for seven and a half million years' work?'

'I checked it very thoroughly,' said the computer, 'and that quite definitely is the answer. I think the problem, to be quite honest with you, is that you've never actually known what the question is.'[1]

The roots of the social audit idea lie within the perceived need to make business more accountable to the community, and to ensure that the impacts of business – beneficial and non-beneficial – are understood. Geddes's definition remains one of the clearest and fullest:

'Social audit is best understood as a reaction against conventional accounting principles and practices. These centre on the financial viability and profitability of the individual economic enterprise. By contrast, social audit proposes a broader financial and economic perspective, reaching far beyond the individual enterprise... Social audit posits other goals as well as, or instead of, financial profitability... Moreover social audit attempts to embrace not only economic and monetary variables but also – as its name suggests – social ones, including some which may not be amenable to quantification in monetary term.'[2]

The social economy sector

The social economy sector was early in the field of developing practical and workable methodology for social accounting and social audit. In Scotland, Strathclyde Community Business (SCB) recognised the need to understand, account for and report on the social benefits of the community businesses which were being established in the 1980s throughout Scotland. SCB's thinking and experimentation led to what became known as 'the Scottish model' which, blended with the experience of the New Economics Foundation working with Traidcraft, was published later in *Social Auditing for Small Organisations: The workbook.*[3]

In England, the Industrial Common Ownership Movement (ICOM), working through its Beechwood College near Leeds, developed during the 1980s a social audit model aimed in the first instance at workers' co-operatives. This model was piloted in the early 1980s and has since been developed by the Social Enterprise

Partnership into the Social Audit Toolkit[4] and used within the community sector, especially in the context of a number of transnational European programmes.

In the 1980s both ICOM and Community Business Scotland included a social audit clause in the model constitutions which they were offering to the co-operative and community enterprises they advised and it is now quite common practice for community-based organisations to include that commitment to do a social audit in their constitution, although that commitment does not necessarily mean that they do undertake a social audit.

In more recent years the practice of social accounting and audit has begun to expand significantly in the social economy sector.

- The Scottish model was tested in the early 1990s with community enterprises in the Lothian Region[5] and also with workers' co-operatives in Nottinghamshire.
- The Beechwood model, as developed into the Social Audit Toolkit, has been used by a number of social enterprises in the Midlands, Bristol, South Wales and elsewhere.
- In Northern Ireland the Social Economy Agency promoted a training course in social accounting and auditing in 1996 which was accredited by the Open College Network (OCN). The model used draws both on the Scottish/New Economics Foundation (NEF)and the Beechwood models and the training programme continues to be delivered regularly.
- In the city of Liverpool a social audit initiative, using the Scottish/NEF model and sponsored by the city council, has been running since 1996.[6] The model was developed into an accredited OCN course in 1999 which is now being delivered by a local facilitation team through the Merseyside Social Enterprise Network (MSEN). More than 35 local organisations have engaged with social accounting, one now into its fifth cycle. A *Social Audit and Accounting Manual* based on the OCN course and including a Workbook and CD-ROM was published towards the end of 2001.[7] A new generation of the programme is now to be extended to the whole of Merseyside and Halton, funded by the North-West Regional Development Agency.
- NEF, in association with the Association of Chief Executives of Voluntary Organisations (ACEVO), attracted lottery funding to run a pilot social audit programme for 13 voluntary organisations throughout the UK (Social Auditing for Voluntary Organisations – SAVO) between 1998 and 2000.[8] NEF was also associated with a pilot programme with four English housing associations, funded by the Housing Corporation.
- In Scotland, CBSN has worked with clusters of organisations in Moray and Aberdeenshire, Edinburgh, Glasgow and Fife. The cluster approach gives the opportunity for peer support and mutual learning as well as being a more cost-effective way in which to deliver training and support. A continuing series of training workshops is organised around the country.
- Other clusters, notably in Devon, Cumbria and most recently in the North-East of England, have been introduced to social accounting, while other

community-based organisations are known to have developed their own styles of social accounting and audit, for example: the Black Country Housing and Community Services Group; Total Coverage (a workers' co-operative in Southampton); the Shetland Community Enterprise Network.
- The GB Social Enterprise Partnership (SEP) has included a component on measuring quality and impact which will examine current practice in the social economy, test various models and develop new tools for social accounting.
- In Europe, social accounting and audit have featured in a growing number of EU-funded transnational programmes using both the Scottish/NEF and the Beechwood/SEP models, with increasing evidence of cross-over or 'convergence' between the two. In some countries such as Italy and France, with their 'social balance sheets', other forms have been devised.
- Further afield, COMMACT Aotearoa runs a social audit programme for social economy organisations in New Zealand, having adapted the Scottish/NEF model to local needs. Community organisations in India, the Philippines, South Africa, Canada, Australia and the US are amongst the many others also now experimenting with forms of social accounting and audit.

Developments in social accounting and audit are fast-moving within the social enterprise sector. No one can yet claim: 'This is how it should be done.' The experience becomes richer and more diverse all the time and a challenge for those involved is to ensure that lessons learned are lessons shared and to develop common standards that are relevant and appropriate.

The real surprise is that the interest in social accounting has only lately emerged. Social enterprises have come relatively late to understand the importance of effectively measuring impact so that they can report on performance, account to stakeholders and make the case for continued investment in their work. Even more surprising has been the failure of the financers of social enterprises to require real evidence of social impact and benefit. So often their concern is 'are they succeeding as businesses?' without taking the intended 'social added value' into account. Similarly, society has failed to demand to know just what the impacts, bad as well as good, are of business generally. Changes are clearly underway and for social enterprises the challenge is to take the lead in developing ways of reporting which are appropriate to the social economy and which reflect the values of the third system.

Global networks

In September 2000 at a symposium held in Edinburgh for social accounting and audit practitioners in the social economy it was agreed to establish a UK Social Audit Network (SAN).[9] The Network sees its role as being to represent practitioners in the social economy, to develop agreed methods for the approval of competent social auditors and of training providers, and to develop agreed common standards for the content of social accounts and for the verification process. In Ireland, a national institute (Institute of Social Auditing of Ireland) has been established with similar aims by social audit practitioners from the social economy.[10] The same has happened in New Zealand (Social Audit New Zealand)[11] and in Australia (Queensland Social and Environmental Accounting Network).[12]

Additionally there is a global network, established in 1996 in the form of the Institute of Social and Ethical AccountAbility (ISEA).[13] Based in London, ISEA has a worldwide membership and seeks to develop agreed standards for social audit, to accredit training programmes and to accredit the members of what it sees as a 'new profession' of social and ethical accountants and auditors. While ISEA seeks to represent all sectors in the social audit movement its focus has tended to be with the corporate sector and the processes it develops to be driven by corporate needs.

The basics of social accounting

The first basic is the fundamental concept which lies behind social accounting and audit: to understand the impact of organisations on society and on the environment; on people and on the planet.

Social accounting should therefore certainly embrace environmental accounting. No organisation can be socially responsible if it does not consider the effect it is having on the environment. In the early days, social audit discussions referred, rather clumsily, to 'social/environmental/cultural auditing' which came to be abbreviated for convenience to 'social auditing'. Maybe that 'short-handing' of language lost sight of the inclusiveness that lies behind the concept, to the extent that it is now necessary to remind people that social auditing should not be distinct from environmental auditing but should include it.

The overarching context is of course sustainability: sustainability of the organisation itself (the interrelation of the social, the environmental and the financial) and sustainability of behaviour which contributes to a future for the people and the planet. Here is the concept of the triple bottom line: that an organisation should report on its social, environmental and financial performance and in doing so, recognise the relation between the three aspects. Some, indeed, are advocating a quadruple bottom line to ensure that the cultural impact is also considered and reported, an especially important dimension in multicultural societies.

The second basic is the *core principles* which underpin social accounting and audit.

- *Multiperspective:* to ensure that the voices of all the key stakeholders are heard (and where they are not, to ensure that all omissions are satisfactorily explained).
- *Comprehensive:* to ensure that the social accounts report on all aspects of an organisation's work, rather than just on a selective sample. This requires

clarity – and openness – about values, about the objectives and about what is actually done in order to achieve those objectives.

- *Regular:* to ensure that social accounts are prepared regularly (year on year or maybe biennially) so that social accounting becomes embedded within the culture and systems of the organisation, so contributing to:
  - Management of performance
  - Ability to report effectively on what has been done
  - Accountability to stakeholders, and
  - Creation of recognised channels through which stakeholders are empowered to influence the organisation.
- *Comparative:* to ensure that the organisation makes year-on-year comparisons of performance and relates the performance to appropriate benchmarks and other external standards; and also to allow other stakeholders to make comparisons (and therefore choices) between organisations.
- *Verified:* to ensure that the social accounts are verified by an independent auditor or panel.
- *Disclosed:* to ensure that the findings of the social accounts are reported to stakeholders and to the wider community in the interests of accountability and transparency and to develop dialogue with stakeholders about the issues raised.

The third basic is that the social accounting process belongs to the organisation which itself determines the scope of the accounts and prepares them. In this way it empowers the organisation to report on its work and the impact it is having both from its own perspective and from that of all its stakeholders.

The five stages of social accounting

In *At the Heart of the Community Economy* a social audit model which had been evolving within the community business movement in Scotland was outlined.[14] That model has continued to evolve and is summarised in the box below and more fully in Appendix ii.

The core business of community and social enterprises and of community organisations is to achieve some form of social, community or environmental benefit. Financial sustainability or profitability is essential to achieving that benefit, but secondary to it. The organisation – and all the people associated with it or affected by it – need to know if it is achieving its objectives, what impact it is having on society and on the environment, if it is living up to its values and if the objectives and values are relevant and appropriate. The social accounting process facilitates this and enables the production of a social audit report.

Social accounting and audit is a framework which allows an organisation to build on existing documentation and reporting methods to develop a process whereby it can *account* for its social performance, *report* on that performance and draw up an action plan to *improve* on that performance, and through which it can understand its *impact* on the community and be *accountable* to its key stakeholders. Keeping social accounts gives the information needed – qualitative and quantitative – to tell us how the organisation is performing and what people think not only about what it does but about how it does it.

Social accounts which have been audited by an independent social audit panel will have credibility. The information from such audited accounts can then be used to demonstrate not only what the organisation has done but how it intends to improve. Publishing the social accounts allows all stakeholders – those who benefit from what is done, those who do the work, those who pay for it, those who work in partnership – to understand the true nature of the added value achieved. It is a social balance sheet which all stakeholders can use to decide for themselves whether to engage, work for, support, or invest in the organisation. Through the production of audited social accounts the organisation fulfils its accountability to its stakeholders.

Stage One: Introducing social accounting and audit

- What is it?
- Why do a social audit?
- Benefits and snags
- What are the key principles?
- The language of social accounting: understanding the jargon
- What do we already do – towards a social audit?
- History and current practice in different sectors
- Do we want to do it?
- Managing the social audit
- The cost of the social audit

Stage Two: The foundations

- Clarify the social objectives and the activities undertaken to achieve them
- State the values that underpin the purpose and work of the organisation
- Prepare a stakeholder map of the organisation
- Identify the key stakeholders
- Determine the scope of the social audit

Stage Three: The nuts and bolts – social book-keeping

- Agree the indicators which will allow performance to be assessed
- Identify what existing records and data can be used
- Decide what new, additional data will be collected and how
- Agree how and when to consult which stakeholders, and about what
- Organise the resources needed to carry out the social book-keeping and the stakeholder consultation

- Produce a social accounting plan and timetable
- Implement the plan and monitor progress

Stage Four: Preparing and using the social accounts

- Draft the social accounts using existing information, the data collected and the views of the stakeholders
- Identify the key issues on which the organisation should act
- Review the objectives and activities, and the values
- Set targets for the future
- Review the social accounting process and make necessary adjustments
- Plan dialogue and discussion with stakeholders
- Plan how to disseminate the social accounts

Stage Five: The social audit

- Appoint the members of the social audit panel
- Present the social accounts to the social audit panel
- The panel arranges to verify a sample of the data used;
  Assesses the interpretations given in the accounts; and
  Comments on the quality of the social accounting and reporting
- The social accounts are revised in accordance with the panel's recommendations, and the social audit statement is issued
- Publish (a summary of) the audited accounts to all stakeholders
- Continue with the next cycle of social accounting

Evaluating the model

The social audit model outlined above has now been used in a variety of circumstances and with organisations of differing size and complexity, including at the micro end of the scale a voluntary-run community minibus scheme in rural Aberdeenshire. It appears capable of adaptation by small as well as larger social enterprises, and users comment on the value of the step-by-step approach. Nonetheless it can appear a somewhat daunting and complex prospect at the start and there seems to be no way around that other than to give it a try. In that context getting organisations to work together has been found to be beneficial. Not only is it cheaper, but sharing problems and learning together makes the whole process more attractive. Group learning also brings useful peer group pressure to meet deadlines!

It is necessary to have the social audit process 'embedded' in the organisation as a whole, as often the success of the social audit may be overly dependent on one or two determined individuals. It seems that there are considerable personal benefits for individuals working through the social audit process. Participants report that social auditing has changed the whole way they work – 'less intuitive and more organised, disciplined and planned'. Others report how much they learn about consultation techniques, questionnaire design, and so on, and that the social audit had 'systemised the anecdotal evidence and made it demonstrable, reportable...'

An organisation should have sufficient time to prepare itself before embarking on a social audit cycle. This enables it to assess the time and resources that have to be allocated to the tasks, and to agree internal arrangements for managing the social audit process. The social accounting tasks should be written into job descriptions and not just added on to existing workloads. Adequate time and resources (money and people) are essential for preparing social accounts, for writing them and making any changes after the panel meeting. It follows that social auditing should be built into funding applications and routinely appear as a budget line.

It is important not to be overly ambitious in the scope of the first social audit. That in turn may mean prioritising the objectives in order to focus on only the main ones.

Information from the social accounts is used in a number of different ways: appearing in the annual report, in applications for funds, in publicity documents. But the process of carrying out a social audit is more important than the production of a final, glossy report. It is not possible to 'jump' to a short glossy version without the full social accounts having been prepared and audited.

Where social enterprises engage with social accounting and audit it appears that the social accounting tends to absorb other strategic planning and organisational review processes. These all fuse together as one continuous exercise which allows the organisation to manage itself better, monitor its performance and its impact, report fully and so account to stakeholders. As one Liverpool organisation commented: 'We do it because it is what we do.'

A key difference

A key difference has emerged between social accounting in the social economy sector and in the corporate sector and is influencing the way the process evolves differently in the two sectors.

For the social economy sector (and also for truly ethical businesses) the social accounts are about the organisation's core business – its social and/or environmental purpose. Successful commercial performance is a means to achieving that primary purpose. The social accounts are central to the organisation's reporting and accountability needs. Thus, in the social economy, accounting must be truly triple-bottom-line – in order to understand the impact and to know if and how well the social and environmental purposes have been achieved. And, of course, to see if financial performance is sufficiently robust to allow the organisation to continue doing its work and achieve its objectives.

An increasing number of social economy organisations include as one of their key 'social' objectives 'to be financially viable or sustainable' thus tying organisational sustainability into the social accounting process. Similarly, organisations are increasingly likely to adopt a specific environmental objective to ensure that they develop appropriate policies and practices on which they will report in the social accounts. Introduce cultural objectives as well and a quadruple bottom line emerges.

For profit-making and profit-distributing organisations the core business remains whatever it does (manufacturing or service) and reporting on that core business is about growth, return on investment, share value etc. Inevitably, the social accounts become something of an add-on; sometimes an honest attempt to introduce ethical and social values into running the business, though ultimately they will be subservient to the core business; sometimes in order to demonstrate corporate social responsibility and to ensure that they maintain a 'licence to operate' from society by managing stakeholder relations effectively. In a 2000 report, NEF warned against the dangers of social audits becoming no more than 'whitewash' documents driven by public relations departments,[15] and in an article in the *Guardian* newspaper, went so far as to describe corporate social responsibility as 'with few exceptions, simply the icing on a rotten cake'.[16]

We should not in any way infer, however, that social enterprises are perfect – they are not and indeed are often sadly lacking in respect of environmental, and sometimes employment, practices. But it is easier and more likely for social economy organisations to be explicit and straightforward about their values and their true objectives and to report on them in ways that would inevitably be more problematic for the corporate sector. In the second system, the public sector, it should also be easier and more likely but sadly there has so far been minimal engagement by that sector in social accounting and audit.

Social economy organisations should, as well as reporting stakeholder views, report robustly, with facts and figures, on what has been done to achieve the objectives, to what extent the intended activities have been carried out and whether targets have been met. In this way stakeholders can understand the full story. Thus the social accounts must contain both quantitative information as well as the qualitative views of the various stakeholders.

A competent set of social accounts

A competent set of social accounts should include all of the following:

- A report on performance against the stated objectives (how well have we done what we said we would do?)
- An assessment of the impact on the community (can this be measured? what do people think?)
- The views of stakeholders on the objectives and on the values (are we doing the 'right' things? are we 'walking our talk'?)
- A report on environmental performance (are we 'living lightly' and minimising resource consumption?)
- A report on compliance with statutory and voluntary quality and procedural standards (do we do what is expected of us? do we do more?)

Stakeholder consultation must be a genuine process of seeking stakeholders' views and engaging in dialogue with them, not just managing relations. One of the excitements of working in the field is seeking and learning new and imaginative (and cost-effective) ways of consulting stakeholders which go beyond the tried and tested methods of social science, customer and market research. In Scotland social accountants have used to good effect participatory appraisal processes, first devised for work in developing countries. A report on the New Zealand pilot produced by COMMACT Aotearoa however reported a tendency to 'rush to survey', sometimes even before objectives and values had been clarified.[17]

The bottom line of what is done and how it is done to produce the social accounts must be for each organisation a balance between what may be ideal and what can realistically be done given the human resources and the finance available. Here of course is another significant difference between the corporate sector and the social economy, for the corporates can pump substantial amounts of money into the process. A case study describing a single focus group in a private-sector corporation was reported to have cost £4,000 – the sort of budget most community organisations would require to fund the complete process![18]

Any organisation engaging in social accounting must understand that it will incur costs of time and money and must factor that into its plans. More than that, it should factor the social accounting process into budgets along with other budget lines, as well as into work schedules and job descriptions. Ideally funding organisations should also recognise such budget lines as legitimate and be prepared to pay the costs for social accounting and audit. Indeed it is surely in their interests to do so.

Verification – the crucial stage

Verification is crucial because that is what confirms to all stakeholders and to the wider community that what they read is trustworthy, that the social accounts are a fair assessment and a balanced interpretation of the social accounting information which has been gathered and that the information has been collected in a competent and reliable manner. Verification must be done by people with no close or vested interest in the organisation.

Within the social economy sector the process of a social audit panel is used, chaired by someone with experience. The panel examines the social accounts, sample checks to source some of the data used and goes through with the organisation the social accounts they have prepared, probing and challenging interpretations made, looking at the quality and competence of the methods used and ensuring there are no obvious omissions which are not explained or accounted for. The process may include additional, prior visits to the organisation by the panel chair and even some corroborative telephone calls to selected stakeholders. A social audit panel day is a tough day but it is usually a constructive day.

The key questions which a social audit panel will examine are:

- To what extent do the social accounts report comprehensively on all the work of the organisation and how it lives up to its values?
- Have all the key stakeholders been effectively consulted?
- Are any omissions from the social accounts satisfactorily explained?
- Do the social accounts include a report on environmental practices and impact?
- Do the social accounts report on the statutory and voluntary standards with which the organisation should comply?

The purpose of the social audit panel is thus not to evaluate the actual work of the organisation but to assess the quality of the social accounts and verify if they are based on adequate data, competently gathered and reasonably interpreted. Judging the value of the work is the job of the stakeholders, having been informed by the audited social accounts. The panel is a group of independent people whose opinion will be respected and whose names, associated with the process and with signing off the accounts, will lend the credibility that ensures the social accounts are considered trustworthy.

Social audit practitioners in the social economy sector are not comfortable with the apparent trend in the corporate sector to rely on a sole social auditor, often the same firm which acts for them in other consultative capacities, although in the wake of the Enron affair this practice is surely likely to change. Some corporate examples appear to dispense entirely with true external verification. The panel approach keeps a wider, lay, perspective and reduces dependence on a sole professional, in a field which is in danger of becoming too rapidly over-professionalised.

The question of standards

Social audit practitioners in the social economy also recognise that there must be agreed minimum standards for ensuring the quality of the process. Standards will revolve around three key areas:

- Agreement about what should constitute the content of a competent set of social accounts: what *must* be there, what might be optional?
- Agreement about minimum standards for the processes used to gather information (especially the qualitative information) for the social accounts;
- Agreement about how the verification is conducted and what, at a minimum, must be done and how.

There is not yet agreement about these standards, apart from, within the sector, recognition that they must derive from practice and be simple rather than complex, easily applied and readily understood. ISEA's AccountAbility1000

Framework[19] is perceived to be too complex, too academic, too costly, too directed at professionalisation and mostly driven by corporate-sector interests. As a consequence the UK SAN, like its counterparts overseas, has begun to develop its own processes to agree standards and approve competent social auditors and training programmes appropriate to the social economy.

There probably also needs to be a series of 'stepped' social audit 'levels' linked to comprehensiveness and to the quality components. Each level would specify what should be done as regards the social accounting process and then reported in the social accounts. The levels would relate to the size, capacity and complexity of an organisation and reflect the amount of social accounting work that different types of organisation might be expected to undertake. Larger, complex social enterprises would be expected to go for a more comprehensive level than a small, voluntary-run, community enterprise. Organisations preparing social accounts would commit themselves to going for a particular level which would determine what they should be required to do. The larger enterprise might start at level one or two but their serious commitment to social accounting would be challenged if they did not progress through the levels, whereas it would be acceptable for the small, voluntary, enterprise to stick at an earlier level.

A similar standard of verification rigour would be applied to each level; only the complexity and the comprehensiveness would vary. The wording of the social audit statement issued by a social audit panel would reflect the level chosen. The development of agreed standard wordings for social audit statements, related to agreed standards for content and process, would be a major step forward.

A process of approving social auditors is essential if external stakeholders are to be satisfied that minimum standards have been applied in the process of verifying social accounts. This will require a recognised mechanism to be established within the social economy to agree and safeguard quality standards. The UK SAN has now established such an agreed approval process for registering people in the UK who are considered to be competent to chair social audit panels and sign and issue a social audit statement. Later, if the system for regulating social enterprises as suggested in chapter 10 were adopted, there would need to be a clear link between the regulator and the social audit quality mechanism.

Indicators for society

The idea behind regulation for social enterprises is to verify that they adhere to the defining characteristics and in return may qualify for various fiscal and other benefits (chapter 10). Society invests in social enterprises because they are providing added value which society recognises and wishes to encourage. It is therefore essential that such added value is identified, measured and reported.

However, there may be wider objectives which society is looking to social enterprises to fulfil and social accounts as at present prepared do not always address these wider aims. Thus investment in a job creation project for young people may also be seeking to reduce crime in a locality and increase the involvement of young people in civil society and the democratic process.

There is a need to identify what these wider objectives are which society seeks to attain through its investment in social enterprises and then to develop a set of indicators which may be used not only by individual social enterprises but also groups of social enterprises. Reporting on these would allow social accounts to demonstrate the wider, societal impact of individual enterprises and also permit cumulative impact to be measured.

The Conscise action research project[20] has experimented with agreeing two common objectives (in this case to do with the creation and use of social capital) which have been adopted by eight social enterprises in addition to their own unique objectives. In this way the social accounts produced both report on the unique work of each enterprise and, in common format, on their impact on social capital.

Process and tools

The social audit model described in Appendix ii is about process: it is a step-by-step framework which assists an organisation to set about gathering the information needed to prepare social accounts. It builds on rather than replaces the existing mechanisms an organisation will have in place to record data, consult stakeholders and comply with standards, voluntary and statutory.

To make the process work, various tools are required which assist organisations to gather and process data, and to consult stakeholders in ways which really engage and involve them. To be useful such tools must be easy and interesting to use, effective for their purpose, appropriate and relevant for a wide range of circumstances and for all types of stakeholder groups, and they must not demand too much by way of time and finance. This is a tall order, but long-term successful social accounting in the social economy will depend on more such tools being developed. The challenge, then, is not about process but about devising tools which will make the process work.

Current social accounting is constrained by the rudimentary tools available, especially with regard to consulting stakeholders. Often the aspiration to engage in face-to-face dialogue gives way to the use of questionnaires because they are quicker and cheaper, and easier to process. Common consultation themes are emerging which lend themselves to common sets of questions which may be customised for the individual social enterprise.[21] Similarly, methods of recording data can be transferred between organisations. But the bank of tools is as yet incomplete and more investment is required.

Transparency

It is a key principle that the social accounts are disclosed. This is usually achieved through the publication of a social performance report which summarises the full, verified social accounts. It is too easy to see that published report as the main end product, a tendency which is encouraged by annual award schemes for social reports. More important by far than the glossy booklet is the *process*: the process which leads to the social accounts being prepared and to the process of accountability, ensuring openness in the way stakeholders are consulted and opening up varied two-way channels between the organisation and its stakeholders. 'Social auditing is not about reaching a destination determined by someone else. It is about the quality of the journey and the impact of that journey on others. It may also include building the road the organisation travels over.'[22]

Mandatory or voluntary?

A further issue concerns the tricky question of whether social accounting should be mandatory or whether it should remain a voluntary endeavour, and thus voluntarily regulated. There are two powerful reasons in favour of making social accounting compulsory.

First, society has a right to know just what impact organisations are having on people and on the planet. Organisations should be required to demonstrate to society the impact they are making by producing social accounts which not only spell out the benefits to be seen but also the dis-benefits. The requirement to report should identify what should be included in such accounts according to the size, capability and capacity of different organisations. The principle should be that all account and report on their social and environmental (and cultural?) impacts: corporates (big and small), small businesses, the public sector and quangos as well as the social economy and other organisations of the third system.

A system of voluntary, self-regulating reporting will not provide society with the information it needs to moderate the behaviour of organisations. As Ed Mayo has pointed out: 'All of the significant improvements in business responsibility, from equal pay to trade union membership, started as voluntary innovations. But they had to graduate into regulation and law to make a real impact.'[23]

George Goyder favoured 'enforcing' social accounting by requiring companies 'once they reach a certain size...by law to adapt in their memorandum of association a General Objects clause setting out one by one the objects of the company in terms of its own health, the development and the welfare of its employees, consumers, shareholders, locality and the State.'[24] While that would be a useful step forward and lead to an interesting amendment to the Companies Acts it would probably, of itself, not be sufficient. Social audit clauses in the memorandum and articles of social enterprises have not thus far had the required effect. What is needed is legislation; society demanding that social accounts be kept.

That is now the policy of the Co-operative Party which has recognised that 'until social auditing is a regulatory condition for all businesses of a certain size, it is difficult to see how co-operatives could adopt social auditing without incurring extra costs... There now needs to be government endorsement and adoption and eventual statutory compliance.'[25] In April 2002 a private member's bill along these lines was introduced to the House of Commons with the support of over 200 Members of Parliament. Although that bill will not make the statute book and although government has made clear in its Social Enterprise Strategy that it does not intend to introduce social auditing, it is clear that the pressure is beginning to build.[26]

Second, there is an acknowledged interest by public-sector agencies in social accounting as something the social enterprises and voluntary organisations they support and fund might undertake as a means of allowing them, the funders, to understand how effective they are. There is here a distinct danger of social accounting becoming compulsory 'through the back door' or, worse, being seen as something the social economy sector must do, but not necessarily the other sectors. To be truly effective, social accounting and audit should be the means whereby all institutions in society report on what they do, and account to their stakeholders.

The really big game now is to ensure that social auditing becomes mandatory and that in this way society receives sound information about the benefits and the dis-benefits delivered by different organisations. That surely is essential for sustainable policy-making. For social enterprises the social audit will also be the means through which they regularly re-establish their public recognition as a social enterprise and therefore their right to the fiscal and other advantages which should be put in place to ensure the social economy becomes a driver in the British economy.

From social accounting and audit we now look farther afield, to the implications of globalisation for the social economy, and suggest that the values of the third system should be an important influence on the way the world is managed.

NOTES

1. Douglas Adams, *The Hitch Hiker's Guide to the Galaxy* (London, Pan Books, 1979).
2. Mike Geddes, 'The Social Audit Movement', in *Green Reporting: The challenge of the nineties*, 1992.
3. John Pearce, Simon Zadek and Peter Raynard, *Social Auditing for Small Organisations: The workbook* (London, New Economics Foundation, 1996).
4. Freer Spreckley, *Social Audit Toolkit* (Herefordshire, Social Enterprise Partnership, 2000).
5. John Pearce, *Social Audit Study for Community Enterprise Lothian* (Edinburgh, XCEL Consultants, 1995).
6. John Pearce, *Liverpool Social Audit Initiative: Report on the pilot programme 1996–98* (Liverpool City Council, 1999).
7. John Pearce, *Social Audit and Accounting: Manual, workbook and CD-ROM* (West Calder, Community Business Scotland Network and Liverpool, Social Enterprise Network, 2001).
8. Peter Raynard and Sarah Murphy, *Charitable Trust? Social Auditing with voluntary organisations* (London, Association of Chief Executives of Voluntary Organisations and New Economics Foundation, 2000).
9. www.cbs-network.org.uk (click on Social Audit Network).
10. www.isai.ie
11. www.socialaudit.co.nz
12. www.socialaudit.org.au
13. www.accountability.org.uk

14. John Pearce, *At the Heart of the Community Economy: Community enterprise in a changing world* (London, Calouste Gulbenkian Foundation, 1993).
15. Deborah Doane, *Corporate Spin: The troubled teenage years of social reporting* (London, New Economics Foundation, 2000).
16. Ed Mayo, 'Government must try some make-good repairs', in *The Guardian*, 27 August 2001.
17. *Social Audit Pilot Project 1998–99, Final Report* (COMMACT Aotearoa, 2000).
18. Alison Crowther, 'Stakeholder dialogue: The importance of principles and preparation', in *Accountability Quarterly*, Institute of Social and Ethical AccountAbility (ISEA), March 2000.
19. *AccountAbility 1000 Framework: Standards, guidelines and professional qualification* (Institute of Social and Ethical AccountAbility (ISEA), 1999).
20. Alan Kay and John Pearce, *Social Audits of Social Enterprises: Methodology* (Conscise Project, Middlesex University, 2000).
21. See examples on *Social Audit and Accounting* CD-ROM, Pearce (2001), see note 7.
22. Social Audit New Zealand, information leaflet, 2001.
23. Mayo (2001), see note 16.
24. George Goyder, *Some Thoughts on Trusteeship*, C.C. Desai Memorial Lecture, Hyderabad, 1978.
25. *Enterprise Empowerment Accountability: The co-operative agenda for Labour* (The Co-operative Party, 2001).
26. *Social Enterprise: A strategy for success* (London, Department of Trade and Industry, 2002).

12 Globalisation – friend or foe to the social economy?

'I do not want my house to be walled in on all sides, and my windows to be stuffed. I want the cultures of all the lands to be blown about my house as freely as possible. But I refuse to be blown off my feet by any.'

Mahatma Gandhi[1]

This chapter reflects on why community and social enterprises and other community-led activity are important in the contemporary context of globalisation and suggests that we may be mistaken in the way globalisation is defined and therefore frequently demonised.

What is globalisation?

As a term, 'globalisation' has come to mean the way in which the world economy is run, and dominated by multinational corporations and the international institutions they appear to control. Rather like that other excellent word 'enterprise' which has been hijacked to mean simply business, globalisation is now taken to be about:

- The liberalisation of markets to encourage unrestricted profit-making by capital which knows no sense of place, no sense of local community;
- So-called 'free' trade policed by the World Trade Organisation (WTO), its 'level playing fields';
- Structural adjustments determined and enforced by global institutions such as the World Bank and the International Monetary Fund (IMF) designed to make nations play the globalisation game according to the rules laid down by institutions dominated by the rich and the powerful.

This interpretation of globalisation has led, unsurprisingly, to an anti-globalisation movement, campaigning in frustration at the way the world economy is managed, at the way financial institutions appear to assume the role of global government, at the inexorable rise of inequality and social exclusion and at the continuing degradation of the environment.

The positives of globalisation

While it is right to condemn globalisation as defined in this narrow way, that definition has led to something of a blind refusal to perceive any positive aspects in the globalisation process of the past two decades which has led to an ever more interdependent planet. For globalisation surely means those processes and developments which have made the concept of a 'global village' a reality. These are to do with:

- *Communications*: the way we can now communicate with each other across and around the world speedily and cheaply, using e-mail and the web, knowing what is happening on the other side of the planet as it happens.
- *Transportation*: the fact that it is now possible to travel quickly – and at reasonable cost – between continents allowing visits, meetings and conferences to take place which not long since were unthinkable.
- *Knowledge:* and the information technology which allows that knowledge to spread around the globe.
- *Scientific advances and their application:* which can benefit all of humankind (as an extreme example, the possibility of surgical operations being undertaken across continents by remote control using the very latest techniques of robot, digital and information technologies).

These capacities and characteristics of globalisation can give truly positive benefits just as they can also be used in a negative fashion. They may serve for good or for evil, to benefit the many or just the few.

Thus, global capacities permit terrorism to be organised on a global scale. Equally, however, those who combat global terrorism can employ, for example, the capacity to track financial transactions around the globe to clamp down on the assets and the money movements of suspected terrorists.

Simply because we can transport all things around the globe at great speed does not mean it is sensible to do so. It is a political and economic choice which determines that we transport food huge distances at considerable environmental cost to the planet rather than encourage home production and consumption nearer the point of production.

A global institution such as the WTO does not have to be the instrument which exacerbates divisions between rich and poor and which appears consistently to favour the rich trading nations through the fiction of the level playing field. Who wants a level playing field if you are a village team playing a professional club? Playing off a handicap as in golf would be a more apt analogy, allowing equal rather than unequal competition.

Managing the globe

The problem is not in globalisation itself, but in how we, as a global society, manage and regulate the positive capacities of globalisation and set about achieving our global aspirations. It is a question of governance and of values, of who makes the decisions and from what value base. Historically, even in the US, economic growth has depended on the government taking certain initiatives and setting operating or regulatory frameworks. And government is responsible for what it does through the democratic process. Today, we are presented with the notion that only private business and financial institutions are capable of delivering growth and that there should be only a minimal role for democratically elected governments to oversee and manage that process. Furthermore we are told that only economic growth can deliver social progress and justice. On a global scale we are effectively being offered government by financial institutions, which are secretive and unaccountable. It is arguable that the World Economic Forum and its annual meeting in Davos has far greater authority than the United Nations and it appears that the closed shop of the Business Round Table in Europe has a very significant influence on the policies and direction of the European Union. Meanwhile transnational corporations operate across nations such that they are accountable to none, and frequently avoid contributing to the public finances through 'efficient' schemes of tax avoidance. The World Bank and the IMF shape and dictate the economies of poorer nations to ensure that they fit the established global purpose.

So the key question is: how can processes be developed globally – as well as within nations – that can rein in and control the way the world is run and make those global institutions accountable to the peoples of the world? The movement of protest should not be against globalisation as such but against the way the globe is managed.

Subsidiarity – the concept of reverse delegation

In chapter 3 we discussed the concept of subsidiarity which has featured in EU rhetoric and which means that decision-making and power should be vested in the lowest levels of society which, in turn, delegate upwards those tasks which can best be done on a larger scale or at a higher level (reverse delegation). In practice this does not generally happen in Europe, which remains a highly centralised and controlling bureaucracy, but the concept is exciting, dynamic and in essence quite revolutionary. While power to do things can be delegated upwards from the grass roots, those powers which are delegated may, of course, be taken away if the higher level of government or society does not adequately discharge its responsibilities.

In a global context this idea of subsidiarity correctly implies the need for global institutions – as well as global/regional, national, regional and district institutions – but institutions which take on only those tasks and responsibilities which have been handed to them and are always accountable to the levels below them. So we need global institutions, but along with them we need the democratic processes of civil society through which to control them.

The values of community-based development

It surely follows that the community-based structures within the third system, and especially within the social economy, are crucially important as the test-beds for development which is founded on certain values and principles and as the grass-roots levels from which the first responsibilities may be delegated upwards. Subsidiarity, if it is to work, requires a strong and active base at local community level and strong networks between communities to build grass-roots social capital.

In chapter 3 we identified the values which underpin the social economy and the third system generally and they are summarised in the box below. Involvement at community level is a training ground for the development of a civil society which engages the population and is the bedrock of a civilised society. But the values which underpin community-led, grass-roots institutions of the third system and in the social economy are a direct challenge to the values which influence the prevailing status quo.

- *Democracy:* adopting structures and institutions which are accountable to the people.
- *Working for the common good:* having as primary purposes benefit to both people and the planet.
- *Fundamental rights:* recognising that all people have a fundamental right to adequate food, shelter, health, education and work.
- *People before profit:* focusing on improvements to quality of life while ensuring that there is sufficient profitability for financial sustainability of the project or institution.
- *Local economy:* adopting human-scale activity which strengthens the local economy.
- *Harbouring resources:* adopting environmentally sustainable working practices which minimise harmful impacts on the planet.

The terrorist attacks of 11 September 2001 on New York made articulating the challenge to the status quo suddenly very difficult, as any challenge to the way globalisation is managed ran the risk of being interpreted as pro-terrorist. However, in less than one year confidence in the prevailing capitalist structures has been seriously undermined by the revelations of crooked accounting, whitewash auditing and other shoddy practices at the heart of the world's corporate and financial institutions. As a positive result of this sequence of events the values of the global economic project can again be challenged and the record of its stewardship of the world questioned.

A global movement for change

The opportunity exists to build the challenge from the grass roots, from those operating in the third system, to the way the global system is controlled. That means demonstrating that globalisation is controlled in the interests of the few rather than the many, insisting that there are other values which matter, proposing that global institutions can be developed to serve mankind and be accountable to the people and suggesting how that might be done. His Holiness the Dalai Lama has proposed the concept of Gross National Happiness (GNH) as an indicator and the Government of Bhutan has indeed used this concept to screen proposed development initiatives.

The ethics, values and culture of the community development sector must permeate upwards and outwards.

In order to do that third-system activists should work on four levels:

- To strengthen networking and sharing through international associations in order to build up the global movement for challenge and change using the tools which are now available in the global village.
- To engage in civil society at all levels by becoming active in community affairs and in the democratic processes of our nations, and so press for the implementation of subsidiarity.
- To engage with those people in the first (private) and second (public) systems who share concerns about the present global project, but engage without compromise and without being co-opted unsuspectingly to bolster the agenda of others.
- To change the general perception of the third system from being seen as 'third' to being accepted as equal to – if not more important than – the other systems, and whose task is not to prop up the first and second systems but to rebuild mechanisms for controlling them.

It is a major task and maybe time is against us. But there have already been gains which can be noted: the successful campaign against the multilateral agreement on investment; the success of Jubilee 2000 in gaining some concessions on debt relief; the challenges made and for once listened to in Seattle; the partial climb-down on HIV/AIDS drugs by some of the pharmaceutical companies. Small steps perhaps but evidence that global movement and pressure from below can have some impact, that the capacities of the global village can indeed be used to challenge the way globalisation is managed.

The argument can be briefly summarised:

- The global processes and capacities of the modern age are to be welcomed because they can benefit mankind.
- The key issue is not globalisation, but how the globe is governed.
- We do need global institutions. But they must reflect the different, third-system, values and therefore seek to achieve different objectives.
- Those values and objectives should come from the grass roots with tasks and responsibilities delegated upwards.
- Institutions must be democratically accountable.

The social economy in the UK is part of a world-wide movement and it is important that it nurtures and strengthens its contacts with others seeking similar ends around the globe, not just in Europe and the North but in the South as well. In the final chapter we seek to identify the key ingredients for building social enterprise and third-system values into a powerful force in our society.

NOTES

1. Mahatma Gandhi, quoted by Nesar Ahmed and Ginny Shrivastava in *Voices from the Roots of the Grass: Impact of 'SAP' and the New Economic Policy, Globalisation, Liberalisation, Privatisation on the Poor of Rajasthan* (Udaipur, India, ASTHA, 2001).

13 A manifesto for social enterprise

Recent years have seen the emergence of growing support for social enterprises from the government, especially in London. That commitment and the practical proposals which are emerging have transformed the context for social enterprises. It is also clear that a political commitment is building to use the social enterprise way not just at local level but at all levels in society, as evidenced in the discussion not only about 'community interest companies' but also 'public interest companies'. Exciting times indeed.

The previous chapters have explored some of the key issues which the changing context sometimes brings into focus and sometimes blurs. The intention of this final chapter is to focus on the key points made throughout these pages and to offer them as a manifesto for social enterprise. Like all manifestos, it will have achieved its purpose if it stimulates debate and discussion.

Values

Social enterprises are not businesses like any other. They are fundamentally different because of the values which underpin them and guide what they do and how they do it. Those values distinguish social enterprises, from first-system businesses and from second-system organisations.

The values tend to be expressed in fine-sounding but rather general phrases: 'working for the common good', 'putting people before profit', 'taking a holistic approach', 'promoting sustainability', 'respecting cultural differences', 'social justice', 'common ownership', 'democratic structures', 'accountability to stakeholders', 'self-help and mutuality'. These words build up a picture of a way of managing society which one can sense as being quite different, but which is also rather fuzzy, lacking in sharp focus. What does it all mean?

The value base of the social economy needs to be developed into a cross-cutting charter, with a clearly expressed philosophy with which people may identify and which can be seen as leading to practical consequences.

Social enterprises must articulate their values and consider what message they should convey in the way they go about their daily business. Too often social enterprises are coy about their values and play them down, pretending that they are really the same as other businesses, but just happen to have a social purpose.

- It is the values of the social economy which mark out social enterprises as different.
- Those values should be made more explicit.
- Social enterprises should focus on how they live their values: 'walking their talk'.

Building the vision

Social enterprises need to build a shared vision based on their values. That requires that they work together as a movement, to develop the links and networks through which relationships can build, trust can grow and reciprocal help and mutual collaboration flourish. That is the social capital which social enterprises can use to strengthen their place and influence in society.

Social capital research has demonstrated how people and organisations who share a way of thinking and common values may more quickly develop trust and find ways of working together. The lesson here is for social enterprises to invest time and energy in working with others in the social economy and in the third system rather than concentrating on partnerships with players from the other systems.

The social economy has always been fragmented and riven with argumentative tendencies. The establishment of inclusive coalitions and networks of networks are important steps forward to building greater co-operation, and eventually, the social capital which the social economy needs. It is the common ground which is more important than the differences.

Competition can drive a dangerous wedge into this push to build social capital and all too easily fragment the beginnings of coalition. Yet competition is being advocated constantly as the preferred way of making choices. It should not be the third-system way and social enterprises must be wary of competition and find ways of managing it. The consortia being promoted by Social Enterprise London are one way, learning from the first and second systems which have been adept at managing competition to their advantage over the centuries.

- Social enterprises should build social capital within the third system.
- Coalitions and networks can focus on common ground rather than differences and provide the opportunity for trust to grow.
- Mutual help and collaboration will grow from trust and shared values.
- Social enterprises should be wary of competition and learn ways of managing it to the benefit of all.

Celebrating the difference

Social enterprises are part of a wider social economy which, in turn, is part of a distinctive third system in the global economy. Social enterprises are not a subset of the first system, mopping up the misfits and problems of capitalism on behalf of the private and public sectors. They should see themselves as the wealth-creating engine-room of the third system.

Social enterprises should be aware, and proud, of their difference and have the confidence to promote it. The Social Enterprise Movement must lobby and campaign in order to persuade others to understand and adopt its values and to share its vision of the way society could be. The values and the vision are why people and politicians should wish to embrace the idea of social enterprise.

- Social enterprises and the third system are different.
- Social enterprises should promote the difference, and
- Campaign for others to share the values and the vision.

Definitions are important

It is essential to have a clear, unambiguous, definition of social enterprise. A clear definition will allow society to know, not only when an organisation is a social enterprise, but also when one is *not*.

The definition should be based on the six defining characteristics which distinguish social enterprises: social purpose, engaging in trade, no private profit distribution, assets held for community benefit, being democratic and accountable. These characteristics should be embedded into constitutions and monitored through a system of registration and regulation for social enterprises, based on the characteristics defined. A 'social enterprise test' should be devised.

Regulation will be the first step by which society makes it clear that it recognises the distinctive difference of social enterprises and wishes to encourage their formation. Such a system will also serve as a kitemark such that society and government know with confidence whether an enterprise meets the agreed criteria for being considered as a social enterprise. It will also serve to strengthen, for social enterprises, the sense of belonging to a movement; and at the same time will remove that sense of social enterprises somehow being 'odd'.

- Agree a clear definition of social enterprise based on the six defining characteristics.
- Establish a system of registration and regulation.
- Understand both what is and what is not a bona fide social enterprise through the 'social enterprise test'.

Democracy

Democracy is the defining characteristic about which there is most hesitation. Yet the democratic concept is at the heart of our society. It is the way in which people may exert control over the institutions of civil society and, hence, over the way their lives are shaped.

Democracy is not something which relates only to government. Practising democracy should be part of our society from bottom to top, from community organisations to national and European parliamentary elections. Social and community enterprises are part of that democratic weave which gives people a taste for controlling their own affairs and demonstrating that democracy can work.

Democracy does not work simply because there is a democratic constitution. It has to be encouraged, nurtured and facilitated. It is easy to find ways around it, as politicians show, by discouraging participation, by not opening up information, by stifling debate and discussion – and then lamenting that 'people are not interested'.

Making democracy work in social and community enterprises requires effort and investment: to build and encourage membership, to train new and potential directors, to share information, to create and use channels of communication and accountability. One of the dilemmas for social enterprises is how to finance this investment in making democracy work. Maybe facilitating the democratic process within social and community enterprises is another social cost which by rights the state should consider bearing?

- Democratic structures and organisation are one of the defining characteristics of social enterprise.
- Making democracy work is essential to the wider health of society.
- Making democracy work requires the investment of time and effort, and therefore costs money.

Subsidiarity

A further dimension to the democracy issue is that of *subsidiarity*.

Community enterprises in particular are about structures within communities which give people the capacity to engage in trade and develop other economic and social initiatives on a collective basis. They – and other social enterprises – provide a mechanism through which services may be provided at local level.

That means government and local councils agreeing to 'let go' and hand down (or maybe hand back) the power and responsibility to manage local services, including control of physical assets. There has generally been strong reluctance to do this on the part of the public-sector agencies. But it is a clear part of the social enterprise vision: that if something can be organised and managed competently at local level, that is where and how it should be done.

It means specifying contracts in a way that relates to communities and not to convenience. It means recognising the best value inherent in local people doing local work and in local knowledge. It may also mean being more relaxed about an uneven patchwork of services.

Social enterprises undoubtedly have an important part to play in delivering services and managing facilities, but they also have other roles within communities and within wider markets. Most social enterprise practitioners have long argued that social enterprises could and should have a greater say in providing local services and have been frustrated at the reluctance of local government to let go. At the same time many social enterprise practitioners are uneasy about possibly being used as pawns in a game designed to reduce labour costs by shifting the provision of services from the public sector.

It is important that social enterprises are not simply seen as the servants of the state, not just as another way for the public sector to manage its affairs.

- Social and community enterprises are democratic structures to which government can hand down or hand back the responsibility of providing and managing certain services.
- Such transfers require government – at all levels – to let go, and
- To specify contracts such that they may be delivered at local level.
- Social enterprises must not be seen just as servants of the state but valued for the particular strengths and additional benefits they can deliver.

Mutual financing

Financial institutions are required within the third system which have the capacity to make the scale of investments that are needed to seriously grow social enterprises.

The idea of making social enterprise 'bankable' sends out quite the wrong message. It implies that social enterprises are, or should become, like other businesses, which they are not and should not aspire to be. It further implies that social enterprises should somehow fit themselves to the demands of the existing banking system.

The first step must be to consolidate the network of finance institutions which belong to the social economy. That may not mean proliferating small Community Development Finance Institutions (CDFIs) but building institutions of some scale which can both make loans and provide 'patient' equity capital. The emphasis should be on finance institutions which share social economy values rather than on funds which are controlled by the state or by the private sector.

The second step is surely for the existing big financial players from the traditional co-operative sector in the social economy to take a lead in developing a new national institution or supporting regional social economy funds to build up and provide the investment capital which is required. They have the expertise. There is substantial money around the social economy, but most of it is kept and used within the mainstream banking system. Therefore it does not work to benefit the social economy. The Charity Bank, Triodos Bank and others have demonstrated that there is money out there which people are willing to invest in social enterprises and to accept that social returns temper the financial return they may expect.

The third step is to make more sensible use of the substantial funds which the public sector already invests in social enterprises. That means the introduction of 'recoverable grants', paying revenue money as up-front capital, working through social investment funds rather than direct from the public sector, and diverting some of the expensive revenue schemes (Intermediate Labour Markets for example) into capital investment funds.

- The social economy requires its own mutual financing institutions based on social economy values rather than having to become 'bankable' in the style of the first-system banks.
- These mutual finance institutions must build investment funds of a scale which can deliver the growth capital required for social enterprises to make a significant difference.
- The existing co-operative financial institutions should take a lead in developing new institutions and mobilising the substantial funds already within the social economy to work for social enterprises.
- Public-sector investment in social enterprises should be routed through the mutual financing institutions and delivered as 'patient' equity.

Structures of mutual support

Support structures for social enterprises should be of the social economy and accountable to social enterprises.

Because social enterprises are different they require support structures appropriate to their needs. It should not be thought that they may simply tap into services provided by the state and designed to grow the private sector in the economy.

There should be a network of social enterprise support structures at national, regional and local or district levels. National and regional bodies should be accountable to their social enterprise members and should themselves meet the criteria for being bona fide social enterprises.

At local level it will be more appropriate for existing social enterprises to take on the role of giving support to the formation of new community and social enterprises in their area. Social enterprise support should build on the community development approach, not the business development approach. That recognises that the creation of a business is often but one of a raft of integrated initiatives.

Social enterprises do not need business plans, they need *social enterprise plans* which demonstrate how their social purpose will be achieved, how they will be environmentally responsible and how they will achieve financial sustainability. The business plan as traditionally understood addresses only a small portion of the needs of a social enterprise plan.

Within the social economy there is already a wide range of expertise which may be made available. That expertise understands the needs of social enterprise. While it is to be welcomed that public (and private) sector agencies are being encouraged and required to understand the particular characteristics and needs of social enterprises so that they may give helpful advice, it is mistaken thinking to believe that the support needs for social enterprises will be effectively met in this way. There are examples of public/private agencies giving valuable and effective support to social enterprises but that should be in addition to rather than instead of a mutual support structure within the social economy.

The support structure must not conflate support for social enterprises with support for voluntary organisations.

- Social enterprises need their own mutually owned and controlled support structures.
- Those structures should be strengthened at national, regional and local/district levels.
- Social enterprises need social enterprise plans, not business plans.
- Within the social economy there is a wide range of expertise available which should be used to support social enterprises rather than using expertise designed to grow first-system business.
- Voluntary organisations are not social enterprises and, although part of the third system, need their own support systems.

Counting the benefit

The social enterprise plan will articulate precisely what a social enterprise is intending to achieve and how it will achieve it, including being overt about the values on which it is basing its work.

It is essential that a mechanism is in place which will allow performance to be monitored and reported on, and which will, at the same time, allow the social enterprise to plan better for the future and account for what it does by allowing all its stakeholders, including the wider society, to judge the value. That mechanism is *social accounting*.

Social accounting is a framework through which an enterprise puts into place systems to gather hard facts and figures as well as qualitative opinions about what it is doing and the impacts it is having. It ensures the enterprise is clear about its mission, its values and its core objectives as well as being precise about exactly what it does to achieve those objectives.

The social accounts report to what extent the social enterprise plan has been achieved, including not just what has been done (objectives and activities) but how it has been done (values). The social accounts are audited so that outsiders can take what they read as trustworthy and base their judgements on them.

Social accounts allow society to understand the additional benefits – and the costs associated with them – which social enterprises can achieve. Contracts with social enterprises must recognise those social costs and factor them in. Social accounting and audit will play a key role in ensuring compliance and accountability in the system of regulation for social enterprises. It will mediate between social and commercial tensions.

Social accounting and audit should be mandatory, but not just for social enterprises. All organisations should be expected to account for the impact they have on people and the planet, for the benefits they provide and for the damage they inflict. Companies and public-sector agencies, as well as social enterprises, should be required to produce social accounts, including an environmental statement, on a regular basis and to submit them for independent verification.

- Social accounting is the mechanism by which social enterprises can monitor to what extent they are achieving their social enterprise plan.
- Audited social accounts allow all stakeholders to judge the value achieved by social enterprises.
- Social accounts demonstrate the added value of social enterprises, which society must be prepared to pay for.
- Social accounting and audit should become the routine way through which social enterprises are regulated.
- Social accounting should be mandatory, but not only for social enterprises. It is equally relevant for private business and public agencies. We also need to know the impact they have on people and on the planet.

Changing society

Social enterprise is a practical manifestation of an altogether bigger project, namely, changing the way society is run.

Social enterprise has a political purpose. It is about a different way of doing things, based on shared values. It is about a vision of the way people and organisations might work together for the common good, where private gain is tempered always by consideration for the needs of people and the planet.

It is easy for social enterprise activists to lose sight of this bigger picture in the struggle for survival and be tempted to reject the push for radical change and adopt the reformist tendency. Government is saying 'come and help us achieve our purpose'. Business is saying 'you are businesses just like us, come and join the mainstream'.

But social enterprise and the third system are about doing things differently and seeking fundamental changes. It is hard, maybe impossible, to do that and at the same time collaborate to keep the status quo working. Yet that is the role which is being advocated for social enterprises. Come and mop up the problems of society, deal with the disadvantaged, create employment in poor rundown areas, tackle social exclusion and everything else. The dilemma for social enterprise radicals is the age-old one of how to retain the ideals while working in compromising contexts; there can be no survival without compromise.

While the main focus of these pages has been social enterprise in the UK, we must always remember that similar movements exist all around the world. One of the advantages of globalisation has been the way in which social and community economy activists can now network and share information and experience, and organise together. The language changes from country to country and from continent to continent, but the sense of purpose is common and the underpinning values are universal.

'Think global, act local' was Gandhi's dictum and it sums up the social enterprise approach. The danger now is that we concentrate on the 'acting local' and become absorbed in what we can do in our own backyards. That is of course encouraged by those who prefer to think *and* act global, as it gives them a freer rein to use the planet and its people for their purposes. Global alliances and global networks are essential if the ideas and values of social enterprise are to make headway in challenging the world order.

The time is ripe for being bold and for taking the argument to the public. To explain and demonstrate why the social enterprise way is preferable. To promote the values and ensure that social enterprises live them. To make it easier for closet radicals to come out. To make it the norm to celebrate being a social enterprise with firmly held beliefs rather than to work away in the marketplace pretending to be like any other business. To pin our colours to the mast of radical, global change.

Appendix i
Community futures workshops

Community Futures Workshops (CFW) consist of five workshops which take place at roughly two- or three-week intervals so that the process is completed within 10 to 15 weeks. Dates are fixed either in advance or at the first workshop and a commitment sought from all participants that they will attend all five workshops if they possibly can.

A group of between 30 and 40 participants is an ideal number of which at least half might be local residents and the others representative of the other stakeholder groups. Working with a larger group is possible but can be problematic in that the more small working groups there are the longer the feedback process takes and the more time is required to complete the programme for each workshop.

Attendance at the workshops is normally by invitation, although people who turn up out of interest are not sent away. The group promoting the workshop series has the difficult task of agreeing whom to invite and ensuring that the people they do invite are both a good representative section of the different stakeholder interests and are sufficiently motivated to participate. Time spent by both the promoting group and the facilitating body at this preparatory stage will help ensure that the process stands a better chance of success. Participants should be invited personally, at least by telephone and preferably face-to-face, so that they really understand what it is they are being invited to take part in, what the purpose is, what will happen and – very important for most – the extent of their initial commitment: no more than for the series of five workshops. Personal invitations should be followed up and confirmed in writing and it is good practice also to do some telephone reminding in the days before the first workshop.

External facilitation of the workshops is essential and the promoting group needs to engage someone with experience of facilitating community consultation and planning. He or she or their agency should ideally be involved in the preparatory stage, including making some of the personal contacts with the participants. In this way the facilitator gains some understanding of the locality and its context and at the same time, people can be assured that the process is not closely tied to any one particular local faction and that it will unfold in an even-handed, objective manner.

Much of the work within the workshops is done in small discussion groups (of 8 to10 people) and for each of these, there needs to be a facilitator with experience of running a group so that all are able to contribute, none may dominate and the discussion can be focused. The small-group facilitators may be associates of the main facilitator or they may be people from the area nominated by the promoting group but they should all be known to have the necessary ability. The skill of facilitating a small group frequently goes unrecognised (like the writing of minutes) and many who think they can do it are not suited. It is wise to allocate participants to their smaller group in advance of the workshops and to identify them in some way such as a coloured mark on their name badge. In this way, each group can be sure to include a cross-section of stakeholders and obvious caucuses can be split up.

It is good practice for workshops to be held at different local venues. This serves to avoid association with any one agency or organisation, gets the workshops out and about to see different facilities in the community and engages several organisations directly in the process.

Workshops usually take up a full half-day, either starting or ending with lunch. The timing must be sensitive to cater for people with children needing to be collected from school, and if workshops happen during school holidays, some childcare arrangements may be needed. Each series of workshops will have its own peculiarities regarding the best time and some compromises will almost certainly be needed.

The lunch time is important as it gives participants the opportunity to talk informally and for people from different stakeholder groups to get to know each other. When food is provided by the various venues, competitive catering can result in high-quality buffets!

Equipment needed is basic: flip-charts, felt pens, Blu-tack, name badges and maps of the area and (sometimes) post-its. Venues need to be checked to make sure that there are sufficient wall areas on which Blu-tack can be used. A camera allows a photographic record of the process to be kept, evidence that such a mix of stakeholders worked enthusiastically and energetically together. (Maybe a camcorder would be even better!)

The introductions stage of workshops is crucial as it is during this part that the workshop atmosphere begins to be created and people start to relax and feel able to participate. Each series of workshops develops its own unique style and feeling. The explanation of what the process is about must be clear and must emphasise that the workshops should be seen as a 'level playing field' where all participants come with different, but important, skills ready to share their experiences and to bring collective wisdom to bear on the issues facing the community. The explanation must also make clear what people are going to be expected to do.

Participants also need to learn about each other and at the same time 'find their voices' and make a first spoken contribution in the group. All facilitators have their own favoured ice-breaker methods. One is getting people to physically move around to find someone they do not know in order to 'interview' them for two or three minutes about who they are, where they live, what they do, why they are here and to discover something they are passionate about.

Workshop One

1. Introduction

- Why the workshops have been arranged; how they will work
- Who we all are, and why we are here

2. Finding out the facts about the community: building up a Community Profile

A. The community

- Agree the boundaries
- The people: how many residents? Breakdown by age group
- Increasing/decreasing?
- What do we know about the history of the area?

B. Image

- How do others see us? How do we see ourselves?

C. The local economy

- What do people do? Main occupations/employment
- Scale of unemployment; particular groups affected?
- Local skills?
- Who are the main employers?
- Where do people shop?
- What about other commercial services? e.g. banks, post office, building societies
- Are there any community enterprises? What do they do?
- What is the scale of small, self-employed business? What do they do?
- Is the informal economy important?

D. Housing and the environment

- How many houses? What type of housing?
- Council? Housing association? Owner-occupied? Private rented?
- Housing for special needs? Empty houses?
- What is the standard of housing? best/worst areas?
- Where is the housing office?
- What are the distinguishing features of the area?
- Public open space? Street lighting?
- Roads and pavements? Traffic?

E. Education and training; leisure and recreation

- What nurseries? Creches? Playgroups? After-school clubs?
- What schools? Primary and secondary?
- Adult education? Further education?

- Training projects/organisations
- What sports facilities?
- What playgrounds, playing fields?
- Cinemas, bingo halls, function suites
- Pubs, clubs, coffee bars

F. Community organisations and facilities

What community organisations are there? List:

- For senior citizens; for adults
- For children and young people
- For tenants
- Churches and church-based organisations
- Sports organisations
- Where can people meet? Halls?

G. Health, social and public services

- What facilities?
- Doctors' surgeries, clinics, health centres, dentists; nearest hospital
- Social services; DWP/benefit office; police
- Public telephones; post boxes
- Public transport; gas; electricity; water; drains
- What vacant land? Empty buildings?
- Who are the key people locally?

3. What more do we need to find out?

- What plans are in the pipeline: public or private?
- Who will find out what?
- Who can bring what information?
- Who do we need to hear from?
- Who will plan the tour of the area?
- Confirm the dates and venues for the next workshops

Each interviewer then tells the full group about their interviewee. Although it can be a slow process, eating up time, it can also be fun and set up a good tone as well as letting people know something about the others in the workshop.

Community Profile

The main work of the first workshop is to build up a Community Profile. The first task here is to agree the boundaries of the 'community' under discussion. Each small group tackles this task with the help of a (preferably large-scale) map of the locality and groups share their ideas. It is not uncommon that what local people perceive as a community differs from the official boundary lines on the maps. For the purpose of the workshops, it is important to come to some agreement about what is included within the community under discussion. As well as looking at boundaries, the groups will note what they know of the population size, composition and changes, and of the history of the area.

The second task is to consider the reputation of the area: How do others see us? How do we see ourselves?

Third, each small group will take *two* of the profile topics from the previous box and will write on flip charts what they know between them (maybe 20 minutes per topic) – and also note any information they do not know but believe should be obtained. The community profiling process can be assisted if the facilitator or the promoting group primes some people in advance to bring with them bits of information which they know will be needed – such as local unemployment rates, the nature of the housing stock, any existing local development initiatives or other plans known to be in the pipeline. Each group puts its flip chart sheets about its first topic on the wall and shares its part of the profile with the others, allowing other information or comments to be added. The groups then proceed to do their second topic and share and discuss that with the others.

It is not an exact science but in the space of two hours, workshop members can have described the key features of the community, highlighted facts and figures and identified where more information is required. Volunteers are then sought to research the missing information and bring it to the next workshop. Participants are invited to bring information and leaflets about local organisations and services which they think may be of interest to other workshop members.

Finally, there will always be some aspects of the Community Profile which can be completed only by getting someone to come and make a presentation to the workshop. So the workshop will draw up a list of people it wishes to invite to come and make a five-minute presentation to the second or third workshops (it is amazing how much can be said in five minutes if you try!). Some of these presenters may be workshop participants themselves from whom members want to hear more. Some may be people from organisations who have not been invited but who are 'summoned' to 'give evidence'. Interestingly, those who are summoned usually come.

What emerges is an instant picture of the community, and from it begin to emerge the problems and issues which are important. Part of Workshop Two will be to go on a tour of the area, so the final part of Workshop One is to seek local volunteers to plan the tour, usually on foot and by bus, so that workshop members can see all aspects of the area.

Workshop notes

Notes of each workshop are prepared as soon as possible afterwards and circulated to all participants. The notes not only record what was done and said during the workshop but bind in any information material which participants provide. In this way, the collected notes become a detailed dossier about the community. In several cases, it is decided to develop the list of local organisations and services begun as part of the Community Profile into a comprehensive local directory which then becomes one of the first, tangible spin-offs from the workshops.

Workshop Two

1. **Completing the picture**
   - Report back on additional information gathered since the first workshop
2. **Go on a tour of the area**
   - On foot and/or by bus
   - See the good, the bad and the ugly!
3. **Reactions to the tour**
4. **What is already happening in ....? What is already planned for the area?**
   - An opportunity for local organisations and agencies to explain their work, plans and proposals for the future

[Note that this item may continue into Workshop Three.]

The second workshop starts with agreeing (or correcting) the notes of the first and with receiving (verbally or on paper) reports from those members who had volunteered to do some 'homework' and find out additional information for the Community Profile.

Then comes the tour, typically partly by bus, partly on foot and with local residents as tour leaders – using the bus microphone and talking to small groups. Sometimes arrangements may be made to go into some local premises and hear a short presentation from one or other local organisation. There are two main purposes to the tour.

First, it is for all the workshop members to see all sides of the area first-hand, the back streets and the front streets, the good and the bad, the problems and past successes, and to be led through this by people who know the place intimately – although it is usually the case that even residents from one end of the area will discover something new about the other end!

Second, it is an opportunity for workshop members to mingle and share their thoughts with other stakeholders. Facilitators can assist this by themselves always taking a different seat on the bus and aiming to engage in separate discussions with as many workshop members as possible.

Returning from the tour, the workshop participants share their reactions to what they have seen. There is then time for some of the presentations decided upon at the first workshop – continuing to build up the Community Profile and develop a shared understanding both of the community and its context.

The workshop notes are again prepared as soon as possible and circulated, with all the new information bound in. The facilitator may also include information about projects elsewhere which he or she considers to be relevant to the circumstances and the issues which are beginning to emerge.

Arranging an 'away-day'

An additional element of the CFW can be to arrange a visit for the members to another community which has already engaged in a similar development process. If it is agreed to make such a visit, some time around Workshops Three and Four is good timing, perhaps even, if the logistics permit, on the morning or afternoon of one of these workshops.

A visit provides a further opportunity for members to get to know each other as well as to learn about what others have done, and how they did it, direct from the people themselves. Moreover, it is often easier to see one's own community objectively when making comparisons with another, or when away from the home turf, if only for half a day. It is not only about seeing what could be copied, but seeing what you would *not* do, or do quite differently, and sometimes by comparison recognising the value and quality of some of the things you are already doing! For the facilitator and the promoting group a visit gives a good opportunity to get a feel for how the process is going generally.

Workshop Three

Building our Vision for the Future

1. What is our community like now?
- Pros and cons: good points – bad points (strengths – weaknesses)

2. What are the problems and needs?
- Identify the key issues which need to be tackled.

3. What chances are there for the future? and what blocks?
- Opportunities – threats

4. What is our vision?

5. More information about local plans in the pipeline

Workshop Three starts with agreeing or amending the notes of Workshop Two, receiving any further information for the Community Profile and listening to any remaining presentations.

Then it is down to work in small groups discussing what the community is like now (strengths and weaknesses), identifying the key problem issues to be tackled and looking at opportunities and threats. At each stage, the groups share what they have come up with and discuss their different perceptions.

The picture builds and leads to each group formulating a vision for the community. Usually, some volunteers will be sought to take the different vision statements of the groups and weld them into one composite statement for presentation to Workshop Four.

If a visit has been made to another community, then the opportunity must be found for people to share their thoughts and impressions about the visit, not least for the benefit of any members who were unable to go.

Workshop Four

1. Agree the vision statement and prioritise the key issues

2. Ideas for *action*

- Brainstorm…
- What can be done? What must be done?
- Analyse the ideas:
  Benefit to the local community?
  Building on strengths?
  Realistic? Practical?
  Resources available?
  Pitfalls and problems?
  Project or policy?

3. Select the best/preferable ideas

After agreeing the notes of Workshop Three and receiving any further information, Workshop Four will seek to gain agreement over the composite vision statement prepared from the last workshop.

Then the key issues must be prioritised. For this to be done the facilitator will have clustered these under a number of main headings, drawing from and interpreting what has come out from the earlier workshops and especially Workshop Three.

Presenting the clusters enables the facilitator to clarify points which have been raised and ensure that nothing has been omitted. Sometimes in the ensuing debate, additional points have to be added or some clusters divided into two under different headings. Once the clusters are agreed, workshop members are asked to vote on which are to them the most important to address by using five self-adhesive coloured dots.

The four, five or six issue clusters so prioritised are then the basis for the next stage. Small groups are formed to discuss each prioritised issue cluster and workshop members join the group which especially interests them. Sometimes, this 'voting by feet' leaves one of the clusters with no takers, suggesting that it may be less of a priority after all. Throughout, it is important to emphasise that the prioritising is in terms of *devising action* to tackle the issue. It may be that although an issue is of great importance to a community, it is not prioritised because people are reasonably satisfied with what is already being done to try and tackle it.

It is often the case that one of the issue clusters will be to do with local capacity and the need for an organisation to take things forward on behalf of the community. It is also unusual if tackling unemployment or some other aspect of the local economy is not one of the issue clusters to be prioritised.

The issue groups then brainstorm ideas to tackle the problems identified: seeking proposals which build on existing strengths and which adopt a practical approach, recognising what resources may be needed and what are available, and analysing what problems might get in the way. Some action ideas will be to create a project to do something to tackle the problems, others will be more about policy change, trying to get others to modify what they do, or to adopt new practices. Some action projects will be for the community to undertake itself, often via a social or community enterprise, others will be done in partnership with other bodies, and some will be taken up by other agencies.

Workshop Five

1. Turning Ideas into Action

- Who can/should do what?
- Which organisations can do what?
- Should we form a local development organisation?
- What help do we need with: finance, legal matters, project planning, publicity, writing funding applications, business planning, other?
- What help can we obtain? From where?
- What needs to be done: Now, soon, later?
- Can we draw up a step-by-step action plan – or at least an 'action shopping list'?

2. … and who will take it forward?

- Us? Them? Together?
- Wider community consultation: A newsletter? Presentations to local community groups? A community conference?
- Involving members of the community
- Strengthening local organisations
- Ensuring local political support

3. Who will do what next and by when?

After agreeing the notes of Workshop Four, the fifth workshop starts by prioritising which of the action ideas identified at the earlier workshop should be taken forward. The facilitator will have prepared a summary of the action ideas onto flip charts and workshop members are invited to show where they would invest their money, again represented by a number of coloured dots.

Once it is clear what the priorities are for the group's investment, then two, three or four smaller groups convene to consider how, realistically, the priorities can be taken forward: what needs to be done, by whom; what resources are needed and where they may come from. Typically at least one group will be planning how to create the organisational capacity of the community (or to strengthen existing capacity) so that the community can keep control of the development process. Other specific action initiatives may be structured as subsidiary or separate community enterprises. Others will be for other, existing organisations to pick up.

Returning to the plenary session, the workshop will hear the specific plans and discuss some important issues to follow up:

1. What commitments to help take things forward will be volunteered from within the workshop? With luck 'buy-in' from one or more public agencies will have been achieved and they will publicly undertake to support any future organisation and action. Perhaps a private-sector or other body can be encouraged to make a public commitment.
2. How can the proposals of the workshop be shared with the wider community of the area and with other agencies and organisations who may be implicated or affected? After all, the workshop members were invited; they were in no sense democratically representative. Thus it is important to seek the legitimacy of support from the wider community. Producing a special news sheet; arranging a community conference; embarking on a series of explanatory meetings and dialogues with local organisations; arranging an exhibition; press publicity are all effective mechanisms.
3. How should political support for proposals be built up? The local politicians may not have been participants in the workshops. Some people prefer that they do not take part, as councillors often find it difficult not to be seen to have an answer for everything! But in all cases it is important that the politicians are brought on-side.
4. Are there early action projects which can be undertaken? It is important to maintain momentum and to demonstrate to all residents that the workshops were more than talk. Usually, some simple action project will have been identified and some combination of workshop participants will be able to make it happen.
5. Who will be responsible for maintaining momentum and following up the decisions? Will a steering group be formed? Will one of the public agencies provide some pump-priming finance for the steering group?

Where things go well, some effective answers to all these key questions emerge and momentum is sustained. This is more likely to be the case where the promoting group and the body which financially sponsored the workshops have understood that follow-up may be necessary and have made plans to be able to respond to the need for support if it arises. Indeed, it could be considered irresponsible if a sponsoring body has not thought about how to respond to the positive proposals coming from a successful CFW series.

But it will not always be the case that there is a consensus about what can or should be done. It may be that the workshops reveal irreconcilable conflicts or perceptions; that community and external stakeholders cannot work in partnership; that there simply is not the capacity to take anything forward. In such a case the promoting and sponsoring bodies have to take stock and consider how to deal with the problems raised. Usually the issues to tackle will be clear enough: the problem will be to do with local organisational capacity, with the ability of groups to co-operate and collaborate, with getting key external agencies to engage positively and have confidence in community-run structures, or with getting political support. But, whatever the problem, it is important to withdraw and reflect on how to try again rather than seek to push forward with a programme which does not have real support.

Appendix ii
The five stage social accounting model

Stage one: Introducing social accounting and audit

Social accounting is not just another system to be imposed on an organisation. It is more an *approach*, providing a *framework* that permits the organisation to report on its social performance in the fullest and most effective way possible. Therefore social accounts make use of information that an organisation already gathers, reports which already have to be prepared, and consultations which are already carried out. No organisation starts with a blank sheet. Often there is much more 'in the bag' than is realised, sometimes tucked away in different departments or different computers and not brought together or used for only one purpose when it could be used to inform others as a part of the social accounting process. Gaps in existing documentation and information systems will be identified and new methods of capturing information and gathering stakeholder views developed.

It is important that an organisation makes a clear and positive decision to keep social accounts and have them independently verified. Although that decision will be taken by the board or management committee it should be 'owned' and understood at all levels in the organisation. Hence the importance of discussing the concept, of allaying fears and building a commitment and enthusiasm for the idea – not always easy, as people will tend initially to perceive it as added work and more hassle. As part of the 'buy-in' process members of the organisation should become familiar with the key principles and have the opportunity to read social accounts which have been produced by other organisations.

Managing the social audit

Usually someone will be given responsibility to co-ordinate the process and ensure that it is carried through – the organisation's *social accountant*. Some organisations have found it best to nominate two people to work together, which safeguards against the loss of continuity should the social accountant become ill or leave the organisation. It is essential that the workload of the social accountant(s) is managed so that they have the capacity to do the work that will be involved and are not expected to add social accounting to an already full schedule. If the task is assigned to someone of relatively junior status it will be important to ensure that they have someone with a sufficient level of authority within the organisation working with and supporting them.

It is further good practice to ensure that each social accountant has some form of support through a small *social audit group*. This ensures that the task is not 'dumped' on someone who goes unsupported, with the resultant danger that the rest of the organisation loses sight of the social audit, then loses interest and does not engage with the process. It can also help if 'social audit' appears regularly on the agenda of management committee meetings. In this way the social accountant(s) and the social audit group can keep others informed of progress.

The *social audit year* is likely to be the financial year, with the advantage that social, environmental and financial reports can be combined (the 'triple bottom line'). However, this is not essential, and each organisation will determine the social accounting period which best suits it.

The cost of social audit

Undertaking to prepare social accounts and have them audited inevitably incurs costs. For community organisations the scale and costs of the social accounting process have to be managed so that they fit with the resources of time and money which can realistically be made available. It is always better to start modestly and build up than try and do too much to start with and fail.

There are four main areas of *external* cost that may be incurred:

- A facilitator to help plan the process and set up the systems, including necessary training;
- Engaging people to undertake some of the stakeholder consultation that must be done independently and confidentially;
- Obtaining help to draft the social accounts (although, ideally, the drafting should be done by the organisation's social accountant, sometimes it may be necessary to bring in external assistance);
- Arranging for a social audit panel to carry out the verification.

The *internal* costs to the organisation can be summarised as:

- Staff time, both of the social accountant and members of the social audit group, and of other members of staff who have to keep various records, attend meetings and so on, and especially time to pull all the information together and draft the social accounts;
- Administrative (time, copying, postage etc.);
- Printing and publishing the social audit report.

Independent, and usually cost-free, resources which may be sought to help with the social accounting process include: negotiating with a local university or college for a student to come on placement; swapping time with another organisation also preparing social accounts (you do some interviews for them and they for you); involving members of the management or advisory committee (perhaps out and about interviewing stakeholders); seeing if any other local bodies can offer a volunteer (the local volunteer agency, retired business executives); seeking out interested academics from the local university (they may help you get a student placement, or advise on surveys and help with the analysis of data); approaching local public-sector workers (health board, social services) who may be able, for example, to facilitate focus groups as part of their job; seeing if the local sixth form can help (pupils going out with tape machines as roving reporters).

Stage two: The foundations

Objectives, activities and values

If an organisation is to produce competent social accounts it must first be clear about what it seeks to do, why it is doing it, and what the values are which guide the way the organisation behaves.

Objectives should be clear and focused. Existing objectives may have been set some years before by the founders and not revisited for some time. They may have been 'lost' in the hurly burly of keeping going and raising funds. They may even have become subtly reworded to suit successive funding opportunities. An organisation may find that it has implicit objectives which have never been overtly expressed, but which are integral to its activities. Objectives require regular review: are they still appropriate? are the activities relevant to the objectives?

The mission statement is the starting point – usually a vague set of words that describe the nature of the organisation and what it does. These need to be 'unpicked' in order to understand exactly what the core objectives and the underpinning values are, as well as what is actually *done* to achieve these.

It can be easy to confuse activities with objectives: if you are uncertain, ask 'Why do we do that? What is the purpose of doing that?' Identifying all the activities (writing them on post-its for example) and then clustering them under apparent objectives can help with the process of clarification. Remembering some of the half-forgotten things you do may lead to defining an objective you had never before clarified. Sometimes asking 'Why do we do that?' will help decide to stop doing something because it does not fit with the objectives, is not really effective or is simply no longer relevant. It can be helpful to distinguish between *external objectives* (those which are about what is done to/for others) and *internal objectives* (about how the organisation is run).

At the same time as agreeing objectives and identifying the activities, an organisation should list the values that underpin all it does and which it seeks to live up to. There can be crossover between objectives and values. That is unimportant provided that the organisation expresses overtly all that it is aiming to do (objectives and activities) and the manner in which it intends to do them and behave to its stakeholders (values). The aim is to produce a clear statement of *Mission, Values, Objectives and Activities***.** The statement is a public acknowledgement that the organisation will report:

1. on what it does in respect of all its objectives;
2. how stakeholders perceive its performance; and
3. on how well it lives up to its values.

These values and objectives belong to the organisation. Clearly, they must be compatible with the objectives of any bodies who invest in various aspects of the work but they also include those other aspects which the organisation considers important and wishes to report on and consult stakeholders about. The purpose is to give as full and rounded a picture of performance as possible and, if stakeholders are included in the process, they share not only in the assessment of performance but also in the review of objectives.

Stakeholders

The stakeholders are all those people or groups who are affected by an organisation or who are in a position to affect it. The second foundation step therefore is to build up a *'stakeholder map'* so that the extent of the potential impact and the nature of the relationship with different stakeholders is understood. The stakeholder concept recognises that any organisation, and especially a social enterprise, should account for its actions to those people it affects and give them the

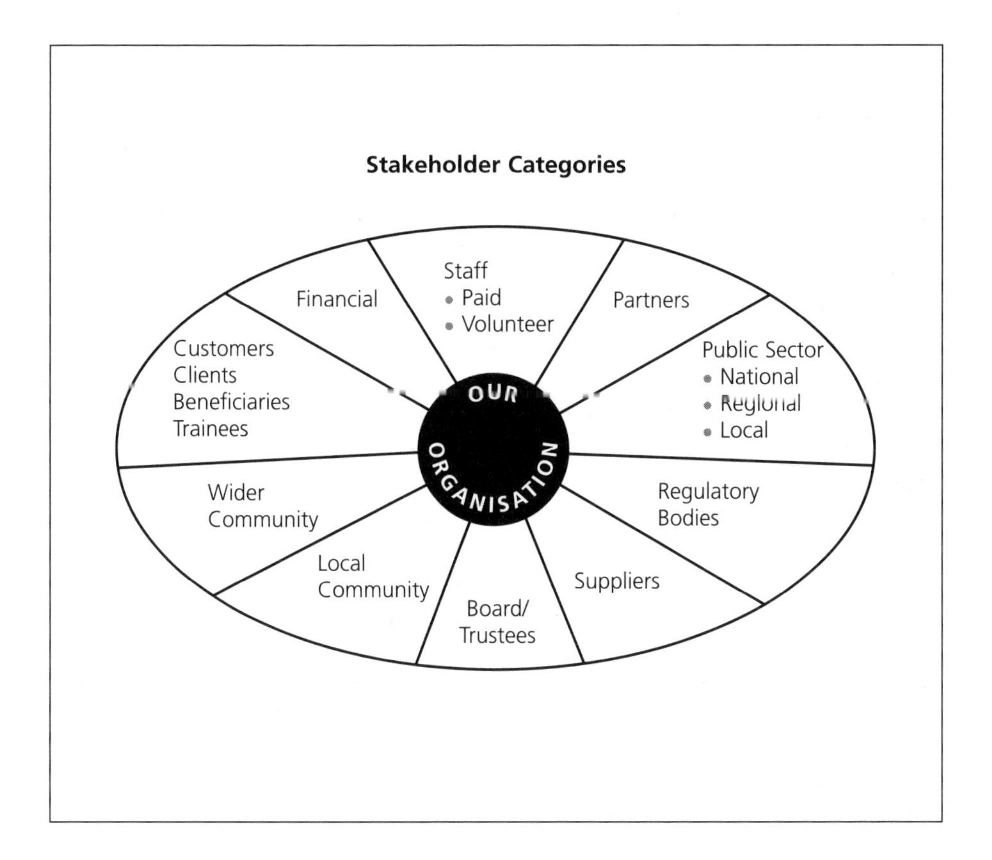

opportunity to influence the way the organisation behaves, at the same time as understanding the pressures of competing priorities and demands.

The diagram on page 169 provides a framework which can be used to help identify stakeholders by grouping them into various categories. Some stakeholders may appear in more than one category, demonstrating that an organisation can have differing relationships with the same organisation. Most organisations discover that they affect many more people than they had realised and sometimes the relationship with a particular stakeholder group suggests an unspoken or hitherto unrecognised objective.

The stakeholder map should be comprehensive, but from that full picture it is necessary to decide which are the *key* stakeholders who must be consulted as part of a credible social accounting process. Key stakeholders will be those with whom the organisation most frequently interacts and those most affected by (or able to affect) the organisation.

Social enterprises which have undertaken the foundation stage, even if they do not proceed to complete their social accounts, invariably acknowledge the usefulness of having submitted their values, objectives and activities to review and of developing an understanding of how they affect stakeholders.

Stage three: The nuts and bolts – social book-keeping

Stage three is about determining what information (indicators) will show whether and how well the activities are being carried out and so achieving the enterprise's objectives. Some of this information will be countable, statistical data (quantitative): how many, how often, how much, etc. Other information will be what people think and feel about performance (qualitative) and what stakeholders think about the objectives and values themselves.

The social accounts should include some information about every activity of each objective, even if it is to say that it has been decided not to report on it or that data is not available (but will be in the next social accounting cycle). For each there should be:

- *Narrative* information that *describes* clearly what has been done; which will be backed up by
- *Quantitative* data which give the *countable* facts and figures about what has been done; and
- *Qualitative* information that tells us what the stakeholders think – their *voices*.

Stage three therefore entails agreeing, first, what quantitative information is required and, if it is not already available, how it might be gathered; and second, what qualitative questions need to be asked and answered; of which stakeholders, and how, when and by whom. In agreeing a practical social book-keeping plan it is important to be aware of the resources available and to devise a plan which may be carried through effectively. Far better to start with modest ambitions and achieve them thoroughly than to aim too high and fail to complete. More can always be added in the next cycle.

It is tempting to get caught up with the fascination of consulting the stakeholders and consequently under-report quantitatively. In the social economy sector it is essential to balance what people think with the hard detailed information about what has been done.

There are no magical ways of consulting stakeholders beyond the tried and tested methods of consumer or market research, of social science investigation, of community or popular participatory consultation. Indeed one of the exciting challenges of social accounting practice in the social economy is to find effective, appropriate and fun ways of consulting the stakeholders which really engage them in the process and which are not too costly to conduct.

Some of the most usual consultation methods are listed in the box below.

- *Feedback/evaluation sheets ('reactionnaires')* completed by trainees, by workshop participants, by clients and others from time to time. It is best to analyse the forms at the time they are completed – both to absorb any necessary findings quickly into practice and to ensure that the data is easily accessible and useable when the social accounts are prepared.
- *Questionnaires* to (selected) stakeholders: these may be sent out by post, delivered and collected by hand, passed round at meetings, put on a clipboard and used in the street or door-to-door, sent by e-mail or posted on your website.
- *Interviews* face to face with individuals or groups, or on the telephone.
- *Focus groups* inviting a group of stakeholders to come together to discuss key questions. The Scandinavians call them *'dialogue circles'* which nicely introduces the idea of a two-way exchange rather than the group simply being a means of 'our finding out what they think'.
- *Participatory rapid appraisal techniques* these were originally developed in overseas development work and make use of visual, participatory techniques to allow groups to express opinions and come to consensus views.
- *Workshops, team meetings, the annual general meeting and other gatherings* any time during the year when groups of stakeholders gather for one purpose or another can be seen as an opportunity to consult and to engage them in the process of assessment and review. Make use of all opportunities.
- *Channels of accountability* establishing clearly known channels through which stakeholders can learn about what the organisation is doing

and comment on it on an ongoing basis. This might be achieved by posting information onto a website with a facility for comment and debate; or through distributing a regular community information sheet with response slips; via regular community meetings; or via a well-publicised AGM which includes debate and the chance to give and take feedback. Establishing such channels of accountability is an important element in the open democracy of social economy organisations and can well complement other aspects of the social accounting system.

- *Community reference group* (or *community jury)* A group of people broadly representative of the wider community, whose opinion you would value and who are in a position to understand what you do, to whom to put key questions about your performance in respect of objectives and values.

It is best to spread stakeholder consultations over a number of months rather than 'bottle-neck' them at the end of the year. The findings of consultations and other facts and figures should be available within the organisation as they are ready, providing social management accounts to go with the financial.

Stage four: Preparing and using the social accounts

It makes the drafting of the social accounts easier if a framework for them is worked out at an early stage rather than at the last minute when people are faced with all the quantitative data and all the reports of the various stakeholder consultations. Most social accountants report that the task is much easier the second time around because they are working from an existing framework and improving on it.

The 13 points in the box below give a practical framework for arranging the social accounts. The list is not necessarily to be followed exactly – and each social accountant has their own ideas – but a comprehensive set of social accounts should include all of the items.

1. *Background information* about the organisation: history, location, structure etc.
2. Explain *why* the organisation decided to prepare social accounts, how the process was managed and who has done the work.
3. State the *objectives* and the *activities* being undertaken to achieve them; and explain the *values* which underpin the work of the organisation.
4. Provide a *stakeholder map* and explain how the *key stakeholders* have been selected for the purposes of the social audit.

5. Spell out the *scope* of the social audit: i.e. what has been done and how (methodology) with particular reference to which stakeholders have been consulted and how they have been consulted. Where particular groups of stakeholders have been omitted from the process or if some part of the organisation's work has been excluded the reasons for omission/exclusion should be given.
6. Report *objective by objective and activity by activity* on performance. The report will cover:
   - descriptive information in narrative form;
   - quantitative information/data which demonstrates what has been done;
   - qualitative information – the views of the stakeholders in respect of the specific objectives/actions;
   - commentary – a brief section on each objective to interpret the findings, explain the context if necessary and summarise the main issues which arise.
7. Report the *views of the different stakeholder groups* you have consulted as regards overall performance, the relevance/suitability of the objectives and activities, living up to the *values*, and any other issues asked of them or raised by them during the consultation processes.
8. Report on the organisation's *compliance* with various statutory or voluntary standards.
9. Report on *environmental* performance, if it is not included already as an objective in section 6.
10. Highlight *the issues that arise* on which the organisation should consider taking action as regards performance and behaviour.
11. Highlight *problems/weaknesses* of the *social accounting process*.
12. Make proposals for the *next social accounting cycle*.
13. Outline what your organisation is intending to do about *publishing* the social audit findings and entering into *dialogue* with stakeholders.

Usually the social accountant(s) will take responsibility for co-ordinating the compilation of the social accounts and will do most, if not all, of the writing. Occasionally an organisation may ask an outsider to draft the social accounts for it. That person is not the social auditor, but someone hired to write the accounts on behalf of the organisation. The ownership of the accounts and the responsibility for what they say rest with the organisation and not with the author.

The turn of the social accounting cycle

Writing the social accounts marks the end of the social accounting year, although of course the next year is already underway as the accounts are being prepared. For this reason some social economy organisations choose to prepare social accounts every second year to give themselves the time to complete one cycle fully before embarking on the next. However, once the process becomes established, preparing social accounts annually is little different from preparing financial accounts on an annual basis – and doing both each year means that there is a triple-bottom-line report each year.

The task at the year-end is to review the findings as presented in the social accounts and ensure that they have either been considered and acted upon, or that a mechanism has been established for considering them. It will of course not always be possible to respond to all stakeholder wishes: sometimes the desires of different groups are not compatible, and sometimes the organisation will assert (and explain) what it believes to be right, notwithstanding the views of its stakeholders.

The organisation will:

- review the stated *objectives* both in the light of reported performance and in response to stakeholder views;
- examine the *activities* through which the objectives are achieved: are they still relevant? Are they effective?
- review how well it is thought to be living up to the *values*: are they still appropriate?
- set *targets* for performance for the year ahead and identify appropriate *benchmarks*;
- modify *practices* in the light of performance and of stakeholder comments, and identify *training and development* needs;
- review the social accounting and audit process itself in order to agree a *social accounting plan for the next year*.

Disclosure

It is a key principle that the findings of the social accounts are disclosed to all stakeholders. In the case of social economy organisations that usually also means the community at large, the general public. The presumption always is that the substance of all findings will be disclosed. However, there may be circumstances when certain findings must be kept confidential for one reason or another. The decision to withhold information rests with the board or management committee and they must satisfy themselves that their decision to withhold information from the published report is justified. They must also be confident that they can adequately explain their decision to the social audit panel in the following cycle. Equally important, of course, is that the organisation takes urgent steps to tackle those confidential and sensitive matters which are the subject of non-disclosure so that the next social accounts can report that the matters have been satisfactorily dealt with.

There is no prescribed format for publishing social accounts. Some organisations publish in full, others prepare a summary, but the full social accounts and the notes of the panel meeting should certainly be available for inspection at the organisation's office. The signed social audit statement should be included in the published version. Increasingly, organisations roll up their annual (statutory) report with their social audit report, producing just the one document which reports on social, financial and environmental performance.

Stage five: The social audit

The social audit panel process has been developed through experience gained in the City of Liverpool's social audit initiative, in the COMMACT Aotearoa programme and by the work of the Community Business Scotland Network. The process derives from earlier experience of Traidcraft plc and the New Economics Foundation.

The verification of the social accounts is carried out by a social audit panel consisting of between three and five people. The chair of the panel should ideally be someone with experience of social auditing. However until the practice of social audit in the social economy sector becomes more widespread the availability of people with practical social audit experience remains patchy.

Social audit panel members are appointed by the organisation itself, although, where a local social audit initiative is in place then the initiative will probably appoint the panel chair. Members of the panel will be people who have no vested interest in the organisation being audited but who know something about the field of work in which it is engaged and about the locality in which it works. The key point is that the panel must be seen to be objective and impartial, for the credibility of the audit depends on whether the opinion of the panel is perceived by stakeholders to be credible.

The chair of the social audit panel has the tasks of:

- co-ordinating the arrangements for the panel meeting, including circulating the agenda and briefing panel members;
- organising the 'audit trail' (see below);
- chairing the panel meeting;
- writing up the notes of the meeting;
- negotiating over and approving subsequent changes to the draft social accounts; and
- eventually, issuing the social audit statement.

The draft social accounts and any attached documents are circulated to the panel members at least one week before the meeting to give them good time to read the documentation and prepare themselves for the panel meeting which typically lasts for the best part of one working day.

Before the panel meeting the chair may arrange a visit to the organisation to carry out a sample check (the audit trail) of the social book-keeping systems and the stakeholder consultation processes. This involves checking evidence of information and views reported in the social accounts and also verifying the existence of data quoted in them. It may include corroborative telephone interviews with stakeholders who have been quoted. The audit visit may be carried by the panel chair him- or herself, maybe with one of the other panellists, or the task may be delegated to some other independent person acting on behalf of the panel. In either event, a report will be submitted to the panel when it meets, detailing which items were checked, whether the records are systematically stored and are accessible, and whether ongoing social book-keeping systems appear to be in place.

If it is not possible to arrange an audit trail visit before the panel meeting, the audit trail may be conducted either as part of the panel meeting or immediately afterwards. This arrangement has the practical merit of conducting all aspects of the social audit on one day and for reasons of cost is the one most usually adopted.

The social audit panel meeting

The purpose of the social audit is to assess:

- the quality and completeness of the social accounting process, and
- the fairness of the interpretations given in the accounts.

The social audit panel does *not* evaluate the work of the organisation: that is for the organisation and its stakeholders to do for themselves, making use of the social accounts in the knowledge that their contents and interpretations have been verified by an independent social audit panel and can therefore be considered as trustworthy.

The panel meeting offers the opportunity for both panel members and the organisation's representatives to go through the accounts section by section, page by page. Usually, the organisation will be represented by the social accountant and his or her social audit group. During the course of the meeting the panel will examine all the questions in the social audit checklist included at the end of this Appendix (see page 179).

Panel meetings will be rigorous, but fair, and often creative. Initial uncertainty and defensiveness on behalf of the organisation usually give way to constructive engagement when it becomes apparent that the role of the panel is not to evaluate the work but only the social accounting process and that both organisation and panel have a common interest to ensure that the social accounts are as full and as reliable as they can be.

Following the panel meeting comprehensive notes will be prepared covering the items noted in the framework. In particular the notes will identify:

- changes which the panel require to be made to the draft before they can agree to issue a social audit statement; and

- recommendations regarding scope, methodology and process for the next social audit cycle.

The notes are circulated to all those who have been part of the social audit panel meeting for comment and approval and then the social accountant of the organisation has the task of incorporating the required changes to produce a revised draft. In the case of disagreement over any of the recommended changes the panel chair will negotiate with the organisation on behalf of the panel. Usually there is little disagreement as all the changes will have been discussed and agreed during the panel meeting and seen to be constructive and contributing to the quality and completeness of the social accounts. In the event of an unresolvable difference, the panel chair will either refuse to issue a statement or will include a relevant qualification in the statement.

The social audit statement

The text of a sample social audit statement is given in the box overleaf. The key words of the audit panel's opinion are highlighted. The statement provides for identifying the key recommendations for the next social audit cycle and lists the names of the panel members.

The note at the bottom of the statement makes clear that the notes of the panel meeting form part of the social accounting and audit process and may in the interests of transparency, along with the full social accounts, be inspected at the offices of the organisation. In this way the social accounts are placed in the public domain and are available for inspection. Many organisations now place their full social accounts on their websites.

The social audit statement

The social audit panel has examined the draft social accounts submitted to us and discussed them in detail with (names of persons) of (name of organisation) at the social audit panel meeting held on (date). We have examined the revised social accounts which were prepared following the social audit panel meeting and which have taken into account various points identified in our notes of the meeting.* We have also examined a sample of the data and the sources of information on which the social accounts have been based.

Although social accounting and social auditing is a relatively new concept and there is no generally accepted code of social accounting and auditing practice we believe that the process outlined above has given us sufficient information on which to base our opinion.

We are satisfied that, given the scope of the social accounting explained in the revised draft and given the limitations of time available to us, the statement of social accounts is free from material mis-statement and presents a fair and balanced view of the performance of (name of organisation) as measured against its stated social objectives and the views of the stakeholders who were consulted.

In our notes of the social audit panel meeting we identified a number of important issues to be taken into consideration during the next social audit cycle. In particular we would refer to the following:

i.
ii.
iii. [to be completed as appropriate]

The members of the social audit panel were:

a.
b.
c.
d.

Signed:..................... Dated:...................
Chair of the social audit panel

* The notes of the social audit panel meeting form part of the social accounting and auditing process and may, together with the full social accounts be inspected, by arrangement, at the offices of (organisation) at (address).

Social audit checklist

Scope and completeness of the social accounts

1.	Comprehensive	Y	N	Comment
1.1	Are the objectives clearly stated?			
1.2	Are the values clearly stated?			
1.3	Do the social accounts report adequately on performance against each activity of all objectives?			
1.4	Are the reasons for any omissions clearly explained?			
2.	**Multiperspective**			
2.1	Has a full stakeholder analysis been undertaken?			
2.2	Have any important stakeholder groups been omitted?			
2.3	Have all key stakeholders been consulted: • about performance and impact • about relevance of objectives • about living up to the values stated?			
2.4	Is the process for selecting key stakeholder groups properly explained?			
3.	**Environmental**			
3.1	Do the social accounts include information on environmental impact/performance?			
4.	**Compliance**			
4.1	Are the statutory and voluntary standards complied with reported in the social accounts?			
5.	**Comparisons**			
5.1	Are internal, year-on-year, targets set?			
5.2	Are relevant external comparisons (benchmarks) used?			
6.	**Social audit trail**			
6.1	Has a sample of items been satisfactorily examined/traced to source?			

		Y	N	Comment
6.2	Were the social book-keeping records fully available and accessible to the panel?			
6.3	Are the records (qualitative and quantitative) stored systematically?			
6.4	Are ongoing social book-keeping systems in place?			

Process

7.	**Regular**	**Y**	**N**	**Comment**
7.1	Are social accounts prepared (intended to be prepared) on a regular basis?			
7.2	Is the understanding and practice of social accounting embedded in the organisation?			
8.	**Disclosure and Dialogue**			
8.1	Are the social accounts organised in a clear and comprehensive format?			
8.2	Do the social accounts report on the follow-up of issues raised in an earlier social audit?			
8.3	Are there clear plans to disseminate the findings of the social accounts to stakeholders and to others?			
8.4	Is it planned that the stakeholders will be included in discussion of the issues arising from the social accounts and the social audit process?			

Learning

9.	**Methodology and Resources**	**Y**	**N**	**Comment**
9.1	What lessons of methodology have been learned from this social audit cycle?	*	*	
9.2	What problems have been encountered in carrying through the process (e.g. resources etc.)?	*	*	

A directory of resource organisations

CBS Network
Princes House
5 Shandwick Place
Edinburgh EH2 4RG
0131 229 7257
info@cbs-network.org.uk
www.cbs-network.org.uk

Charity Bank
PO Box 295
25 Kings Hill Avenue
West Malling
Kent ME19 4WD
01732 520029
enquiries@charitybank.org
www.charitybank.org

Community Action Network
The Mezzanine
Elizabeth House
39 York Road
London SE1 7NQ
020 7401 5311
canhq@can-online.org.uk
www.can-online.org.uk

Community Development Finance Association
80–84 Bondway
London SW8 1SF
020 7820 1282
info@cdfa.org.uk
www.cdfa.org.uk

Community Enterprise Wales
36 Union Terrace
Merthyr Tydfil CF47 0DY
01685 376490
cewunion@aol.com
www.communityenterprisewales.com

Co-operative Union, incorporating ICOM the worker co-op federation
Holyoake House
Hanover Street
Manchester M60 0AS
0161 246 2959
enquiries.coopunion@co-op.co.uk
www.coopunion.coop

Development Trusts Association
2/8 Scrutton Street
London EC2A 4RT
0845 458 8336
info@dta.org.uk
www.dta.org.uk

Industrial Common Ownership Finance
227c City Road
London EC1V 1JT
020 7251 6181
icof@icof.co.uk
www.icof.co.uk

Local Investment Fund
123 Minories
London EC3N 1NT
020 7680 1028
information@lif.org.uk
www.lif.org.uk

New Economics Foundation
Cinnamon House
6–8 Cole Street
London SE1 4YH
020 7089 2800
info@neweconomics.org
www.neweconomics.org

New Sector
1 Red Hill Villas
Durham DH1 4BA
0191 375 0101
editor@newsector.co.uk
www.newsector.co.uk

Radical Routes and Rootstock
Cornerstone Resource Centre
16 Sholebroke Avenue
Chapeltown
Leeds LS7 3HB
0113 262 9356
info@radicalroutes.org.uk
www.radicalroutes.org.uk
www.rootstock.org.uk

School for Social Entrepreneurs
18 Victoria Park Square
Bethnal Green
London E2 9PF
020 8981 0300
kevin.simmonds@sse.org.uk
www.sse.org.uk

Social Audit Network
Princes House
5 Shandwick Place
Edinburgh EH2 4RG
0131 229 7257
info@cbs-network.org.uk
www.cbs-network.org.uk (click social audit network)

Social Economy Agency NI
2 Bay Road
Derry BT48 7SH
028 7137 1733
info@socialeconomyagency.org
www.socialeconomyagency.org

Social Enterprise
11 Stanley Road
London N10 2HU
020 8442 1623
news@socialenterprisemag.co.uk
www.socialenterprisemag.co.uk

Social Enterprise Coalition
C/o Coin Street Community Builders
99 Upper Ground
South Bank
London SE1 9PP
020 7401 3166
info@socialenterprise.org.uk
www.socialenterprise.org.uk

Social Enterprise London
1a Aberdeen Studios
22–24 Highbury Grove
London N5 2AE
020 7704 7490
info@sel.org.uk
www.sel.org.uk

Social Enterprise Partnership GB
Aspect House
2–4 Monson Road
Redhill
Surrey RH1 2ET
01737 773919
shines@cqm.co.uk

Social Enterprise Scotland
C/o Social Firms Scotland
Unit 1 Block 3
Peffermill Industrial estate
Edinburgh EH16 5UY
0131 539 7374
karen.maclean@socialfirms.org.uk

Social Enterprise Unit
Department of Trade and Industry
Fourth Floor
1 Victoria Street
London SW1H 0ET
020 7215 0397
socialenterpriseunit@dti.gsi.gov.uk
www.dti.gov.uk/socialenterprise

Social Entrepreneurs Scotland (Senscot)
54 Manor Place
Edinburgh EH3 7EH
0131 220 4104
mail@senscot.net
www.senscot.net

Social Firms UK
2–4 Monson Road
Redhill
Surrey RH1 2ET
01737 764021
socialfirms@cqm.co.uk
www.socialfirms.co.uk

Triodos Bank
Brunel House
11 The Promenade
Bristol BS8 3NN
0117 973 9339
mail@triodos.co.uk
www.triodos.co.uk

Wales Co-operative Centre
Llandaff Court
Fairwater Road
Cardiff CF5 2XP
029 2055 4955
walescoop@walescoop.com
www.walescoop.com

List of persons consulted

Jackie Baillie	*MSP*
Liam Black	*Furniture Resource Centre, Liverpool*
Jonathan Bland	*Social Enterprise London*
Jackie Brierton	*Independent consultant (formerly of Wellpark Enterprise Centre, Glasgow)*
David Coulter	*Scottish Enterprise*
Mark Cullens	*BRAG Enterprises, Fife*
John Duncan	*Social Enterprise Network, Merseyside (formerly of Liverpool City Council)*
Mel Evans	*Institute of Social and Health Research, University of Middlesex, and Community Economy Limited*
Murdoch Gatward	*Traidcraft Exchange*
Alastair Grimes	*Community Enterprise in Strathclyde*
Chris Hart	*The Eldonians, Liverpool*
Ian Hughes	*Independent consultant (formerly of Queens Cross Group, Glasgow)*
Conal McFeely	*Social Economy Agency, Northern Ireland*
Richard Meegan	*University of Liverpool*
Martin Meteyard	*The Co-operative Group (formerly of Green City Wholefoods)*
Gareth Nash	*Independent consultant (formerly of Lancashire Co-operative Development Agency)*
Barbara Phillips	*Social Enterprise Unit, Department of Trade and Industry*
Stephen Phillips	*Burness lawyers*
Judith Reynolds	*Co-active, Devon*
Andrew Robinson	*Head of Community Development Banking, NatWest and The Royal Bank of Scotland*
Helen Seymour	*The Co-operative Group (formerly of the Industrial Common Ownership Movement)*
Dave Turner	*Independent consultant*
Alan Tuffs	*CBS Network*
Alison West	*Community Development Foundation*
Bruce Wood	*London Rebuilding Society*
Steve Wyler	*Development Trusts Association*

Glossary of social enterprise and social audit terms

Accountability: where an organisation recognises and accepts that it should honestly and openly explain to its stakeholders what it has done and why, so that they can make their own judgements about continuing to support, use, trade with or work for the organisation. *AccountAbility* is also the name of the quarterly journal published by the Institute of Social and Ethical AccountAbility.

Activity: the detailed work that an organisation undertakes in order to achieve its objectives.

Added value: an economics term increasingly used in the social economy to refer to the social or community benefit which social enterprises deliver; sometimes 'social added value'.

Audit trail: checking/verification by the social audit panel of the data, social book-keeping systems and stakeholder consultation processes on which the social accounts are based.

Benchmark: an external standard or reference point against which performance may be compared.

Bottom-up: an initiative or development within a community which is led from and directed by the community itself.

Building society: originally a co-operative society where members saved collectively in order to lend to their members sufficient funds to build a house and which was often wound up when all members had achieved that; now finance institutions which retain a co-operative or mutual structure and which take in savings from the public and specialise in making loans for the purchase of houses.

Capacity building: the process by which individuals and groups acquire the skills, confidence, information and knowledge with which they can turn their wishes and aims into practical action.

Charity: an organisation which is recognised by the Charity Commission in England and Wales (Inland Revenue in Scotland) as meeting the requirements laid down by the Charities Acts. Charities are generally not permitted to engage in straightforward commercial trading, nor are their beneficiaries or employees permitted to serve on the management committee. Co-operatives may generally not be charities, except for those societies established specifically for the benefit of the community (sometimes referred to as 'bencoms').

Charity trading arm: where charities wish to trade, for example to raise funds, they may establish a separate company for this purpose.

Collective: a co-operative organisation with a 'flat' structure which permits all members to play a full part in decision-making.

Common bond: the definition of the area or constituency to be served by a credit union.

Common ownership company: where the constitution states that the assets may not be realised and distributed amongst the members, but shall be held in trust for a defined community or membership constituency.

Community-based economic development: economic development focused on usually compact local communities and directed and controlled by the local community.

Community-based housing association: a housing association which is locality-based and -focused, in contrast to larger associations covering a wider geographical district, region, or even nation.

Community benefit corporation (CBC): a generic term used for all social and community enterprises which operate for the common good, and which was promoted by the community business movement in the 1980s. The term is resurrected here (see chapter 10).

Community business: the term adopted in 1982 in place of 'community enterprise' when the Conservative government adopted the latter for the job creation scheme that succeeded the Special Temporary Employment Programme (STEP). Community business is now generally taken to mean a community-based commercial organisation with strong roots in a specific locality.

Community business venture: the term first adopted when 'community enterprise' was hijacked by the government, but quickly shortened to 'community business'.

Community co-operative: a community enterprise or community business with strong local roots which has adopted the legal form of a co-operative rather than that of a company.

Community credit union: a credit union which has a relatively small local geographical area defined as its common bond.

Community development: in the UK, the process of working with groups of people and communities to define needs, agree strategies and plans for tackling them, and to take action to carry through those plans using local organisations controlled by and accountable to the community. In the US the term is more to do with applying an economic edge to the development of poor communities and therefore focusing on business-led development, and with the physical regeneration of property in a neighbourhood.

Community development corporation (CDC): an American term for what in the UK would be known as a development trust or a community enterprise.

Community development finance initiative (CDFI): a relatively small-scale loan fund which specialises in lending to enterprises in disadvantaged areas.

Community enterprise: a social enterprise which is linked to a particular locality from which it draws its members and which it seeks to benefit.

Community housing trust: a local community enterprise which manages a small amount of, usually specialist, social housing.

Community interest company: the term proposed by the review of Charity Law for a new legal form for social and community enterprises.

Community trading organisation: an alternative term for 'community enterprise' which was used in the Highlands of Scotland in the early 1990s but which never caught on.

Community transport: community-owned and -controlled transport services designed to overcome mobility and access problems faced by particular groups.

Community trust: a neighbourhood- or area-based development organisation that is a charity; an alternative term for 'community enterprise' or 'development trust'.

Company limited by guarantee: a company formed under the Companies Acts and registered with Companies House which has members rather than shareholders; members guarantee a nominal sum towards final debts and (usually) pay a regular membership subscription.

Company limited by shares: a company formed under the Companies Acts which is controlled by its shareholders.

Consumer retail co-operative society: the 'Co-op' store in the high street, or any other co-operative which is a retail organisation.

Co-operative: an organisation, owned and controlled by its members, which is incorporated under the Industrial and Provident Societies Acts and regulated by the Registry of Friendly Societies, now part of the Financial Services Authority. Otherwise known as mutuals, friendly societies, industrial and provident societies.

Corporate social responsibility (CSR): the term which is increasingly used within the corporate sector instead of 'social accounting and audit'. It tends to lay greater emphasis on what companies do to discharge their perceived social responsibilities rather than on accounting for all their impacts, good and bad.

Credit union: a savings and loans co-operative society regulated under the Credit Union Act and, more recently, the Financial Services Authority.

Data: information that is gathered as part of the social book-keeping and stakeholder consultation.

Development trust: the term popularised by the Development Trusts Association (DTA) for a community enterprise which is locally based, serving a defined geographical area and which is usually multifunctional, engaged in a wide range of trade and service delivery.

Dialogue circle: an organised and recorded process of bringing together a group of stakeholders to discuss issues which relate to or emerge during the social accounting process.

Disclosure: publication to the stakeholders of the findings of the audited social accounts.

Employee common ownership plan (ECOP): a legal structure whereby the workers in an organisation and the local community may hold (some of the) shares in an operating company which employs all the worker members and on the management committee of which both workers and the local community are represented.

Employee-ownership business: an alternative term for a workers' co-operative.

Employee-ownership share plan (ESOP): a legal structure whereby a workers' co-operative may hold (some of the) shares in an operating company in which all the members are employed and on the board of which they are represented.

Equity finance: funds invested in a business in the form of shares which usually give investors a say in the control of the company in relation to the size of their shareholding and which pay profits (known as dividends) to shareholders, again in proportion to their shares. As the advertisements say, the value of shares may go down as well as up, and equity investment does not necessarily expect immediate returns.

Ethical investment: where funds are invested in companies which have been screened to ensure that they are not engaged in activities which the investor would not wish to support.

Exit strategy: the process through which a top-down and time-limited initiative in a community seeks to withdraw; the establishment of a social enterprise is often seen as an appropriate way of continuing the work initiated.

Fair trade company: a business established with the particular remit of trading with enterprises in the developing world and paying fair rates for goods and products, ensuring that working conditions are acceptable, and offering equitable terms of trade. Many fair trade companies are established as social enterprises.

Focus group: an organised process of bringing together a group of stakeholders to discuss issues which relate to or emerge during the social accounting process. 'Focus group' suggests less a 'dialogue', more 'our finding out what they think'. The results are recorded.

Food co-operative: a voluntary-run organisation which buys food in bulk for sale to its members at low prices.

Friendly society: another term for organisations set up under the Industrial and Provident Societies Acts and otherwise known as co-operative or mutual societies, which are based on memberships with a common interest and where each member has one vote regardless of the size of any shareholding they may have.

Holistic development: where a process of development seeks to ensure that all aspects (social, economic, environmental, health etc.) of a community are considered and strategies devised which recognise and build on the inter-connections between these.

Housing association: a form of industrial and provident society established especially for the provision of social housing.

Housing co-operative: like a housing association but likely to be smaller and locality- or special needs-based and to emphasise co-operative practices in its management.

Indicator: information which allows performance to be measured.

Industrial and provident society: organisations incorporated under the Industrial and Provident Societies Acts and regulated by the Registry of Friendly Societies, now part of the Financial Services Authority. Otherwise known as mutuals, friendly societies, co-operatives.

Industrial credit union: a credit union based on the common bond of a workplace.

Intermediate labour market company (ILM): an organisation which offers subsidised salaried training (work experience and vocational training) to unemployed people for up to one year and seeks to assist them obtain employment in the wider labour market. Some ILMs are established as social enterprises.

Job-ownership company: another term for a workers' co-operative.

Limited liability: Organisations incorporated as companies or as industrial and provident societies (co-operatives) are recognised as distinct legal entities such that the liability for any debts remaining on the winding up of the organisation is restricted to the organisation; members or directors are not personally liable (unless they are found to have wrongfully traded or knowingly traded when the organisation was insolvent).

Loan stock: funds loaned to an organisation in such a way that the lenders receive a fixed dividend, subject to performance, but do not have any rights of control in the way that holders of equity shares might have.

Local exchange trading scheme (LETS): a system which allows members to trade using a local, non-sterling currency, for the multilateral exchange of goods and services.

Managed workspace: a building which provides workshops and offices to several enterprises and organisations and which offers various services to the tenants. Many social enterprises run managed workspaces.

Marketing co-operative: a co-operative society established to provide a marketing service for its members who may or may not be themselves co-operatives.

Mezzanine finance: a 'half-way house' term used for funds invested in an enterprise which are long-term and accept deferred payments like equity but, like loans, do not demand a controlling interest.

Mission statement: a simple statement which briefly describes the nature of an organisation, clearly setting out why it exists, its ethics and what it does, in readily understood and remembered terms.

Mutual society: another term for an industrial and provident society, or co-operative, or friendly society.

Neighbourhood co-operative: a co-operative society which is located in and serves a relatively small neighbourhood.

Not-for-profit company: a company (or co-operative) which has in its constitution a clause preventing the distribution of profits to members and stipulating that profits should be used for social or community benefit or for some other charitable purpose.

Objective: defines what the organisation aims to achieve. Objectives will be achieved by undertaking a number of activities.

Outcome: the 'soft' consequence of a programme, which is not easily measured.

Output: the 'hard' consequence of a programme which can readily be measured, usually quantitatively.

Partnership: where the three different sectors – public, private and community – are brought together to implement a programme. Although designed to involve local people in decision-making the community input is often no more than token.

Patient finance: funds which are invested in an enterprise but which are not seeking an immediate return on that investment.

Preference shares: funds which are invested as equity in an enterprise but which forgo rights of control for a guaranteed regular dividend payment and have priority over ordinary shares in the case of an enterprise being wound up and its assets distributed to creditors and shareholders.

Private limited company: another term for a company limited by shares.

Public interest company: a recently introduced term for a non-profit-distributing company which is running a service for the benefit of the public (see also community benefit corporation and community interest company).

Public limited company (PLC): a company limited by shares where the shares are offered for purchase by the public.

Quadruple bottom line: where a report on cultural performance and impact is added to a triple-bottom-line report.

Regeneration: although originally referring specifically to physical improvements, this term has come to mean any process or programme of local development, embracing social and economic aspects as well as physical and environmental, in both urban and rural settings.

Scope: an explanation of what the social accounts include (and therefore what they do not include). The 'scoping proposal' is the initial suggestion by the social accountant (or social audit facilitator) about what an organisation might realistically aim to include in any one social audit cycle.

Secondary co-operative: a co-operative society established to provide a service for a group of other organisations which may or may not be co-operatives or social enterprises.

Social accountant: the person within an organisation who is charged with the task of co-ordinating the social accounting process and preparing (most of) the social accounts.

Social accounting: the process whereby the organisation collects, analyses and interprets descriptive, quantitative and qualitative information in order to produce an account of its performance.

Social accounts: the document which is prepared as a consequence of the social accounting process and submitted for audit to the social audit panel.

Social audit: the process of reviewing and verifying the social accounts at the end of each social audit cycle The term 'social audit' is also used generically for the concept and for the whole process.

Social audit cycle: the agreed period for which the social accounts are prepared. This may be for 12 months and coincide with the financial year, or it may be for a longer period.

Social audit facilitator: a person who advises and supports an organisation in its planning, and sets up and implements its social accounting process. (Social audit facilitators also often act as social auditors, but not for the organisations for whom they are facilitating the social accounting process.)

Social audit panel: the group of independent people appointed by an organisation to work with the social auditor to review the social accounts in detail and on the basis of which a social audit statement may be issued.

Social auditor: a person who chairs the social audit panel and manages the audit at the end of each cycle, including the examination of the data and the sample checking to source (the audit trail).

Social book-keeping: the means by which information is routinely collected during the year to record performance in relation to the stated social objectives.

Social business: a social enterprise which tends to emphasise its business aspect and plays down any distinction from private business; often established without a democratic constitution to involve the beneficiaries.

Social capital: a term popularised in recent years to describe those resources, and in particular trust, reciprocity and the sharing of values or norms of behaviour, which allow a community or society to function more effectively (see chapter 6).

Social co-operative: a social firm which has been set up as a co-operative society.

Social economy: that part of the third system or sector which is made up of organisations who to some degree engage in the sale of goods and services.

Social enterprise: the generic term for all trading enterprises which have a social purpose, are non-profit-distributing and have a democratic, accountable and common-ownership structure.

Social entrepreneur: an individual who establishes and runs an enterprise with social objectives. Some such enterprises would meet the defining characteristics of social enterprise as described in chapter 3, others may not.

Social entrepreneurship: any activity which uses entrepreneurial skills and techniques for a social purpose.

Social exclusion: where particular groups of people in society find themselves, for various reasons such as poverty, ethnic origin, criminal record, age etc., excluded from normal life and opportunities.

Social firm: a social enterprise which specialises in the employment of people with some form of disability (at least 25% of the workforce) and which earns at least 50% of its income from trade.

Social inclusion: policies and programmes designed to combat social exclusion.

Social investment: where funds are invested in an enterprise (or a social investment mechanism) specifically to support a particular social purpose. Sometimes social investors will agree to accept a lower than market rate of return on their investment.

Society for the benefit of the community: a form of industrial and provident society which is established for the benefit of a designated community and which may be accorded charitable status (sometimes known as a 'bencom').

Stakeholder engagement: the process of entering into dialogue with stakeholders and consulting them as part of the social accounting process.

Stakeholders: those people or groups who are either affected by or who can affect the activities of an organisation.

Subsidiary company: a company which is owned by another company or co-operative.

Sustainability: a) ensuring that an enterprise can generate sufficient revenue to be financially viable; and b) adopting environmental policies and practices which minimise the impact of the enterprise on the environment and the future of the planet.

Target: a desired level of performance to be aimed for.

Third sector: often used to designate those organisations which are not part of either the private or the public sectors.

Third system: used in this book as a preferred designation for the third sector in that it recognises the existence of a different way of organising and managing economic activity (see chapter 2).

Time bank: a system through which people can do voluntary work to assist others and thereby 'bank' hours which they may later cash in to be helped themselves or which they may donate so that some other person or organisation receives the benefit.

Top-down: where a local development initiative is instigated and delivered by agencies from outside the area with little input from the local community.

Transparency: where an organisation, in the interests of being accountable, openly discloses the findings of its social accounts so that stakeholders have a good understanding of how the organisation performs and behaves, and why it does what it does.

Triple bottom line: when an organisation produces an annual report covering financial, environmental and social performance, giving equal weight and importance to each of the three aspects.

Value: a key principle which underpins the way an organisation operates, and which influences the way it and its members behave.

Verification: the process within the social audit whereby the social audit panel examines the social accounts and the information on which they are based in order to say if they are a reasonable statement and based on competent, reliable data.

Vision statement: as for mission statement.

Voluntary enterprise: a social or community enterprise where all the workers are volunteers.

Voluntary organisation: an organisation, usually charitable, established to achieve a social purpose and which depends on grants and donations and other forms of fundraising for its revenue.

Workers' co-operative: a co-operative society which is owned and controlled by the members who work for it.